SCUBA DIVING

P29 *Patrol Boat.*

MALTA • GOZO • COMINO

SECOND EDITION

PETER G. LEMON

Planned and produced by
Peter G. Lemon and Sue Lemon
7 Earls Hill Gardens, Royston
Herts SG8 9DA

www.scubadivingmalta.co.uk
www.scubadivinggozo.co.uk
www.scubadivingmaltagozocomino.com

PUBLISHER Peter G. Lemon

PROJECT MANAGER Sue Lemon

PRINT PRODUCTION George Lanham

Printed in Malta by Gutenberg Press Ltd

THANK YOU
Peter and Sue would like to thank all persons
who helped in any way to the production of
this book

ACKNOWLEDGEMENTS
A list of names appear on page 208

ISBN 978-0-9541789-1-8

Migra Ferha, Dingli Cliffs

Contents

Lantern Point.

The Author!

FRONT COVER: *MV* Um El Faroud, *Malta.*
INSERT: *Tugboat* Rozi.
BACK COVER: *Blue Hole, Drewra, Gozo.*

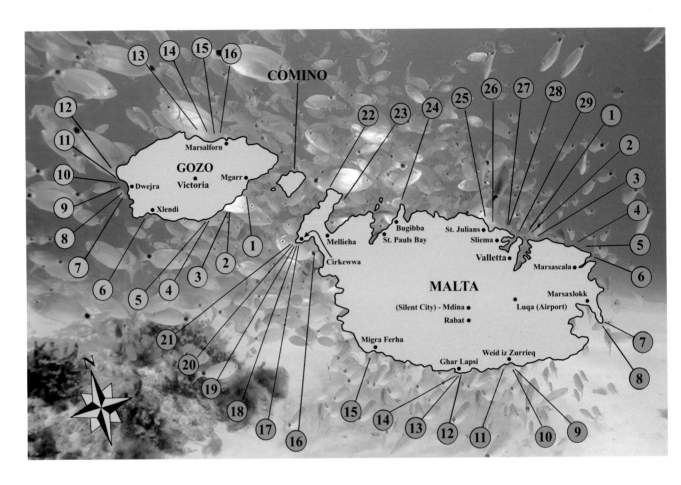

Blue Hole, Gozo

Malta

Gozo

Boat diving site locations

There are many dive sites around Malta, Gozo and Comino which are not accessible from the shore. The following wrecks and off shore reefs which I have selected are just a few of the many areas/dive sites which are available as boat dives.

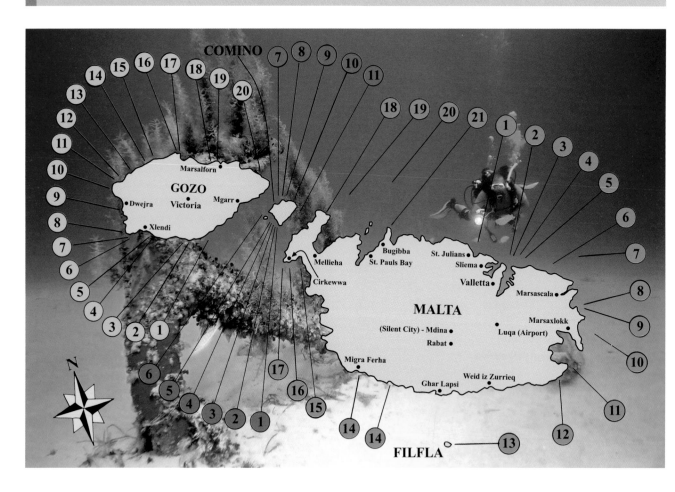

Malta

Gozo

Comino

Shore diving plays an important part of the attraction of diving Malta and Gozo. The entry points do vary considerably, some are reasonably easy, the more difficult ones some divers prefer to boat dive, and it is really down to personal choice. Gozo dive centres will sometimes boat dive some of the dives I have listed on Malta as shore dives, likewise Malta dives centres will boat dive some of the Gozo dive sites.

MALTA HIGH COMMISSION
Malta House
36-38 Piccadilly
London W1J 0LE
Tel: 020 7292 4800
Fax: 020 7734 1831

THE HIGH COMMISSIONER

FOREWORD

My most sincere congratulations to Peter Lemon and his wife Sue for presenting the Maltese and visiting diving community with a much enhanced update of their seminal work on Scuba Diving in the Maltese Islands.

Was it simply luck and coincidence that we met again seven years to the day I signed off my foreword to Peter's first edition? Whatever the reason we were glad to renew old friendships as we reminisced about past chapters in our life. For a quarter of a century Peter Lemon has made an annual pilgrimage to our islands, painstakingly gathered information, sketched and measured the best most secluded dive sites and as I had written at the beginning of the third millennium, shared the delights and excitement of his adventures and the underwater discoveries that Malta offers.

This edition contains more than two hundred pages of informative text, pictures, photographs, graphs and sketches. More importantly it updates the reader with the latest on wrecks since placed on the seabed and transformed into veritable marine attractions.

Peter and Sue Lemon bring to life a fascinating, twenty-five year love affair with Malta and the azure world that bathes our island home – one of Malta's most successful tourist market niches. They do not keep knowledge to themselves but are content to parade their secrets to anyone wishing to enjoy their favourite pastime and treasure and protect our marine environment.

This publication is yet another gift to Malta, to our country's tourism industry and particularly to the thousands that practise deep sea diving and underwater photography. It is moreover a valuable *vade mecum* for all travellers to Malta and prides the right level of information and detail to make visitors' stay more pleasurable.

This is a book for all divers, young or old, tyros or experienced, amateur or professional, that I recommend most strongly to first time and regular explorers of the secrets of the marine world around Malta and its Islands.

MICHAEL REFALO
29th June 2007.

Notes from the Author

It was shortly after I retired from the Hertfordshire Fire & Rescue Service, in which I served thirty seven years, I decided to write a guide book for scuba diving the Maltese Islands. With the support of my wife Sue, agreeing to spend our retirement fund on publishing a book instead of purchasing a 4 x 4 or one of those special things you do when you retire. Five years later the book was launched just before Christmas 2001.

Shortly after the first book came onto the market we decided to prepare for a re-print, but it soon became clear that we wanted to fully re-design the whole book, once again I had to call on my two buddies Chris Gray and Bent Matusiak for their help. Thanking them again for their time and patience during our many hours spent below and above the water, in the monotonous task of preparing underwater dive site plans and of course posing for many photographs. To their credit they have become excellent subjects.

Now a further six years on the second edition is in print. It has been an interesting time and I have progressed from a diver to diver and author, receiving help and making many new friends whilst researching this project.

With further help, encouragement and support from my wife Sue, it has been produced and I hope you enjoy making use of it to get the most out of the excellent diving to be found in the Maltese Islands.

I would like to dedicate this, my second book, to my family.

Katie, John, Hannah and Ben. Michael, Rebecca, Jessica, Verity and Constance.
Ann, also my brother John, who sadly passed away in 2006.

PETER G. LEMON

In the early hours of Wednesday 2nd September 1998, the Um el Faroud leaves Grand Harbour on her last journey before slipping slowly beneath the surface at Wied iz Zurrieq, to form Malta's largest artificial reef.
PHOTO: ANTHONY CHETCUTI

Safeguarding Malta's Underwater Heritage

The Maltese Islands are blessed with a clear unpolluted sea, boasting an underwater visibility in excess of 30 metres. In this limpid sea one finds a prolific variety of marine life around the Maltese coast with many wrecks and caverns making the islands a very popular destination for scuba diving enthusiasts. Scuba diving has been around since the sixties and many diving centres have sprouted around the islands to cater for the numerous scuba diving visitors. One can easily say the majority of these divers come to explore our wrecks and the marine life that is abundant around them.

The spectacular arch at Cirkewwa visited and enjoyed by many divers.

In view of this a foundation was set up to Protect Promote and Preserve the many historic wrecks and their inhabitants. A group of dive centre owners together with representatives from local dive clubs, dive equipment distributors and the Malta Tourism Authority, gave birth to the Malta Marine Foundation. The foundations aim is to protect our underwater heritage and the abundant flora and fauna that coexist with the manmade reefs and the superb natural underwater topography. Our heritage will therefore be safeguarded and promoted to our local and overseas scuba diving visitors whilst making certain that our sub marine wonders are preserved for generations to come.

The Malta Marine Foundation, which is a non profit making organization, believes strongly in action not words. Since the outset in January 2005 the foundation set up a number of tasks to deliver and commenced with a public relations mission to promote our cause to locals and abroad. We strongly believe in lobbying to get the authorities concerned involved in our plans and set up a structure and laws safeguarding our heritage. One such issue is to stop fishing from wrecks by any means, whether spear fishing or nets. The numerous historic wrecks must be protected from unscrupulous people who pillage artefacts and even slaughter the large fish that inhabit these monuments.

We regularly organise a number of activities such as underwater and beach clean ups together with the international organizations such as CORAL and Project AWARE. These two bodies are, like us, committed towards the sea's well being. Among the work that the foundation is involved in is the monitoring of the artificial reefs that were recently placed strategically around our shores, for instance the studies which were carried out on the Imperial Eagle in Qawra and the two tug boats at Marsascala. Another of our objectives is to place more reefs underwater for the proliferation of marine life. These come in two main forms which are both very popular with scuba divers, the fish and animals that make them their home.

One way is scuttling wrecks; the other is placing concrete structures strategically on the seabed, the most popular and costly is the scuttling of wrecks. These environmentally friendly wrecks have to be stripped clean from any toxic material and rendered safe for divers to visit; fish are instantly attracted to the wrecks like magnets. Marine life will start to inhabit these reefs from day one. In a matter of a few years the wreck will resemble a reef with myriads of new inhabitants swarming around it. This makes diving wrecks very popular with visiting divers, wrecks, besides being photogenic, provide the diver

The Karwela, scuttled off Gozo in August 2006 as a diver attraction, on the seabed at 42m PHOTO: JON MITCHELL, DIVE DEEP BLUE

Diver surrounded by saddle bream (Oblada melanura) not far from the Santa Marija caves on Comino.

Replica amphora pots placed on the seabed as a diver interest.

with a dramatic backdrop to the dive. Close encounters with the marine life is guaranteed not to mention the wealth of historical information one can gather about the submerged vessel. Divers are fascinated with wrecks and their previous life as vessels sailing the oceans. One cannot but delve on the human drama that was once part of the ship that now lies quietly on the seabed.

The other type of popular manmade reef is manufactured from building waste and cement. These concrete structures can come in any shape or form. The most common ones that can be found are spherical in form, hence the name 'Reef Balls'. The surface of these balls is rough and the pH is that of sea water making it very easy for marine life to attach to them as there are numerous appendages for life to hold on to as opposed to the smooth surface of new shipwrecks. Both wrecks and the reef balls are extremely successful ways to help the seas to regenerate the dwindling fish population. Besides the artificial reef program the MMF has many other projects in the pipeline such as establishing a permanent mooring buoy program around the islands. These mooring buoys are for dive boats to use, making diving safer while protecting the seabed from chafing caused by the chains and anchors.

For more information regarding the Malta Marine Foundation one can visit our website www.marinefoundation.org

Here one can find a detailed list of wrecks that lie around the Maltese islands, photographs of wrecks and marine life and the foundation's projects. For the foundation to succeed we need your help. Membership is encouraged from all sea dwellers and land lubbers alike. Donations are kindly accepted on line.

Malta Marine

Foundation

info@marinefoundation.org

The Blue Lagoon on Comino is a popular place for local people and tourists alike. In the foreground is a Wignacourt watchtower built around 1618.

PHOTO: BDR. ALFRED AZZOPARDI/AFM PRESS OFFICE

The helicopter and crews that took part in a number of flights for the aerial photographs.
ABOVE LEFT: *Left to right: Paul Mizzi, Photographer. S/Sgt Norman Sciberras, Pilot. Peter Lemon, Author/Photographer. Gnr. Philip Mallia, Technician.*
ABOVE RIGHT: *Left to right: Bdr. Sunclair Douglas, AFM Cameraman. L/Bdr. Phillip Mallia, Aircraft Technician. Capt. Anthony Zammit, Pilot. Peter Lemon, Author/Photographer. S/Sgt Ivan Marmara, Pilot. S/Sgt Loreto L. Spiteri PRO. Bdr. Alfred Azzopardi Photographer – AFM Press Office.*
RIGHT: *The author Peter Lemon presenting a book to Major Joseph Abdilla on the 8th July 2005.*

The author wishes to acknowledge the collaboration of the Armed Forces of Malta's Press-Media & Public Information Office, as well as the helicopter crews from the AFM's Air Wing.

Introduction

This guide to diving the Maltese Islands has been written by a diver for divers who wish to make the most of their time underwater. Not only for the experienced diver to use as a guide, but also for the new diver as a souvenir to remind him or her where they had their first dive in the Maltese Islands.

Although the Islands are small, navigating your way to some of the dive sites can be difficult, due to the lack of road signs in some areas, although this is improving. Therefore I would suggest that you arm yourself with a good road map and confirm your directions with the dive shop before you leave.

At the end of Stoney Path in the training area at Cirkewwa is the drop off where the two divers have selected one of the many dives which can be found in this popular location.

Each dive location begins with a short text giving information on how to arrive at your chosen destination; to assist you with this there is a map of the local area. These road maps have been surveyed and drawn by myself, they are not to scale, but you will find details of times and distances within the text. They show details of parking, entry/exit points, nearest telephone (**phone card advisable**) and amenities. It should be noted that in some areas mobile phones do not work. There is also a brief description given on the area of the dive site, followed by my suggested dive plan with a recommended minimum dive time. It is important before selecting your dive site and making a dive plan that the accompanying text is read and understood.

There is an aerial photograph for each dive site and below it an underwater dive plan, both will show your entry/exit points which will enable you to relate one to the other. I feel sure that all experienced divers would check the immediate coastline for entry/exit points to be used other than those identified. You can of course make your own dive plan.

These underwater dive plans, which are to compass bearings and not to scale, have also been surveyed and drawn by myself; you will find details of times taken to cover distances within the text of each dive location. They are based on my average speed under the water which is, whilst exploring and moving slowly, approximately 11 to 12 metres per minute.

A party of divers returning after a morning boat dive trip aboard a traditional Maltese boat.

Although every effort has been made to obtain the correct depths, you may find that they may vary by one or two metres. This is due to the undulating seabed and of course you could be slightly off the position of the depth marked on the plan.

There is a small section in this book giving a brief description of the boat dives available around the islands, also an identification map showing their locations.

If you have not chosen or pre-booked your dive centre and wish to find the nearest one to your accommodation, refer to the dive centre map which shows their locations, for all further information and details enquire at your chosen dive centre or school. An index can be found at the back of this book.

Emergency telephone number	
Police – Fire – Ambulance	**112**
Marine Life Rescue Team	
Nature Trust – Malta	**99422085**
	99422086

Dive Centre Licence Authority

All diving centres in the Maltese Islands must be authorized by the Malta Tourism Authority, which is the official agency responsible for issuing operating licenses to diving centres, who offer Recreational Diving Services. This is defined in local legislation as training, education, accompanied diving and the provision of equipment for unaccompanied diving. Diving centres are inspected by officials of the Authority at least once a year; the centres must conform to the highest standards. The legislation which had been designed around the European standard for recreational diving service providers EN14467. Full details of the Maltese scuba diving legislation may be found on the website at www.mta.com.mt/index.pl/legislation -LN 153(2004)

Inspectors visit the dive centres on a regular basis.

Instructors must be officially registered to act as such through a licensed dive centre, where all training, education will be undertaken. Equipment will be issued by a licensed dive centre where you can be assured that it has undergone regular maintenance, servicing and testing by technical qualified persons, unless of course you have brought your own. Officials from the Enforcement section of the Authority have the executive powers which enable them to stop any activity from taking place if it is considered to be illegal. Legal action would be taken against that individual, not yourself as a consumer, if they are found to be providing illicit recreational diving services, your dive would be ordered to cease. Freelance instructors would not operate from licensed premises and therefore their operations are not open to inspections by the local government agency. This is all planned with the best interest of the consumer in mind and there are some 50 licensed diving centers to choose from around the islands.

In order to enjoy the crystal clear waters of the Maltese Islands make sure you take along your Certification card and your Dive Log. These will be required when you register at any of the licensed diving centers, for equipment rental, training courses, accompanied or unaccompanied dives, to confirm your qualifications and experience. Any diver who is in possession of a diving qualification less than CMAS Two Star, BS-AC Sports Diver, PADI Advanced or its equivalent must dive in the company of a certified diving instructor, who will be solely responsible for the safety of these persons.

With this group there is an eleven year old undertaking training.

PADI Bubble maker can be undertaken at the age of eight within an enclosed environment and must be accompanied by a parent or guardian, at the age of ten Junior Open water may be commenced. BS-AC allow minors to 'try dive' at the age of twelve and continue training to Ocean Diver. These are the regulations of PADI and BS-AC and are accepted at the majority of dive centres in the Maltese Islands.

At the dive centre you will be asked to fill in a short Registration Form with your personal details and a self-assessed medical form. If the form indicates any illnesses or conditions which may hamper the safety of your planned dive, you will be required to undergo a direct medical assessment conducted by one of the hyperbaric doctors available on the Islands. Medical checks are inexpensive and can be done within hours of registration. You may be required by the director of the dive centre to undergo a medical check to ascertain that you are medically fit to dive. The Maltese Islands have a strong and positive track record for safety in diving and all do their best to ensure that you have the safety you require.

Regulatory Officer i/c Diving Sector,
Malta Tourism Authority

www.visitmalta.com
www.maltatourismauthority.com

Travelling information

To the Maltese Islands

Luqa is Malta's International Airport; it is very modern with all amenities. Air Malta and major international airlines operate regular scheduled services from most major European cities. Scheduled flights by Air Malta operate from most UK airports; some of these services are not available in the winter months. Flying time is approximately 3 hours, Malta time is 1 hour ahead of GMT. It is normal for Air Malta to offer an extra 10-15 kilos baggage allowance for sports equipment, but confirmation should be sought before you purchase your ticket.

Passport and Visa regulations

British nationals need a full passport to visit the Maltese Islands; it must have at least 3 months to run before it expires. No visa is required for a stay less than three months. Where a stay longer than three months is envisaged application should be made, in Malta, shortly before the three months are up, to the Immigration Police, Police Headquarters, Floriana.

The ferry Melita, *owned by the Gozo Channel Ferry Service, entering Mgarr, Gozo. In the background is the island of Comino.*

Ferry Service – Malta Gozo

There is a regular passenger/car ferry service between Malta's northernmost point at Cirkewwa and Gozo's harbour at Mgarr, a journey that takes approximately 30 minutes. During public holidays and the summer season extra trips are organised, often on a shuttle basis. The fares for both passengers and cars are very reasonable.

Public Transport – buses

Malta and Gozo's public transport systems offer a very reasonable and efficient way of getting around the Islands. The main bus terminus is in Valletta in Malta and Victoria in Gozo from where the buses operate to all parts of the islands.

The bus service on the islands are extremely good and very reasonable, a good way of touring the islands of Malta and Gozo.

Car hire and traffic laws

Car hire can be booked with your holiday or alternatively, you will find many companies hiring cars and you just may find a better deal. The requirements for hiring a car are, minimum age of 25, if the hirer is over 70 proof of a medical from a doctor is required. Remember to take your driving license and passport when hiring a car; the laws are almost the same in Malta as the UK. If requested to produce your license by either the Police or a Traffic Warden, you have 48 hours to present it at the nearest Police Station. If you are unfortunate enough to be involved in an accident, vehicles must not be moved until the Police /Traffic Warden arrive. There are couple of points to note, do not park within 5 metres of a corner and do not cross a single white line even to park on the opposite side of the road, these actions could result in receiving a fine/ticket.

A more traditional way to travel is the Kartozzin; this is a traditional horse drawn carriage and can be found in the most popular tourist areas.

The Maltese Islands

You or your group will not be the first to land in these delightful Mediterranean islands. You will be following a tradition that started some 6000 years ago. Throughout recorded history, Malta has been at the heart of world events. The islands have been a haven, battleground, home and refuge to a host of famous figures through various episodes of European history. It is this essence of history, which has helped forge their unique Maltese character.

The Maltese archipelago consists of three inhabited islands; they lie in the middle of the Mediterranean Sea approximately 93km south of Sicily and 230km from the North African (Tunisian) coast. Malta, being the largest of the three with a total land area of 246 square km. Gozo is somewhat smaller with a land area of 67 square km. The smallest is Comino, which lies between the two and has a land area of 2.7 square km. There are also a number of small un-inhabited islands, such as Filfla, Cominetto, and the most well chronicled St. Paul's Islands where the Apostle Paul was shipwrecked in AD 60.

St. Pauls Island with the small chapel, where in AD60 the apostle Paul was shipwrecked.

The People of Malta and Gozo

The rare sense of hospitality and friendliness of these people invariably strike visitors to the Islands.

The Apostle Paul, who was shipwrecked off Malta in AD 60, was probably the first long stay winter visitor to the Island and the hospitality shown him by the locals is well recorded in the Acts of the Apostles. Two thousand years later their hospitality remains as warm and as unaffected as it was then. They welcome the company of foreigners and being helpful to them comes naturally. Also, they take great interest in what is happening to the rest of the world, and, with their flair for languages, communication with visitors is easy. They have an admirable sense of humour and like most Mediterranean people, tend to be rather jovial. These qualities endear the inhabitants of the Islands to the foreign visitor. It is generally said that foreigners are tourists to the Islands only on their first visit; on their second and subsequent visits they return as their established friends.

They are proud of their independence, having one of the highest electoral turnouts in the world. Their patriotism was at its most evident during World War II, when they fought so bravely that Great Britain awarded them its highest award for civil bravery, the George Cross, in 1942.

The bus terminus in Valletta is always busy with buses leaving for every part of the island of Malta.

The pace of life is very relaxed by European standards. They enjoy life and their broad smiles tell you they are a happy people. They find great strength and unity in their common language, religion and strong family ties.

One of the favourite sports of the Islanders is football, and their National Stadium is on the island of Malta at Ta'Qali. There is strong support for world and European football, especially the English and Italian Premier Leagues, supporters clubs are to be found in many towns and villages. The matches can be seen live, here on television and if the team they support wins, they celebrate in style by driving around the streets waving team flags and blowing their hooters.

The Islanders love festivals and the warm climate makes it possible to enjoy these colourful events throughout the year.

The church of St. Phillip in the village of Zebbug is illuminated with hundreds of multi coloured light bulbs for the festa, the most important event in any village's calendar.

Between May and October every town and village in Malta and Gozo celebrates the feast day or 'festa' of its patron saint. The festa is the most important event in each village's annual calendar and the villagers eagerly look forward to this very special day. Considerable preparation goes into these celebrations. The village church is draped with red damask and decorated with beautiful flowers. All its gold and silver treasures are put on display thus creating a fitting setting for the statue of the patron saint, which is placed in a prominent position in the Church. The church façade is illuminated with hundreds of multicoloured bulbs, as also are the streets, across which are suspended massive and colourful drapes. Hundreds of flags are flown from rooftops whilst drapes and light bulbs are hung across the width of the covered balconies, which are typical of the traditional houses.

Visitors to a village market held on the festa weekend, admire the local produce for sale, the proceeds of which are given to a local children's charity.

On the festa day, as the statue of the saint is carried shoulder-high along the streets of the village the church bells ring and massed bands play marches. Children throw confetti from balconies on to the passing procession. The nougat and candy floss stands do excellent business whilst the crowds walk up and down the village streets stopping every now and then for a drink or to greet an old friend. The noise reaches a crescendo, as the statue is about to re-enter the church; at this point there is normally a colourful fireworks display. The Maltese people specialise in the manufacture of fireworks and, in the inter-village rivalry, fireworks often constitute the benchmark for comparing the success of the various festas. During the summer season there is a festa practically every weekend and no holidaymaker should leave the Islands without visiting one.

Language
Most of the local people speak Maltese, the national language that is closely related to Arabic. However, they also have English as a second official language, and Italian is widely spoken as well.

The weather
The climate is warm and healthy. There are no biting winds, fog, snow or frost. Rain falls for only very short

Chadwick lakes which are at their most picturesque in the spring, also the surrounding countryside with colourful flowers in bloom.

periods, mostly during the late autumn and mid-winter, averaging about 578 mm (20 inches) in a year. The average temperature is 14°C in the winter months and the sun shines for an average of 6.4 hours each day. During the summer the average temperature is 32°C with the sun shining for an average of 10-11 hours each day, with the hottest period being from mid-July to mid-September. Normally the temperature will not rise above 35°C, even in the height of the summer, as the hot summer days and nights are regularly tempered by cool breezes from the sea.

A fishing boat returns to harbour at the end of the day to a perfect sunset.

Medical care

The Maltese Islands enjoy a high standard of medical care. There is a large General Hospital; Mater Dei in Malta and Craig Hospital Victoria in Gozo, there are also government health clinics in various towns. British nationals holidaying on the islands are entitled to one month's free medical and hospital care in Malta and Gozo. It is advisable to carry your EU Health Insurance card. Persons who are receiving medical treatment and who may need to carry medicine into the Maltese Islands or purchase fresh supplies locally would be well advised to carry a letter of introduction from their family doctor. Most British drugs are available.

Religion

Predominantly Roman Catholic but the Maltese Constitution guarantees freedom of worship. There are also churches belonging to various other religious denominations.

Taking a walk through the countryside these two young boys are being shown something of interest by their mother.

Shopping

Shops are usually open between the hours of 9 am and 7 pm. with a three or four-hour lunch break (siesta). Most well known brands of all items you may require are available in pharmacies, shops and supermarkets. In commercial areas frequented by tourists however, most shops remain open until approximately 10 pm but close earlier during the winter months. Half the joy of planning a day out in Malta or Gozo is that it is easy to combine both sightseeing and shopping; there are many bargains to be had. You may be able to pick up a painting by one of the many local artists or find an unusual piece of jewellery, made from gold or silver and very reasonably priced.

Maltese lace can be bought in the form of shawls, soft furnishings or trimmings. Hand knitted woollens and Arran styles can be purchased and are of exceptional value and anyone who is fond of glass or pottery is spoiled for choice. If you want to get all your shopping out of the way in one go, visit the Crafts Village at Ta'Qali in Malta or the Craft Village near San Lawrenz in Gozo. At both these villages you can watch potters, glassblowers, and filigree craftsmen at work.

Currency

The local currency is the euro. Major credit cards can be used, other currencies can be exchanged at banks, hotels, most retail outlets and restaurants.

Many of these greengrocery stalls are to be found at the side of the road selling lovely local fresh fruit and vegetables.

Phone card

A phone card is a useful purchase, as most telephones boxes are card only. Cards can be purchased from most retail outlets.

Electricity

Electricity supply is 240 volts, single phase, 50 cycles. The square fitting standard three-pin British plugs and sockets are used.

Water

Although the tap water is perfectly safe to drink I would recommend that you use bottled water for drinking, which is reasonably priced and can be purchased almost anywhere, and use tap water for making hot drinks and cooking.

Sea salt is still gathered from the salt pans and locally, in the photograph above the gentleman has carved a small shop from the sandstone cliff. Xwejni Bay, Gozo.

Key to symbols

Dive centre			Location pointer
Camp site		**P**	Parking
Church			Playground
Cinema			Pleasure boats
180°	Compass bearing		Restaurant
Sea grass			Telephone
Short marine growth			Toilet (WC)
32 m	Depth in meters		Viewpoint

Information

(32m)	Depth in meters		
Directional arrows			Building
Distance marker		NOTE:	Information notice
E1	Entry & exit points		One way system
Footpath or route			Rough road or track
Information marker		BEWARE	Warning notice

Chadwick Lakes in the spring.

Month	Hours of Sunshine	Rain		Temperature (in °F/°C)				Sea	
		ins	mm	Max		Min			
				°F	°C	°F	°C	°F	°C
January	5.46	3.5	90.1	59	15.1	49	9.5	58	14.5
February	6.36	2.4	60.8	60	15.3	49	9.3	58	14.5
March	7.33	1.8	44.7	62	16.5	51	10.2	58	14.5
April	8.46	0.9	24.0	66	18.8	54	11.9	62	16.1
May	9.99	0.4	8.9	71	23.1	59	15.1	65	18.1
June	11.23	0.2	3.8	82	27.4	66	18.6	70	21.1
July	12.15	0.04	0.9	83	30.2	70	21.2	75	24.5
August	11.36	0.3	8.8	84	30.6	70	21.8	76	24.5
September	9.00	1.6	40.0	82	27.8	69	20.4	77	25.0
October	7.22	4.9	123.6	67	23.8	63	17.2	72	22.2
November	6.50	3.1	76.8	69	20.0	57	13.9	67	19.5
December	5.2	3.9	100.2	63	16.6	52	11.1	62	16.7

This table gives monthly averages taken over a period of 30 years for hours of bright sunshine, temperature and rainfall

MAIN PICTURE: *A diver with a torpedo above the Um el Faroud*

These small fish, pilchards (Sardina pilchardus) are abundant on this wreck during certain times of the year.
PHOTO: COLIN STEAD

Divers on the bow of the Um el Faroud acting out a scene from the film Titanic

Islands for divers

The Maltese Archipelago – the main Island of Malta, the smaller Island of Gozo and the tiny Island of Comino – is a real paradise for divers and snorklers. These Islands have fortunately retained their natural state due, to a large extent, to the sea and its fauna.

Apart from other positive aspects, one of the most important is that the Maltese Islands are an all year round centre for the diver. Throughout the spring and summer the sea temperature will normally rise to a maximum of 25°C however, from November to March the temperature will gradually fall, rarely going below 14°C. The climate and duration of sunshine at this time of year is similar to an average North European summer, sometimes even better. In stormy weather, these Islands still offer a sufficient number of sheltered interesting dive sites.

Entry point below the lighthouse at Cirkewwa.

Diving Centres/Schools

The islands offer a well-developed infrastructure for divers, representing a high standard and are capable of coping with the most sophisticated demands. A number of Maltese diving centres have organised themselves into the Association of Professional Diving Centres, with the result that the staff are well trained and responsible. Courses leading to international dive qualifications can be undertaken with a majority of dive centres on the islands. It is not necessary to take along your own equipment, as it is possible to hire all your diving equipment at favourable rates.

The Government have official inspectors who regularly check the centres and their equipment. Beginners and advanced divers will receive all help and assistance from the centres to ensure that their diving holiday in Malta is trouble-free and enjoyable. Diver safety is of primary concern.

Diver below the dive boat in the crystal blue waters which surround the Maltese Islands.

The diver, who wishes to dive independently and hire equipment, has to present a qualification certificate to the chosen dive centre, equivalent to at least the CMAS/2-Star (BSAC Sports Diver). You will be required to complete a self certificated medical form, any queries arising from completing this form could require a doctors medical, the cost of this is minimal. The dive centres have the right to request a doctors medical. This also applies to the individual who is undertaking dive guiding or training.

This young Damselfish (Chromis chromis) is an almost fluorescent shade of blue, the adults are a brownish colour

PHOTO: VICTOR FABRI, SUBWAY DIVE CENTRE

Diving for the disabled in Malta

The International Association for Handicapped Divers is an association whose aim is to promote, develop and conduct programmes for the training of the physically disabled in scuba diving. Since its introduction in 1993

Instructors being put through their paces on their IAHD course at Cirkewwa. There are a number of dive centres on the island of Malta who offer diver training for the disabled.

the IAHD has conducted numerous professional and non-professional programmes around the world. There are a number of centres in Malta who offer introductory dives and diver training for the disabled.

Government: protection of the sea and divers

Diving has a prominent position in the Maltese Islands, and with the assistance of the Maltese Government three aims are being followed

1. **Safety Standards for Diving.**
2. **Protection of the sea, its flora and fauna.**
3. **Protection of finds of cultural value.**

Spear fishing is absolutely forbidden. There are heavy fines and possible expulsion and/or confiscation of equipment according to the severity of the case.

Removal and non-reporting of any cultural finds is unlawful. It is a criminal act, which will lead to prosecution. Do not let temptation spoil your holiday, report any such findings to the officials directly or to your dive centre.

Speedboat traffic becomes increasingly busy in the height of the summer season. It is mandatory for dive boats to fly the 'A' flag when people are diving. Permission must be obtained for diving in a main harbour where the use of a Surface Marker Buoy is mandatory and I would also suggest it is used for your own safety when away from the protection of a reef.

These guidelines are in the diver's main interest and are practically self evident to any serious sports diver and coincide with regulations of practically all international diving clubs and centres. All of which are

Possibly the best wreck in the Mediterranean the bridge of the Um el Faroud.

pledged to maintain the fascination, freedom and contribution to the protection of the sea and its fauna and flora, also for the safety of this wonderful sport for future generations.

The sea around the Maltese Islands

The seas around Malta are virtually tideless; however sometimes there are underwater currents even when the sea is calm. At times these underwater currents will travel in the opposite direction to the wind and the surface sea conditions. The waters are still extremely clear and clean around the islands and for that reason certain rare species of fish can be found which unfortunately have vanished from other parts of the Mediterranean.

Brown Grouper (Epinephelus guazza) has a large oval body with a well developed head and large mouth. Lives on rocky bottoms with plenty of crevices measures up to 1 metre.

PHOTO: VICTOR FABRI, SUBWAY DIVE CENTRE

The individual diving site and the weather conditions influence the visibility under water in the Maltese Islands. But thanks to the overwhelmingly rocky coasts and the unpolluted water the visibility is often around 30 metres.

The rather strong topographic structures of the Maltese Islands continue beneath the surface. In this most bizarre underwater landscape of the Mediterranean you will find many caves, some large enough for a double decker bus, grotto's, crevices and undulating reefs with their magnificent and dramatic drop-offs, all these areas are home to many species of fish and an abundance of rich marine life. During recent years the government has arranged for nine ships, which have been made safe for divers to visit, to be scuttled. These have become artificial reefs and now conger, moray eels, cuttlefish and a multitude of other marine life live and hide within these wrecks; they have of course become an attraction for divers. Add these to the number of existing wrecks and the variety of reefs and caves; it is no wonder these islands are a mecca for divers.

Small shoal of Saddle bream (Oblada melanura) check out their new home where the Um el Faroud *has broken in half.*

Marine life

It would be difficult to list and comment on the many various species of fauna and flora to be found in the waters around the islands. It is important to say that the chance of meeting 'Big Game' fish or certain species of shark which maybe dangerous to man, is almost non-existent. Very seldom does anyone see tuna, dolphins or turtles as they rarely come close to shore.

Species which the diver will find around the Maltese Islands are barracuda, groupers, amberjack, various bream, various wrasse, damsel fish, octopus, squid, flying gurnard, stingrays, meagre, bogue, red mullet, painted combers, cardinal fish, parrot fish to name but a few. Conger and moray eels can be seen, the structure of the coast and the rocks seem to offer ideal living conditions for them, and they tend to be more visible during night dives. Also John Dory can be watched here occasionally, mostly during winter time since normally it lives at greater depths. Sea horses are

here too, possibly the best time to see them is July and August, but they are so small and very well camouflaged, you have to be very careful and patient to find them.

There are a few sea animals, which are beautiful to watch but dangerous to touch; they are not deadly but could be very painful. These include scorpion fish, jellyfish, the bristle worm, the weaver and the stingray.

Underwater photography

Maybe it's the crystal blue waters of the Mediterranean and the visibility below the surface that entices divers to the shores of the Maltese Islands, bringing with them their cameras to capture the delights of this underwater world. But first of all you need a buddy with good buoyancy skills and the patience to match. He needs to be a hunter to find some of the elusive marine life, gently persuading it towards the waiting camera, and in the meantime keeping himself as part of the backdrop if required. Around the islands' coastline there are a variety of underwater landscapes and artificial reefs, ranging from areas of sand, fields of sea grass tall and green, shallow reefs where the marine growth sparkles in the rays of the sun to the dramatic sheer drop-offs that disappear into the abyss.

In the clear waters around the Maltese Islands there are many opportunities for the underwater photographer, reefs, marine life, wrecks and caves. PHOTO: ALAN JAMES

The wrecks that have been scuttled to create artificial reefs are now inhabited by fish of many species, for they offer them a safe haven from predators. There is a kaleidoscope of colour to be found amongst the corals and marine life. Here the coral is not of gigantic size – sometimes small can be beautiful – with the vivid red and orange colours of the soft coral and sponges together with the not so colourful hard coral. Together with the many species of tubeworm gently swaying to catch their prey, and many other wonderful sights, all this adds up to the underwater photographer's paradise. Many of the local divers take very seriously the art of underwater photography; they enter many competitions within their dive clubs.

Divers enter the cave at the rear of the Blue Hole, Gozo, like many cave dives this simulates a night dive.

One of the most popular competitions called The Blue Dolphin has not been held in recent years, but is hoped to be revived in the near future. You may find at your dive centre that your instructor/guide is also an excellent underwater photographer.

Although there is a good selection of cameras to be hired or purchased, and some spares are available for emergency repairs of popular brands, I would suggest that you bring a spare set of O-rings and any other small items you may require for running repairs.

This excellent boat dive, on HMS Stubborn *which is still totally intact, a diver explores the area around the conning tower.*

Diving in winter offers the advantage that many species of fish move inshore to shallower, slightly warmer waters and as they are not disturbed by swimmers during this season the diver has even better opportunities for observation and photography than in summer.

Night diving

Night diving opens a whole new dimension for the experienced diver, and Malta is ideally suited for this kind of diving. At night the diver sees an entirely different variety of fish and the colours seen are more vibrant under a diver's torch. Most dive centres feature night diving in their programme and in the right conditions competent divers should enjoy this experience.

Not only a diving paradise

The Maltese Islands are in no way only a diving paradise. They are in many other respects real islands of adventure and stimulating experiences. Their thousands of years old history is documented to the visitor of today in the form of many exciting findings and attractions. Starting with the 6,000 year old megalithic temples of the earliest inhabitants, there are many artefacts dating back to the time of the Phoenicians, Greeks and Romans. The proud buildings and cathedrals of the Knights of St. John and their relevant heritage, down to the many remnants of the last war in which Malta again was a dramatic centre-point of activities in the Mediterranean – a role Malta has had to bear throughout its age old history. Further information on places of interest to visit on Malta, Gozo and Comino can be found from page 197.

SPECIAL NOTES

If this is your first visit to the Maltese Islands or you have any doubts in your dive planning or navigational skills I would strongly recommend that you visit a local dive centre for an orientation dive or escorted diving. You will find that they are friendly and only too pleased to assist you in any way they can.

It is a requirement of Maltese law that a Surface Marker Buoy should be used when diving in a harbour and in some cases permission must be granted from the Harbour Master to dive there. I would also strongly recommend when your dive plan takes you away from the reef into open sea that you carry a DSMB

Would readers please note that the illustrations of the underwater plans and road maps to be found in the following pages have been made as accurate as possible. They are to compass bearings: but not to scale, information for distance and time can be found within the text.

Although every effort to ensure that the information given on the dive sites was as accurate as possible, other information given in this book was correct at the time of going to press, the author accepts no responsibility for any loss, injury or inconvenience sustained by any person using this book.

PGL AERIAL PHOTOS

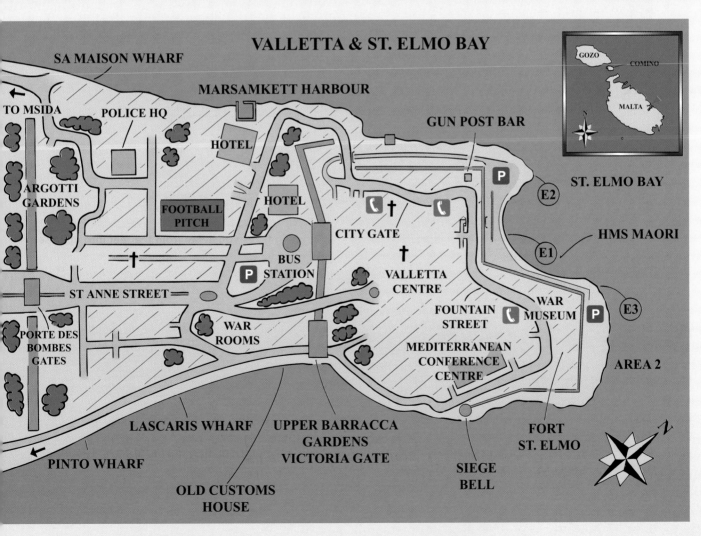

VALLETTA & ST. ELMO BAY

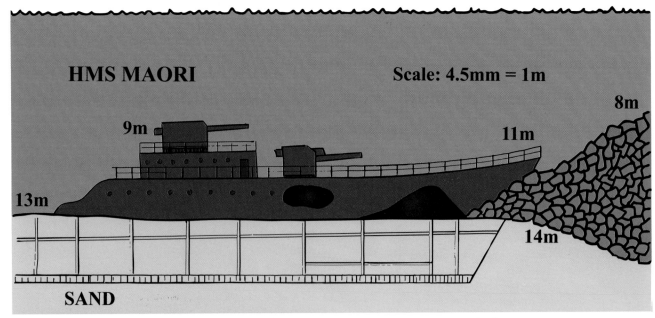

HMS MAORI

Scale: 4.5mm = 1m

Details of HMS Maori *under the water showing the wreckage which is above and below the seabed.*
The two guns shown in the diagram were removed and used as shore batteries.

HMS Maori *outside Grand Harbour and in the foreground two Maltese gondolas.*
PHOTO: BY KIND PERMISSION OF JOSEPH BONNICI,
AUTHOR OF "A CENTURY OF THE ROYAL NAVY IN MALTA".

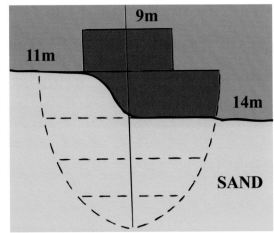

HMS Maori *leaving Grand Harbour with Fort St. Angelo in the background. Numerous attempts have been made to trace the owner of this photograph, which is displayed in many dive centres in Malta.*

St. Elmo Bay – Valletta

St. Elmo Bay is situated on the south side of the entrance to Marsamxett harbour, on the lower level road, below the city walls on the northern side of Valletta.

Divers normally use this dive site when the weather conditions do not permit diving at the more popular dive sites, but in my opinion the *Maori* should be dived when the sea conditions elsewhere are good, your reward would be to find that you are the only divers here. Sometimes it is used for training purposes, for example compass navigation and the use of a Surface Marker Buoy, to and from the wreck. In the early spring or late autumn this site is best dived before the sun begins to set behind the city walls, causing a giant shadow over the bay, therefore reducing the natural sunlight at the end of the dive, also making it quite cool when changing.

Divers at the most popular entry/exit point for HMS Maori.

HMS *Maori*

This 1959-ton Tribal Class British Destroyer, built by Fairfield in Govan, England, was launched on 2nd September 1937, with an overall length of 115m, breadth 11m, main armament 8 x 4.7in guns, 4 x 21in torpedo tubes, twin screws with a speed of 36 knots and a crew of 190 men. During World War II HMS *Maori* was involved in the following campaigns: April/May 1940 – Norway; Bismark – May 1941; Malta Convoys during 1941 and 1942. She was one of the four destroyers which sank two Italian cruisers near Cape Bon on the 13th December 1941.

During the early hours of 12th February 1942 HMS *Maori* was moored in Grand Harbour, Valletta, when a parachute flare dropped by enemy aircraft became trapped in her foremast. Soon after the illuminated destroyer received a direct hit by a bomb and caught fire. She was abandoned and shortly afterwards the aft magazine exploded. The destroyer sank stern first causing the bows to rise out of the sea. During that afternoon she slowly filled with water and sank.

In 1945 she was cut in two and the forepart was re-

The main deck and part of the upper structure of HMS Maori *as she is today.*   PHOTO: IAN FORDER, SUBWAY DIVE CENTRE

floated, then towed to St. Elmo Bay near the entrance to Marsamxett harbour and is still there today. The aft section was re-floated and sunk in deep water off the island.

Area 1 – Route 1

THE DIVE   Minimum time – 30 mins

Route 1 is to use the most popular entry point E1 at the bottom of the steps, which can be very slippery; the depth here is less than 2m so care must be taken when entering the water. From this point take a compass bearing of 20°-30°. The distance is some 120 metres to the wreck and it will take you around 6 minutes at a slow fin to reach the top of the rocky slope, here the depth will be 8 or 9m. Continue down and over the rocky slope onto the sand. Your direction now depends on the depth, if you find yourself at 13m or more, turn right or if less than 10m turn left. The *Maori*'s bows are against the rocky slope (see plan).

A shell case uncovered by rough seas on the starboard side.

Area 1 – Route 2

■ THE DIVE   Minimum time – 30 mins

If you have parked your car opposite the café and you are intending to exit at the bottom of the steps, E1, then once you are kitted up follow the footpath that runs in a westerly direction to the end of the sea wall. From here you will have to walk over the rocks to the most northerly point, where you will find a gentle slope giving easy access to the water, E2. When under the water take a north compass bearing and in less than 2 minutes you will reach the top of the rocky slope at 10m. Continue down and over the rocky slope to your chosen depth or to the sandy bottom at 30m. Once you have reached your chosen depth, keeping the rocky slope on your right, head in an easterly direction. It will take you approximately 10 minutes at a slow swim to reach the *Maori* at 14m. At a depth of 18m you will find a smooth step/slope in the sand, turn away from the rocky slope and head out over the sand for about 2 minutes, you will find a single rock called Photo Rock – a great place for macro photography.

Exploring HMS *Maori* and return route

The deepest part of this dive is on the starboard side of the wreck; here you will find two large holes, which will enable you to enter the forward hold. It is possible to swim through the whole length of this wreck if the conditions are favourable, but remember that silt can be a problem, also keep in mind that the wreck has been here for well over sixty years, so the weak structure could be dangerous. If the visibility is good, move away from the main structure and explore the wreckage, which lies on the sand in an area at the rear of the *Maori*.

Then return, swimming above the deck towards the front, here you will find the brass base of the front gun; unfortunately both guns were removed and re-used as shore battery guns during the Second World War. Do not leave the wreck without visiting the upper structure; here the depth is 9m.

The marine growth, the many small fish and occasionally young morays' are to be found here, with good visibility and sunlight it makes this an ideal spot for photography. Leave the wreck by the bows and continue up the rocky slope, from here your exit point has a compass bearing of 200°.

This shallow area allows you to spend time, if you have the air, to look around on your way back, if you are lucky you may see large shoals of salema fish. The best place to exit the water is just to the right of entry point E1, where there are two smooth flat steps in the rock below the water level, which I call the 'Throne', making an easy exit, even when there is a small swell. You can of course plan your own dive to *Maori* using alternative routes.

Marine life

Marine life that can be found here are small morays', cuttlefish, red mullet digging in the sand, scorpion fish, flatfish, little blue neon fish and occasionally large shoals of salema fish. This site is good for a night dive, a time to catch sight of the little commensal anemone, almost always with the hermit crab.

A diver enters the wreck of HMS Maori *from one of the various openings.*   PHOTO: JESPER KJØLLER, DYK MAGAZINE

Exploring HMS Maori, *hoping to find some unusual marine life.*   PHOTOS: JESPER KJØLLER, DYK MAGAZINE

PGL AERIAL PHOTOS

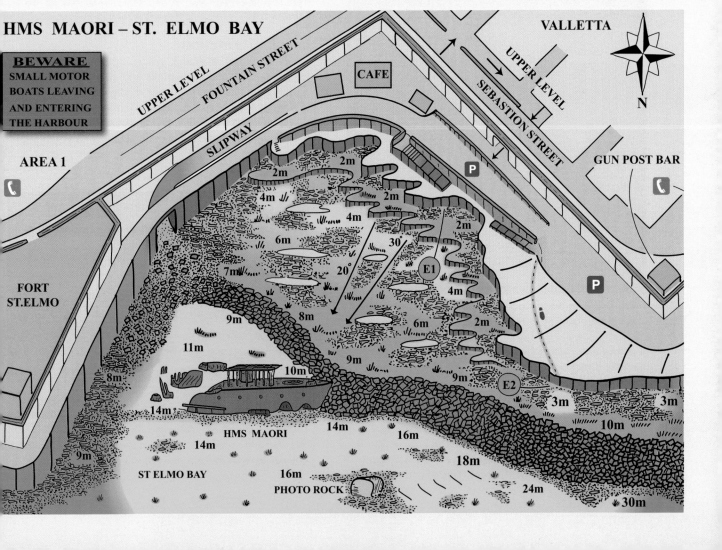

HMS MAORI – ST. ELMO BAY

BEWARE
SMALL MOTOR
BOATS LEAVING
AND ENTERING
THE HARBOUR

VALLETTA

UPPER LEVEL

FOUNTAIN STREET

CAFE

UPPER LEVEL

SEBASTION STREET

N

AREA 1

SLIPWAY

P

GUN POST BAR

2m
2m
4m
2m
4m
6m
30°
2m
7m
20°
E1
8m
4m
FORT
ST.ELMO
9m
6m
2m
11m
9m
10m
E2
8m
9m
14m
3m
3m
14m
16m
10m
HMS MAORI
14m
18m
9m
ST ELMO BAY
16m
24m
PHOTO ROCK
30m

Fort St. Elmo – Valletta

This dive site is situated between the entrance to Grand Harbour and Marsamxett Harbour, to find this site, continue along the lower level road past the café to the furthest point. This dive should not be attempted in rough sea conditions, as exit would be difficult.

Area 2

THE DIVE   Minimum time – 30 mins

The entry point I would normally use would be E3, it is almost on the corner right by the car parking area, where you will find a number of steps cut into the rocks, however it is extremely difficult to exit the water here even with a de-kit exit routine. Your exit points, of which there are three, are marked with an E on the plan. Normally I would exit the water from one of the two little pools, one each side of entry point E3, they both have steps cut in the rock to enable you to exit the water. The exit point to the south of your entry point, E3, requires the use of a stepladder to enable you to reach road level. Be sure to check that the ladders are there, as they are usually removed during the winter months.

A diver explores the reef on this less frequented dive location in the waters off Fort St. Elmo.

Using entry point E3 surface swim round in an easterly direction until in front of the black post, descend to the seabed, from here take a north to northeast compass bearing and within 3 minutes you should reach a depth of 12-13m with a drop off down to 20m, this is the start of the main reef. From here travel in an easterly direction follow the base of the drop off, after some 6 minutes you will reach a valley which runs to the top of the reef. This of course can be

A baby moray (Muraena helena) at home in a large rock surrounded by a red sponge (Crambe crambe).

your turning point or you can continue until reaching a depth of 35m then ascend to the top of the reef, now head in a westerly direction until reaching the top of the valley. A compass bearing from here of 180° will take you to the coastline reef and a depth of 9m; from here to your exit point keep the reef on your left.

Alternatively you could plan your own dive using the same entry/exit points and the coastline reef for your navigation. I found this site to be a place to explore and rummage with a maximum depth of approximately 16m, within this large area there are many gullies, small rocks and boulders to explore. This dive would also be suitable for a second dive or training. A wide variety of marine life can be found here, such as moray octopus, groupers, damselfish, red mullet and shoals of salema fish.

Local information

There is a small cafe here, which is quite reasonable; they serve hot and cold drinks and also snacks. Once again it is advisable not to leave any valuables in your car, unless you have a non-diver with you.

Please note that it is a requirement of Maltese law that a Surface Marker Buoy should be used when diving in the harbour.

This type of tubeworm (Serpula vermicularis) is brightly coloured and uses the tentacles around its head for feeding. Any passing shadow or contact causes instant retraction of the fan into its tube.   PHOTO: DEREK CHIRCOP

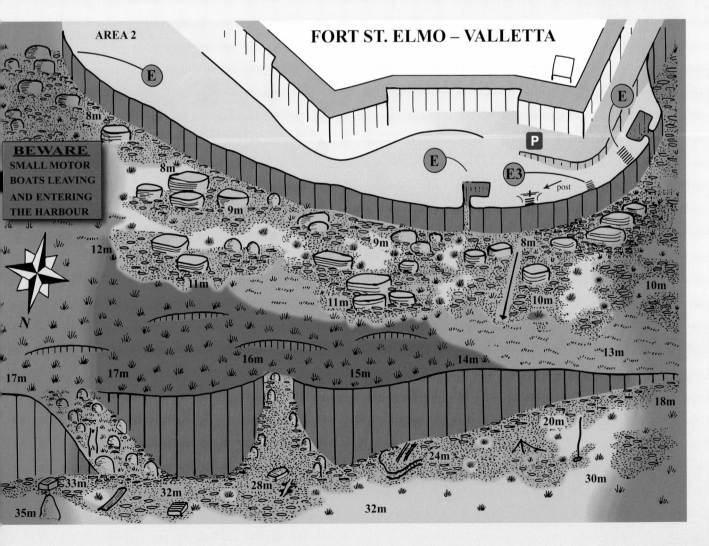

AREA 2

FORT ST. ELMO – VALLETTA

BEWARE
SMALL MOTOR
BOATS LEAVING
AND ENTERING
THE HARBOUR

PGL AERIAL PHO[TO]

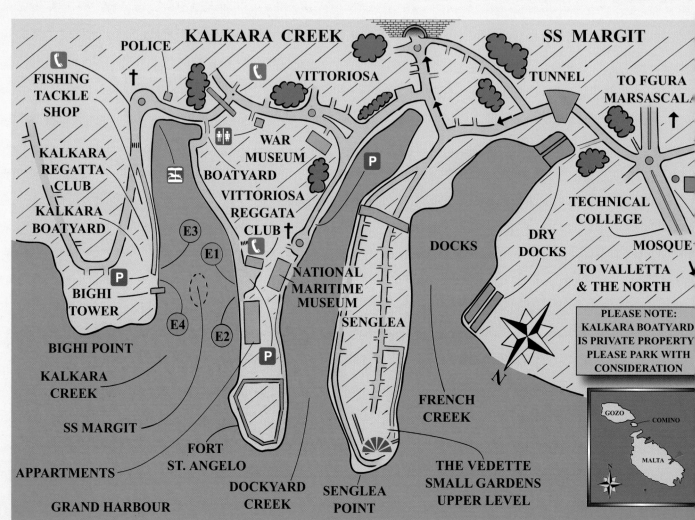

KALKARA CREEK

SS MARGIT

POLICE

FISHING
TACKLE
SHOP

VITTORIOSA

TUNNEL

TO FGURA
MARSASCALA

KALKARA
REGATTA
CLUB

WAR
MUSEUM

KALKARA
BOATYARD

BOATYARD

VITTORIOSA
REGGATA
CLUB

TECHNICAL
COLLEGE

E3

DRY
DOCKS

MOSQUE

E1

DOCKS

BIGHI
TOWER

NATIONAL
MARITIME
MUSEUM

TO VALLETTA
& THE NORTH

E4

SENGLEA

PLEASE NOTE:
KALKARA BOATYARD
IS PRIVATE PROPERTY
PLEASE PARK WITH
CONSIDERATION

E2

BIGHI POINT

KALKARA
CREEK

FRENCH
CREEK

SS MARGIT

GOZO

COMINO

APPARTMENTS

FORT
ST. ANGELO

MALTA

GRAND HARBOUR

DOCKYARD
CREEK

SENGLEA
POINT

THE VEDETTE
SMALL GARDENS
UPPER LEVEL

N

Kalkara Creek

Kalkara Creek is situated on the eastern side of Grand Harbour on the opposite side of the water to Valletta. On one side of the creek is the city of Vittoriosa and on the lower level road is the home of their regatta club, here is a very convenient car park right next to entry points E1 and E2. I personally prefer this side due to the parking. Over on the north side of the creek is the disused lift tower to the old Bighi Hospital, next door is the Kalkara boat yard, although it is private property they will allow you to park here if space is available, please park with consideration for others. Then there is the Kalkara Regatta club house; both of these clubs will allow you to use their facilities when open. The SS *Margit* sits upright at a depth of 22m on a silty seabed and lies almost in the centre of the creek, parallel with the shore line and her bow faces towards the entrance of the creek, so which entry point you choose is up to you.

SS *Margit*

This 3496 ton passenger ship, 105.5 metres in length with a 13.7 metre beam, was built in 1912 by Forges & Chantiers de la Mediteranee at La Seyne (Yard No. 1055) and named 'Theodore Mante' over the next twenty seven years her name was changed several times, *Mustaapha II*, *Djebel Antar* and *Gatun*, in 1939 she was re-named *Margit*.

She arrived in Malta at 1700hrs on 17th April 1939 from Marseilles under a Panamanian flag. She stayed in Malta for the next two years and whilst waiting for a crew, war broke out. During the early hours of 19th April 1941, while moored to buoy No. 14 at the entrance to Kalkara Creek, an air raid by Ju87s took place between 0310-0557 hrs, she was hit, set on fire, listed to port and sank. Only her two masts remained sticking out of the water to mark her grave. In 1943 the two masts and her funnel were removed by explosives, this was to make No 14 berth available for use during the forthcoming invasion of Sicily.

Wreck No 37448 Admiralty Chart HN/52.

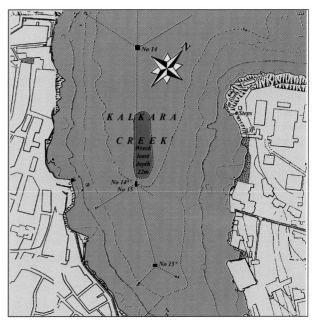

This old chart shows the wreck site of the SS Margit *and the network of massive chains which I am led to believe were moorings for battle ships and aircraft carriers.*

SS Margit *moored on buoys number 14 and 14a in Kalkara Creek, in the background is Fort St. Angelo.*

PHOTO: BY KIND PERMISSION OF JOSEPH CARUANA, THE MALTA MARITIME MUSEUM

Puzzle of names

SS *ODILE* – SS *MARGIT*

Many Maltese in post-war years claimed that the ship sunk at buoy No. 14 on the 19th April 1941 was the ex-Italian *Odile*. In the mid 1980s the National War Museum Association of Malta made an investigation about merchant ships named Odile in World War II. There was no Italian ship named *Odile* during the war – indeed there was no ship of that name in World War I. Only one *Odile* could be traced, a 3206 GRT steamer built in 1907 which was re-named *Katvaldis* in 1929 or 1930; as *Katvaldis*, she was torpedoed and sunk in the Atlantic on 24th August 1942.

How did this name *Odile* come about?

On the 9th June 1940 an Italian steamer named *Rodi* arrived in Malta under arrest of the Contraband Control Service. When Italy declared war, on the 10th June she was still in Malta and she was seized. She was moored to buoy No. 14, when on the 9th July 1940 the Royal Navy took her and other merchant ships to Alexandria so that they were not caught up in the war. The *Rodi* was taken away; she was renamed the *Empire Patrol* and was sunk in 1945. She was replaced at buoy No. 14 by the *Margit*. **Up to here is fact.**

What follows is conjecture!

Note: *Rodi* has 3 letters in sequence ODI – **R**ODI
 Odile has 3 letters in sequence ODI – **ODI**LE

Now in June 1940 the British authorities suspected Malta was a hive of Italian spies. So, perhaps, to mislead these spies, they painted out the R of RODI and added LE, thus making the ship apparently to be named the ODILE and was so seen by the Maltese. Shortly after this time most of the inhabitants of Bighi and Kalkara were evacuated to the country, so that when they returned they failed to realise that the ship which was moored at buoy No. 14 was not the same ex-Italian ship that was there before they were evacuated – one could well imagine that 2 years of rust had made the ships' name unreadable. So they continued to think that the ship was the one they knew as the ex-Italian named RODI.

Research for this puzzle was kindly conducted by Joseph Caruana

A diver explores inside the hull where some of the wreckage stands 5 metres proud of the seabed.

Even in the, sometimes dark waters of Kalkara Creek the bright colour of the little nudibranch (Flabellina affinis) stands out.

THE DIVE
Minimum time – 30 mins

This is an interesting dive, although within the harbour it is still possible to get good visibility but not if there is a strong north easterly wind or you are following a group of divers. The best time to dive this wreck is when sea conditions are good elsewhere. The normal rule is if you can see the seabed at your entry point then the viz should be reasonable.

Depending on which side of the creek you have decided to enter the water it is the same procedure: surface swim to your transit points. You can of course descend at your entry point and swim under the water to the wreck, to do this you will need the following compass bearings: from E1 30° from E2 60° and from E3 270° (**beware of boat traffic, a few of the smaller pleasure boats pass over the wreck, so an SMB is essential**).

If you get your transit right, you should land some 25m along the wreck from the stern, if the visibility is not too good, the starboard side of the wreck is the easiest to navigate along, and in places it is proud of the seabed by as much as 5 metres. Points to note or look for are: the stern mooring chain, prop shaft, gangway and supports, engine room with the piston rods, upper structure of the forward deck, the bow

The end of the prop shaft housing where the propeller has been removed.

mooring buoy and chain. There are a variety of fish on the wreck, but look out for nudebranchs, to see these colourful little creatures on this silt covered wreck is quite remarkable.

These huge mooring buoys were once floating on the surface and chained to mooring blocks and massive chains which laid on the seabed.

A fire extinguisher lies in the wreckage of the SS Margit.

Remains of a lifeboat on the SS Margit.

Return route to the Kalkara side

Your route to this side will also take approximately 5 minutes to clear the silty seabed and a further 5 minutes to reach 9-6m, compass bearing 60°. Around this depth you will find what wreckage remains of the Hunt Class Minesweeper HMS *Abingdon*. In April 1942 she was hit during an air raid and she began to take on water, she was beached in front of Bighi tower, probably to save cluttering up the valuable space along the wharf. She was discarded as a total loss on the 2nd June 1944.

After completing your dive your best exit point is E4 in front of the tower, it means a short walk but it is better than going over the large slippery rocks near to entry point E3.

This entry point is next to the Kalkara boatyard, there is no real difference in distance to the wreck, as to which entry is used, it is just a matter of choice and normally depends on which shallow waters you wish to end your dive. In the winter months it may be more pleasant on this side due to the sun position.

Return route to the Vittoriosa side

Once you have left the wreck it will take you at least 5 minutes to clear the silty seabed and a further 5 minutes to reach a depth of 9m and more shallow water, an approximate compass bearing of 230°.

Just off the harbour wall around this depth are small areas of wreckage, small rocks and also a little reef – lots to explore and the wall itself is alive with marine life, soft corals, cuttlefish, small morays, sea hares and many other small fish – a really good area for macro photography. If your planned exit is E1, a de-kit will be required or you can exit at the steps at E2.

This entry point is situated on the Vittoriosa side of Kalkara Creek which is opposite the old Bighi Hospital and lift.

ABOVE: *Conger eels (Conger conger.Linnaeus) are experts in finding good hiding places within wrecks.*
PHOTO: KEVIN DEBATTISTH, SUBWAY DIVE CENTRE

LEFT: *Exploring the engine room; a diver locates a piston.*

PGL AERIAL PHOTOS

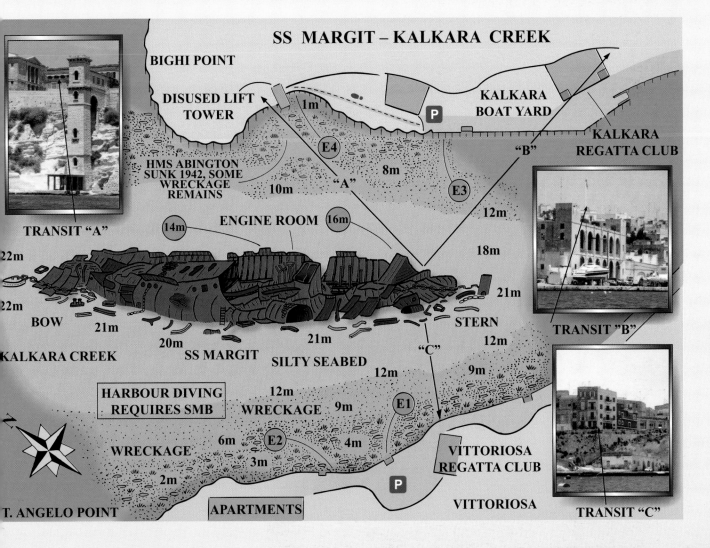

SS MARGIT – KALKARA CREEK

BIGHI POINT

DISUSED LIFT TOWER

KALKARA BOAT YARD

KALKARA REGATTA CLUB

1m

E4

"B"

HMS ABINGTON SUNK 1942, SOME WRECKAGE REMAINS

8m

"A"

10m

E3

12m

TRANSIT "A"

14m

ENGINE ROOM

16m

18m

22m

21m

TRANSIT "B"

22m

BOW

21m

STERN

12m

KALKARA CREEK

20m

SS MARGIT

21m

SILTY SEABED

"C"

12m

HARBOUR DIVING REQUIRES SMB

12m

WRECKAGE

9m

9m

E1

WRECKAGE

6m

E2

4m

VITTORIOSA REGATTA CLUB

3m

2m

APARTMENTS

VITTORIOSA

T. ANGELO POINT

TRANSIT "C"

PGL AERIAL PHO

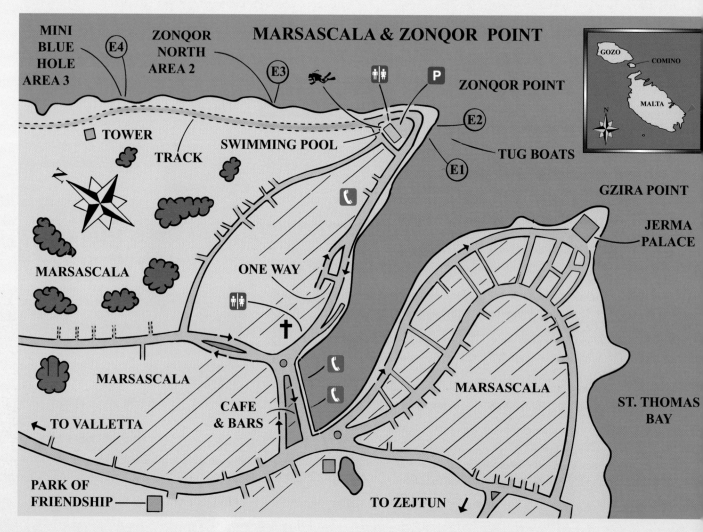

MARSASCALA & ZONQOR POINT

MINI BLUE HOLE AREA 3

(E4)

ZONQOR NORTH AREA 2

(E3)

ZONQOR POINT

(E2)

TUG BOATS

(E1)

□ TOWER

TRACK

SWIMMING POOL

GZIRA POINT

JERMA PALACE

MARSASCALA

ONE WAY

MARSASCALA

MARSASCALA

ST. THOMAS BAY

← TO VALLETTA

CAFE & BARS

PARK OF FRIENDSHIP ──☐

TO ZEJTUN ↙

GOZO

COMINO

MALTA

N

Marsascala – Zonqor Point

Situated on the south east coast of Malta, on the north side of the entrance to Marsascala Bay is an area of land jutting out into the sea, this is called Zonqor Point. When driving into Marsascala from Valletta watch out for the central reservation, here you will need to turn left into a one-way system before you reach the harbour, this route will take you along the north side of Marsascala bay to Zonqor Point. On your return the one-way system takes you past the cafes and little bars on the water front. At Zonqor Point there is a large swimming pool, often referred to as the National Pool, a new Olympic sized pool and complex is now situated between Valletta and Sliema. Within this area there are a number of dive sites, I have selected three: the tugboats *St. Michael* and *10*, Zonqor Point North and the Mini Blue Hole. These dives add to the variety of diving on the island, it is an ideal venue, for training, second dive or just want to be away from the crowd. It tends to be more crowded especially when sea conditions are not perfect on the north and west coasts.

Marsascala harbour with many pavement cafes to sit at and pass the time soaking up the sun.

Tugboats – *St. Michael* and *10*

The tugboats *St. Michael* and *10* were scuttled on the 16th May, 1998, as part of a plan to create an artificial reef at Zonqor Point in Marsascala. At a maximum depth of 22m they are both upright on a flat sandy bottom and have created an oasis for marine life, transforming an ecologically barren area into a shore dive location which is accessible to divers of all levels. The site is particularly well chosen because it is protected from the prevailing north-westerly winds and can therefore be dived when other areas are unreachable due to bad weather conditions. The tugboats, 20 and 16 meters in length – the *St. Michael* being the longer – saw many years of service towing vessels around Grand Harbour, until they were moored at Jetties Wharf and left partially submerged. They underwent a clean up operation to be made environmentally and diver friendly – all glass, doors and hatches were removed and passageways opened to prevent divers who venture within from becoming trapped. The preparation, towing and scuttling operations were funded by Charles and Anthony Cassar Boat and Ship Repair Ltd of Marsa.

The tugboat St. Michael *being towed out of Grand Harbour towards its last resting place at Zonqor Point.*

PHOTO: BY KIND PERMISSION OF MARK BALUCI

▌THE DIVE — Minimum time – 40 mins

Here you have a choice of entry points. Using the nearest entry point E1, turn right after walking through the gap in the wall, when a small ridge appears on your left-hand side, follow it down to the waters edge, from here you will need a compass bearing of 140°. A slow swim, to reach the sand, will take you some 6-8 minutes, here the depth could be 19-20m and you will need to turn left, from here it could take you up to 2 minutes to reach the wreck. Your second choice E2, is to walk towards the salt pans at the far end, passing between the two little buildings, you will find a distinct cut-out in the shoreline from here your compass bearing is 180°.

Possibly the best way to do this dive is to use the nearest entry point E1, and surface swim out until you can just see the reef below you, then descend and follow the gently sloping reef down to the sand. If your depth is 21m you will be very close to the first tug. If your depth is 17m or less, turn left, more than 22m, turn right following the line where the reef meets the sand. Beware; the first area of sand may be covered by dead sea-grass making it difficult to determine where

the reef ends and the sand start especially in areas where the depth is 17m or less. The bows of tugboat *10* lie up against the base of the reef, with its stern some 3 metres away from it. The tugboat *St. Michael* lies some 60 metres off the bow of the first tugboat, taking a compass bearing of 90°, once moving off the wreck.

The *St. Michael* is situated approximately 15 metres from the reef, it is easy to see where the reef meets the sand, if the visibility is good it can be seen from the reef. Sometimes there is a line attached between the two tugs. When it is time to head for shallower waters, especially from the *St. Michael*, take a compass bearing of 330°-300° and follow the reef up to your required depth. At 9m and 6m below the furthest entry point, E2, the rocks and seabed are covered with marine growth of many colours and this makes an excellent area for photography. This is also an ideal place to test your skills in finding octopus and other marine life. To the west of the nearest entry point, E1, the reef becomes more rugged, but beware of the local fishermen if you travel too far along the reef in this direction before you exit the water.

The propeller and rudder of the tugboat St Michael.

The hull of tugboat 10 *is also covered in marine growth after sitting on the seabed since 1998, during my last visit there was a large electric ray resting on the deck.*

The hull of tugboat 10 *resting on a sandy seabed at a depth of 22m.*

The St Michael, *largest of the two tugboats, sitting upright on a sandy seabed at 22m.*

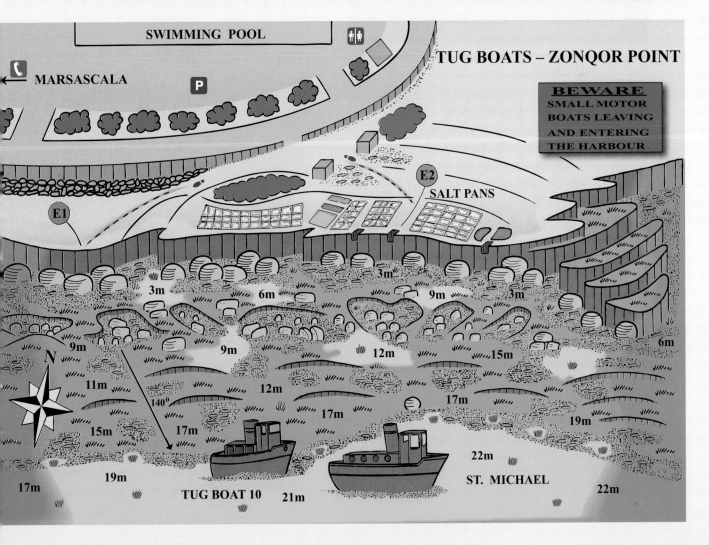

SWIMMING POOL

MARSASCALA

P

TUG BOATS – ZONQOR POINT

BEWARE
SMALL MOTOR
BOATS LEAVING
AND ENTERING
THE HARBOUR

E2

SALT PANS

E1

3m

3m

6m

9m

3m

9m

9m

6m

N

12m

15m

11m

12m

140°

17m

17m

19m

15m

17m

22m

17m

19m

17m

ST. MICHAEL

22m

TUG BOAT 10

21m

Zonqor Point North
Area 2

To find this site, follow the road round to the north side of the swimming pool, turn right along the single track for no more than 200 metres. Do not go too far along, as there are steps which lead down on to the smooth rocks below. See aerial photograph.

The entry point and parking area of this out of the way dive site north of Zonqor Point.

▌THE DIVE   Minimum time – 40 mins

Once you have kitted up go down the steps, turning slightly to the right, walk across the smooth rocks, here you will find a very small cove where there is an area of flatish rock just above sea level, entry point E3, here the depth is about 3.5m. The rocks by the sea are covered by a short soft marine plant, which makes it easy for exit, but be careful, as it can be slippery. Close to the shore are a number of large boulders with gullies to explore; you can of course head north or south along the coastline, I personally prefer to go north, this is what I consider to be the best area.

The further away from the shore you go, the boulders and gullies reduce in size, some 10 minutes out depth 9m, 20 minutes out depth 14m, you will be on the sandy seabed it will now take you a further 15 minutes to reach a depth of 20m. These times allow for looking around and exploring. Bear in mind that your entry point will also be your exit; if you try to exit the water at any other point you may find it to be quite difficult. There are many marine animals to identify, such as sea hares and octopus, once out on the sand keep an eye out for the different species of rays and flying gurnards.

TOP TO BOTTOM:
The flying gurnard (Dactylopterus volitans) does not fly above the surface like the flying fish, but opens its wings when threatened or to swim. Lives on sandy sea beds, usually in the shallows   PHOTO: GRAHAM OWEN
The red scorpion fish (Scorpaena scrofa) is the largest of the scorpion fish and lives among rocks at depths down to 100m or more. The dorsal fin is poisonous.
A flatfish almost circular in shape with the eyes on the left side of the head, the turbot (Psetta maxima) lives on sandy or fine shingle sea beds.
The turbot covers its body with fine shingle or sand with only its eyes visible. This camouflage enables it to hide from predators also to surprise its prey.

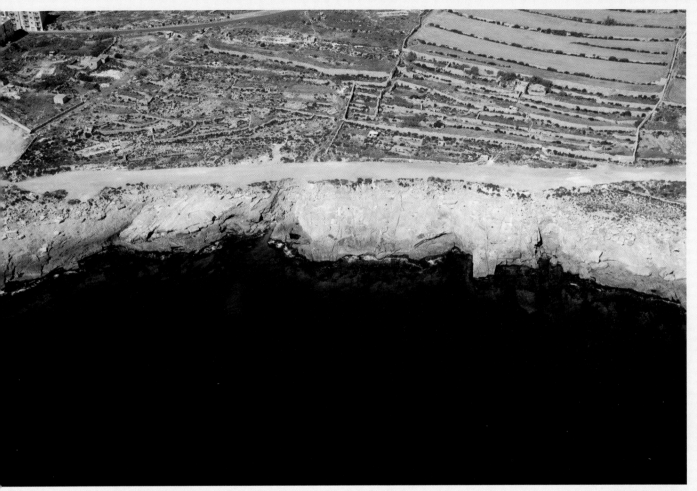

PGL AERIAL PHOTOS

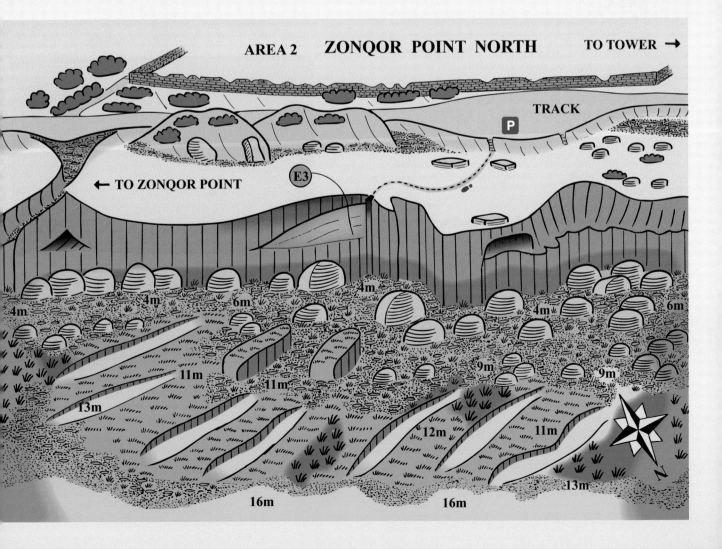

The unique mini blue hole north of Zonqor Point has a cave which leads out to the open sea.

The Mini Blue Hole

Area 3

This unique mini blue hole and the tunnel leading to the open sea, has been eroded by the sea over thousands of years. This site is some 700 metres from the entrance of the track and 100 metres south from the tower, the vehicle shown in the aerial photograph is where I suggest you park. It is important that you walk your route to the entry point before you rig. Entry point E4, here there is a shallow reef covered in some short reddish marine growth which makes for easy and soft access.

THE DIVE   Minimum time – 30 mins

Once you have entered the water move away from the reef and descend, a short way from the tunnel entrance you will find a depth of 7m. From here I suggest you enter the tunnel and explore, continue to the end, you will then find yourself at the bottom of the Mini Blue Hole at 4m, here you can admire what the sea has created or just take photographs. When you return to the entrance it is your choice which way you decide to go. Immediately along the shoreline in both directions, there are many rocks and boulders giving you interesting areas to explore especially if you have a camera. Here the seabed has a variety of depths, moving away from the shoreline the seabed starts to flatten out but within this area there are many little gullies with sandy bottoms and small reefs on each side making this a good habitat for hiding octopus and moray. Further out from the shore the seabed is mainly sand. Just bear in mind that your entry point is also your exit.

The pretty little nudibranch (Flabellina affinis) comes in varying shades of pink. Found on rocky beds from 5 to 50m. The maximum size is 4cm.   PHOTO: SHARON METSON, H2O DIVERS

After your chosen dive you will find there is a small cafe in the car park next to the swimming pool, this is normally only open during the summer months. Alternatively, the short journey to Marsascala centre is where you will find a choice of small bars and cafes which overlook the harbour where you can sit, soak up the sun and enjoy a much-deserved rest.

The moray (Muraena Helena) hides in holes and fissures in rocks with the head protruding, mostly nocturnal, the bite can be dangerous. This one has a cleaning shrimp (Lysmata seticaudata) who obviously is not afraid to clean the inside of this predator's mouth.   PHOTO: IAN FORDER, SUBWAY DIVE CENTRE

PGL AERIAL PHOTOS

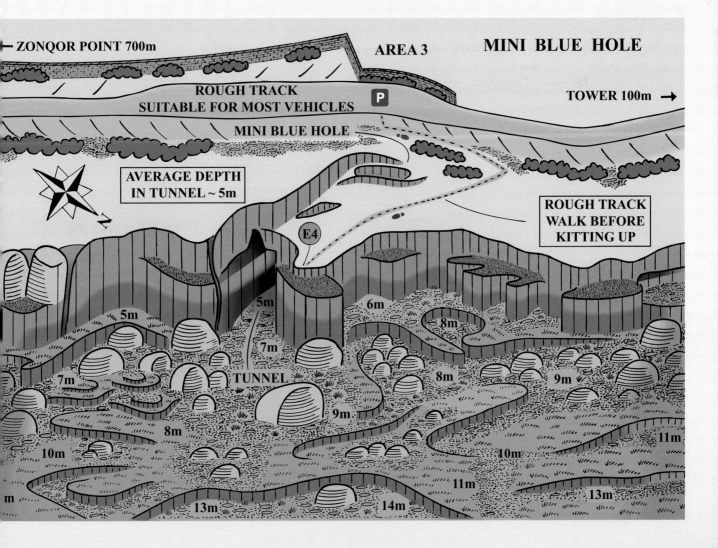

PGL AERIAL PHOT

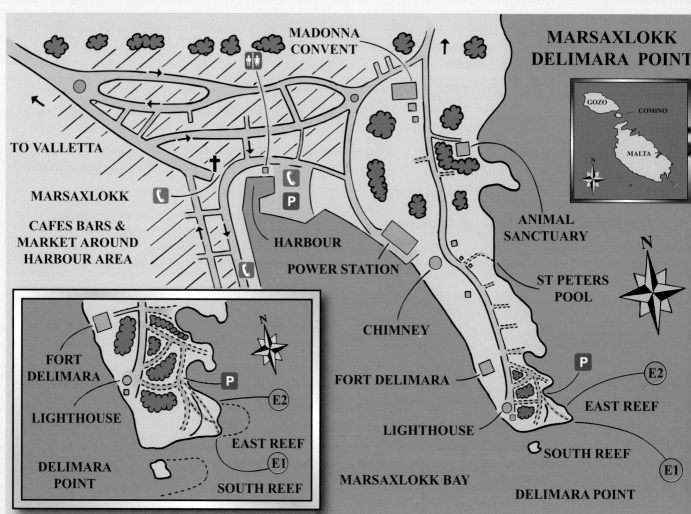

MADONNA CONVENT

MARSAXLOKK DELIMARA POINT

GOZO
COMINO
MALTA

TO VALLETTA

MARSAXLOKK

CAFES BARS & MARKET AROUND HARBOUR AREA

HARBOUR

POWER STATION

ANIMAL SANCTUARY

ST PETERS POOL

N

CHIMNEY

FORT DELIMARA

LIGHTHOUSE

SOUTH REEF

P

E2

EAST REEF

E1

MARSAXLOKK BAY

DELIMARA POINT

FORT DELIMARA

LIGHTHOUSE

DELIMARA POINT

P

N

E2

EAST REEF

E1

SOUTH REEF

Delimara Point

This dive site is situated on the south of the island, approximately 4.2km or a 15 minute drive from the town of Marsaxlokk, which is popular with visitors for its market, colourful boats and harbour. Once here, follow the signs out of the town leading to Delimara Power Station. At the large roundabout do not turn right to the power station, but keep straight on to Madonna Convent, here, turn right to Delimara Point, past the rear of the power station and keep going until you reach a small cross roads. The right hand track takes you to Delimara Fort; the left-hand track leads down to a derelict house and the sea. Continue straight on, after about 50 metres, fork left down a track, for a distance of approximately 500 metres. On your left you will pass two small brick built viewing platforms, next a little track off to your right and a short distance after this the track you require bears to the right. Follow this along and when you come out into the open with the sea on your left your parking area will be in front of you (see aerial photograph).

There are a number of ways that you can plan and dive this under rated dive site with excellent reefs, many over hangs and places to explore at depths of 30m plus. There are two main reefs in this area, for easy reference I will refer to them as East or South Reef. For the East Reef I have three dive plans and one for the South Reef. All dives start at entry/exit point E1. To reach your entry point there are two routes, both involve getting down onto the lower level where the salt pans are, by steps or steps and stones. See insert of local map. Once on the level with the salt pans head to your entry point E1. (I suggest that you check this out before you kit up) It requires a walk of 200 metres once you have kitted up, but in my opinion is well worth the effort, it was here that my buddy found the largest octopus that I have ever seen in Maltese waters, also a good area to locate the locust lobster. Depending on your required dive time it may be worth considering using a 15-litre cylinder for this dive site. Alternatively you can plan your own dive, but always use the reefs for your navigation.

The Delimara lighthouse and the tracks leading to the parking area of this out of the way dive location.

The Valley, which is part of South reef, a diver enjoys the excellent visibility often found here.

It must be noted that there is a possibility of strong currents in this area; if this is combined with poor visibility navigation will be extremely difficult. A good guide for visibility is that you should be able to see the seabed from your entry point.

East Reef

THE DIVE	Minimum time – 50 mins

The East Reef is shaped like the letter U and runs out from the furthest point of land in an easterly direction.

Dive plan 1. Once in and under the water follow the top of the reef in an easterly direction all the way along to the corner, where your depth will be 13m, this will take approximately 6 minutes. At this point there

Pilot fish (Naucrates ductor) a diver makes eye to eye contact with this energetic, inquisitive fish.

are normally large shoals of fish to see or photograph. Descend to the shelf at 17m and down to the bottom at 23m, continue your dive in an easterly direction. Within this area of grass, rugged boulders and sand you will find many places to explore. At a depth of approximately 30m and some 12 minutes into your dive you will find another small reef, if you follow this reef it will lead you in a northerly direction.

At this point you should bear in mind that to reach a depth of 10m or less on the East Reef, will take 8-10 minutes. If you travel along this small reef for approximately 50 metres or 4-5 minutes, then a westerly compass bearing will take you back to the East Reef, any further and you will require a more south-westerly bearing. Once you reach the East Reef, bear to your right, the end of this reef runs in a north-westerly direction, after a short time the direction changes to westerly until it reaches the coastline where you will have to bear right. After a short time the seabed below you will open up to a flat area of sand and small rocks with a depth of 9m, here you will be very close to E2 entry/exit point.

Octopus (Octopus vulgaris) lives in all types of marine habitats, usually hiding in holes, has excellent camouflage.

PHOTO: SHARON METSON, H2O DIVERS

Dive plan 2. Using entry/exit point E1 descend to the seabed at 13m, once away from the reef, head in an easterly direction keeping the main reef on your left, take your time to explore this area with its large boulders, overhangs, grass and small sandy patches. This is a good area for locating the locust lobster. After some 15-20 minutes, depending on the time taken exploring, you will come to an open area and a reef on your right dropping away to 30-35m. Continue along the ridge for approximately 3 minutes until you find a lone boulder at 25m, from this point take a northerly compass bearing to the corner of the East Reef, which should take no more than 3 minutes.

Tube dwelling anemone (Cerianthus membranaceus) this beautiful anemone exists on the sandy seabed: can be found from 5m down to 40m.

This is an excellent area where you normally find large shoals of fish, bring your camera. Now follow the reef, in a northerly direction, either at its base or on the top, after a short time the bearing of the reef will change to north-westerly towards the coastline, here turn right towards entry/exit point E2.

Dive plan 3. Using the same entry/exit point E1, descend to the seabed at 13m, leaving the main reef behind you, swim in a southerly direction and within 5 minutes another reef will appear in front of you, here your depth will be 16m. If you turn right the reef will take you to the little island just off Delimara Point, **but you need to turn left**. Now the dive will take an easterly direction until you reach the end of the reef, where the depth is 20m; to reach this point will take approximately 10-12 minutes. Continue in the same direction down over the grass and small rocks to an area of sand and a number of small boulders at 34m. Here the reef will be on your left, it is quite steep and rises up to 25m and to assist you with your bearings keep it in view. When it is time to return, ascend the reef to the top, follow it in a westerly direction along its ridge, until you reach the single boulder at 25m. When the visibility is good, from this point you will be able to see the corner on the East Reef, if not, take a northerly bearing and within 3 minutes you will reach the corner of the reef. At this point I would ascend to 13m at the top of the reef, then follow the ridge, on the south side of the East Reef, in a westerly direction to my entry/exit point E1.

PGL AERIAL PHOTOS

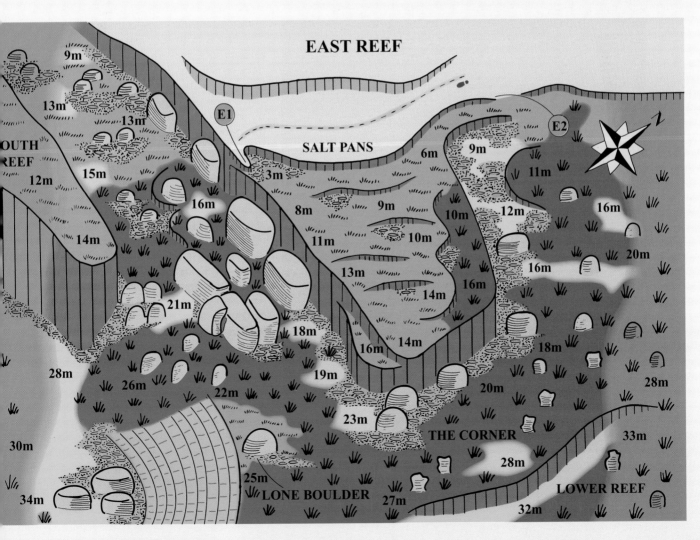

EAST REEF

9m

13m

13m

SOUTH REEF

12m

15m

14m

16m

21m

28m

26m

22m

30m

34m

E1

SALT PANS

3m

8m

9m

11m

13m

14m

10m

16m

16m

18m

19m

23m

25m

LONE BOULDER

27m

6m

9m

10m

12m

16m

14m

14m

16m

20m

THE CORNER

28m

32m

E2

11m

16m

20m

18m

28m

33m

LOWER REEF

South Reef

▊ THE DIVE
Minimum time – 55 mins

In my opinion this dive is for the experienced diver and should not be attempted from the shore in strong currents and/or bad visibility. For this dive the entry/exit point will be E1, once in the water, surface swim in a southerly direction for some 3 minutes, here you should be able to see the South Reef at 12m, if the visibility is reasonable. If you cannot see the seabed when entering the water, drop down to a depth of where you can and then continue in a southerly direction until you reach the reef. Continue over the top of the reef in the same direction until you can see the drop-off, which goes down to 26m. Descend onto the top of the reef, from here head in a westerly direction, slowly descending the reef and in this area you will find three large boulders which I have called the Three Peaks.

You can of course take time to explore this area; or continue along the base of the reef, which now runs in a southerly direction, its gentle sloping bottom will take you to a depth of 33m and onto the sand. If you wish to reach the cave from here, follow the reef in a southerly direction until you reach the end of the reef, at this point your depth will be 22m. From here when

Salema fish (Sarpa sarpa) can be found at depths between 2 to 20m feeding around the rocks and ledges which are rich in vegetation. PHOTO: VICTOR FABRI, SUBWAY DIVE CENTRE

the visibility is good you will be able to see Arrow Head Rock, otherwise a southerly compass bearing will take you across the valley to its base at 24m. The next reef is shaped like a U, follow it all the way round to its bottom, keeping it on your right hand side, your depth here is 23m continue to follow the reef it will curve into a southerly direction and in a short time you will see two large boulders on your right, they will be slightly obscuring the entrance to Abigails Cave at 18m.

Once inside the cave it is quite light due to two openings in the roof, fromwhich you will be able to exit easily onto the top of the reef at 16m. Your dive time is now possibly 35 minutes, bearing in mind that you are at least 20 minutes from your exit point. Your choice of return route depends on the time and air you have remaining, you can either reef hop from one to the other taking a north to north-easterly bearing which would be the most direct route to your exit point or you can navigate the tops of the reefs, only crossing at their narrowest parts back to your exit point. Of course at any time during your dive, if you wish, you could ascend to the top of the reef and return to your exit point

Remember that this site is well away from any amenities therefore if you require refreshments it is advisable to take them with you. **The nearest telephones are in Marsaxlokk; the Military post near the lighthouse will allow you to use their communications in an emergency, but it is not always manned.** If you do not have any non-divers with you do not leave any valuables in the car. You can of course after your dive, drive into Marsaxlokk, where there are a wide variety of cafes and bars situated along the harbour front. In the evening you may wish to return to one of the many restaurants that serve excellent local fish at reasonable prices. The market is a daily event, but the Sunday fish market is very popular, with not only the local people but also tourists, so you can expect heavy traffic and crowds of people in Marsaxlokk.

Part of South Reef and in the background Arrowhead Rock can clearly be seen

PGL AERIAL PHOTOS

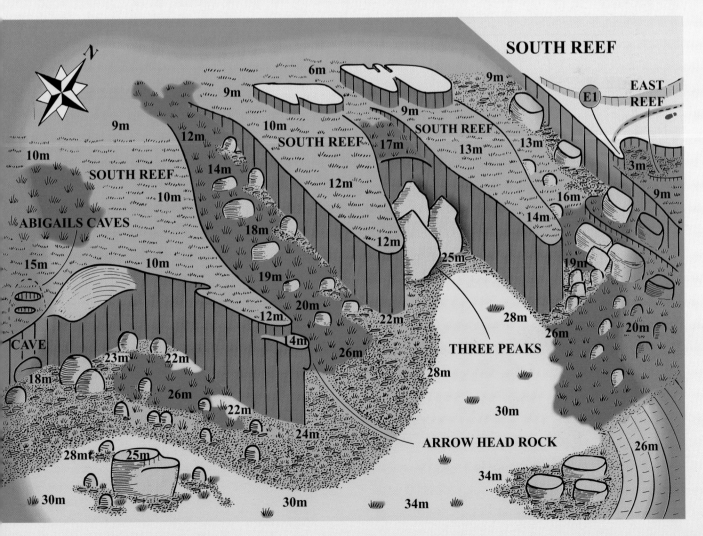

PGL AERIAL PHO

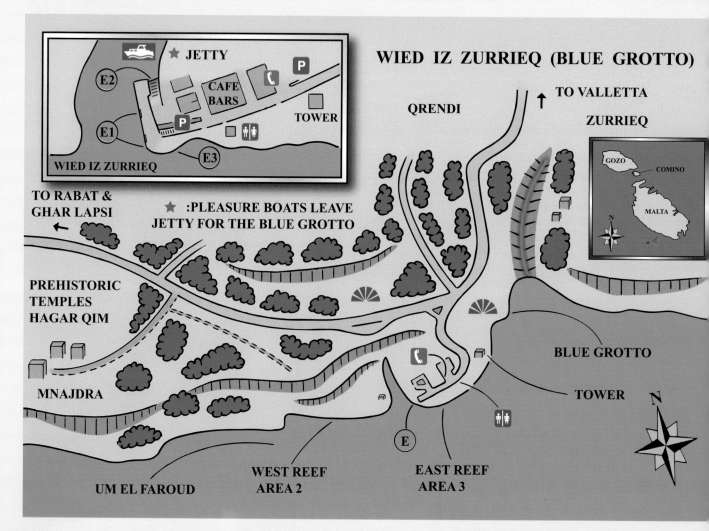

JETTY

CAFE
BARS

P

P

TOWER

E2

E1

E3

WIED IZ ZURRIEQ

WIED IZ ZURRIEQ (BLUE GROTTO)

QRENDI

TO VALLETTA

ZURRIEQ

GOZO

COMINO

MALTA

**TO RABAT &
GHAR LAPSI**

★ :PLEASURE BOATS LEAVE
JETTY FOR THE BLUE GROTTO

**PREHISTORIC
TEMPLES
HAGAR QIM**

MNAJDRA

BLUE GROTTO

TOWER

N

E

UM EL FAROUD

**WEST REEF
AREA 2**

**EAST REEF
AREA 3**

Wied iz Zurrieq (Blue Grotto)

Wied iz Zurrieq is a small village situated on the south coast, there are two main routes to this site, one from Rabat 10km along a country road, or from Luqa 7km along the road which passes under the airport runway. The village is very popular with divers for the *Um el Faroud*, possibly the best wreck dive in the Mediterranean, and with tourists' for the beauty of the Blue Grotto.

The inlet and quayside at Wied iz Zurrieq where the small boats leave for the Blue Grotto. This is also the entry /exit point for the dives listed in this area.

This dive site is normally referred to as the Blue Grotto, but the Grotto is approximately half a mile to the west of the inlet and can only be reached by sea, there is a viewing area up on the main road above the Grotto (see plan). Parking for divers is at the bottom of the hill where the road ends, here it is close to your entry/exit points please note it can be extremely busy at peak times. The sea conditions must be checked here, for although there is virtually no tide, sometimes there are currents even when sea conditions are calm. Maybe if there are divers leaving the water you could ask them if they have experienced any currents during their dive. Remember the small inlet is your only exit area, and depending on the sea conditions you might have to consider use of the slipway, E2, which is sheltered from the open sea.

Beware of the boats taking tourists to the Blue Grotto, they travel quite fast so if you intend to surface swim across the inlet be careful, stay together and keep a look out. There will normally be fishermen here so take care and enter the water away from their lines. There are three diving areas here, but the dive plan can be varied depending on experience and depth required. Please note that due to weather conditions or the possible removal of stepladders, near E1 entry point during the winter period, the slipway is the only exit point E2, but be careful for this is where the boats leave from.

Um el Faroud

The ill fated tanker *Um el Faroud* was scuttled on Wednesday 2nd September, 1998. three and a half years after the explosion that killed nine dockyard workers in Grand Harbour, Valletta. This tragic event shocked the people of Malta. Her final voyage started in the early hours of the morning, arriving off Wied iz Zurrieq around 9.30am. It then took over three hours to get her into position, due to a moderate south-easterly swell. At about 12.30pm the special valves that were fitted for the scuttling were opened and the ship started to take in water, then around 3.30pm she sank quietly beneath the surface, down onto the sand at 35m. Currently she is upright on the seabed with the bow separated from the stern just in front of the bridge. In the centre of the bridge by the window there is a brass plaque in memory of the dockyard workers who sadly lost their lives.

The 3,147 gross ton vessel is a single screw motor tanker, built by Smith Dock Co. Ltd., Middlesbrough, England, in 1969. The port of registry was Tripoli and owned by General National Maritime Transport. The engine room, bridge and accommodation are arranged aft. The cargo section is sub divided into four centre tanks and four wing tanks on each side. The overall length is 110 metres and the breadth is 16m metres, still in place are the propeller and rudder.

A diver on the bows of the Um el Faroud *which was scuttled in September 1998.*

TOP & ABOVE: *The* Um el Faroud *being manouvered into position prior to sinking at Wied iz Zurrieq on 2nd September, 1998*

CUSTOM AERIAL PHOTOS

At 3.30pm on 2nd September, 1998, the Um el Faroud *sinks slowly beneath the surface. She now sits in an upright position on the sand at 35m*

PHOTO: ANTHONY CHETCUTI

A diver explores the waters below the bow where the anchor chain is still in place.

The propeller and rudder of this large ship is the ideal place to take a souvenir photograph.

▌THE DIVE   Minimum time – 50 mins

There are number of ways to reach the *Um el Faroud*, you could of course go by boat, for if they are not too busy the pleasure boatmen will take you out and drop you off over the wreck but they will not wait for you. For this there would be a fee. I personally have two different routes for reaching the *Um el Faroud*, and for both, my entry point is the same, E1 just to the left at the bottom of the steps, they are as follows:

Route 1 If sea conditions are perfect, surface swim taking a compass bearing of 240° until you have a 20° compass bearing on the flat faced sandy coloured rock, which can clearly be seen in the aerial photograph. The surface swim is approximately 200 metres from your entry point, E1 and will take some 8-15 minutes, do not attempt this route if there are any currents.

Route 2 In my opinion the best way to dive this wreck is to surface swim across the inlet entrance, west along coast for approximately 100 meters until you reach a little cove, even at a slow swim, this will take no more than 8-10 minutes. If you are facing out to sea, behind you will be a large sandy coloured flat faced rock and below you a 10m ledge. From this ledge, take a compass bearing of 200°. Your distance from here to the wreck is about 70 metres and takes about 3-4 minutes.

The bridge and main deck of the aft section with the steps leading to the rear gangways.

For the depths on this ship, see plan. If penetration is in your dive plan ensure that all diving safety procedures are carried out. For your safety all doors and windows have been removed and holes have been cut in the hull for entry and exit. Do not be tempted to stay too long, I recommend that you leave the wreck with a minimum of 100 bar which will give you time to explore the reef on your return journey. When it is time to return, leaving from the bridge and once away from the wreck, take a compass bearing of 330°. This compass bearing will not lead you directly back towards the inlet, but to the reef closest to the wreck, which is approximately 50 metres, here the depth will be 18m. To ascend this reef to a

In the bow section of the ship the huge hold can be explored.

depth of 6m will take approximately 5-6 minutes from the bridge of the wreck. Once you have reached your required depth, bear right heading in an easterly direction; follow the reef all the way round back to the inlet and your planned exit point. You should allow for this return journey some 20-25 minutes, but it can be done quicker if you do not explore the reef on the way. If you do not have sufficient air when leaving the wreck, take a compass bearing of 60° this will lead you directly back to your exit point, take care not to miss the inlet entrance. In my opinion, unless you have boat cover, this dive is for experienced divers only and a 15 litre cylinder should be used.

The rear deck and the stern of the Um el Faroud.

PHOTO: JON MITCHELL, DEEP BLUE DIVE CENTRE

PGL AERIAL PHOTOS

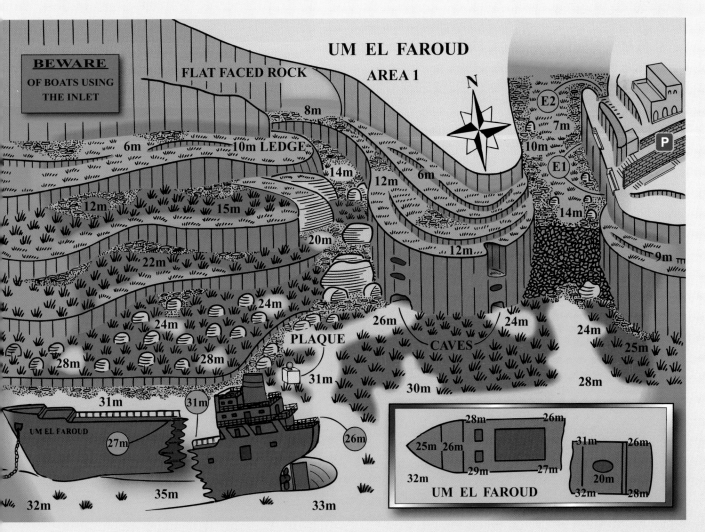

UM EL FAROUD

AREA 1

BEWARE
OF BOATS USING
THE INLET

FLAT FACED ROCK

N

E2

7m

10m

E1

14m

P

8m

6m

10m LEDGE

14m

12m

6m

9m

12m

15m

20m

12m

22m

24m

24m

24m

26m

CAVES

24m

24m

25m

28m

28m

PLAQUE

31m

30m

28m

31m

31m

26m

31m

UM EL FAROUD

27m

26m

32m

35m

33m

28m   26m

25m 26m

29m   27m

31m   26m

20m

32m

UM EL FAROUD

32m   28m

Weid iz Zurrieq – West Reef

Area 2

This dive site is situated on the western side of the inlet and there are a number of different areas to explore. There are drop offs, ledges, gullies and boulders surrounded by sea grass and sandy areas. There are also two caves, the walls of which are covered in a wide variety of brightly coloured corals and inside many cardinal fish using them as their home.

Red Mullet (Mullus surmuletus) normally found in groups on the sandy/shingle seabed. The long barbs are used to disturb the seabed to reveal small animals on which it preys.

PHOTO: VICTOR FABRI, SUBWAY DIVE CENTRE

▌THE DIVE   Minimum time – 40 mins

Enter the water at E1 and descend to 10m, cross the inlet to the western side, down over the rocky slope onto the small area of sand at 24m. Follow the reef around to the right heading west; over the sea grass, the first of the two caves is at 24m, further round you will find a small area of sand where you will find the entrance to Bell Tower Cave at 26m, the cave has enough room for two divers. When entering the cave be careful not to kick up the sand. You can exit the cave at 21m. On the left hand side of the cave is a large rock, from this point follow a line where the grass, rocks and boulders meet the sand at an average compass bearing of 240°. This will lead you to the divers helmet plaque at 30m, placed there by BSAC Atlam Dive Club to commemorate fifty years of their club.

When it is time to return, ascend the reef to your required depth. Follow it along and on the ridge, just before the inlet you will find a fissure, which runs from 16m to the top, another good place to explore. If you intend to cross the inlet underwater, leave at least 6m between yourself and the surface, until you reach the opposite shore.

Divers admiring the plaque which has been placed by 'Atlam Divers' marking fifty years of their diving club. A good pilotage mark for the Um el Faroud.

Cardinal fish (Apogon imberbis) usually found in shoals below 10m, in crevices and overhangs, which act as a refuge when a predator passes by.

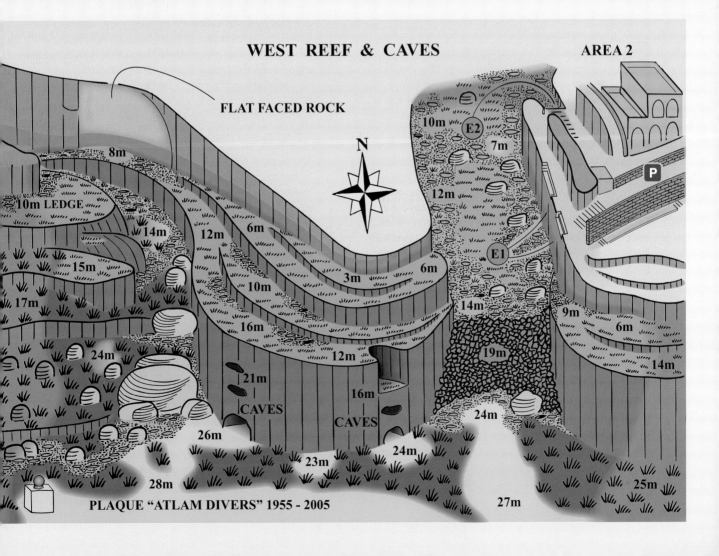

WEST REEF & CAVES
AREA 2

FLAT FACED ROCK

8m
10m LEDGE
14m 12m 6m
15m
17m
10m
16m
24m
21m
26m CAVES
28m
PLAQUE "ATLAM DIVERS" 1955 - 2005
3m
6m
12m
16m
CAVES
23m 24m
27m
10m E2 7m
12m
E1
14m
19m
24m
9m 6m
14m
25m

Weid iz Zurrieq – East Reef

Area 3

This single line reef continues in an easterly direction for 300-400 metres. At the start of this reef is a large ledge with depths from 9m to 16m, the maximum depth to the seabed is 36m. Of course on moving away from the reef the depth will increase, but this area is mostly sand and sea grass. The visibility here can be excellent, with clear water up to 40 metres plus. Usually large shoals of small fish can be seen on the reef, so keep an eye out into the blue for those larger fish that may be coming in to feed.

Sea Hare (Aplysia depilaus) this gentle creature is great to photograph, found in bays and sheltered inlets where it feeds on algae.

▌ THE DIVE   Minimum time – 40-50 mins

Entry for this dive can be made directly below the steps E1, or further round to the east there is another entry point E3, bearing in mind that exit is not possible from the latter. Once under the water you can follow the ledge along for some 60 metres at varying depths of 9m to 16m. at the end of the ledge descend the drop-off down to 28m plus, if you have decided to use entry point E1 descend to 9m then down over the rocky slope to 24m. and out of the inlet bearing left and heading east, follow the bottom of the reef at 28m, **here both routes meet**. Continue to follow the line where the bottom of the reef meets the sand past the small overhang, staying close to the base of the drop off the seabed in front of you will begin to rise, passing a number of large boulders on the seaward side until you reach a depth of 9m you are now immediately beneath the overhang on the surface. This could be your turning point, from here return to the ledge at your required depth. Follow the reef all the way along heading west, round into the inlet and your planned exit point.

Alternatively if you wish to be a little more adventurous, the best way to dive the reef is to surface swim to the overhang (see aerial photograph) be sure to check for currents and keep to the shoreline, as the pleasure boats also use this route to the Blue Grotto. Once you have reached the surface overhang, which

should take you 6 to 8 minutes from E3, descend to 8m on the eastern side of the reef, from here you will be able to descend a drop off to 35m. Follow the line of the reef staying at a depth of 30m keeping the reef on your right and heading in a westerly direction, once you meet the main reef ascend to your required depth until you return to the inlet and your exit point.

The brightly coloured fan worm (Spirographis spallanzani) has a spiral arrangement with a diameter of about 15cm. Tube made of papery material secreted by the worm itself

PHOTO: VICTOR FABRI, SUBWAY DIVE CENTRE

Night diving

Wied iz Zurrieq is an excellent venue for a night dive, for there is an abundance of marine life to see around the small overhangs and rocks within the inlet. There are reef walls to navigate by, safe exits, lighting and footpaths, and if you are very lucky a full moon will shine down and glisten over the sea while you sit and enjoy a drink of your choice after the dive.

There are many fish to see here during the day or night, just to name a few – damselfish, red mullet, cardinalfish within the caves, painted combers, scorpionfish, moray eels, cuttlefish, wrasse, John Dory, and it was here at 6m in the inlet, I saw my first seahorse in Malta.

Restaurants, cafés and gift shops are open during the day and evening over the summer period but close earlier in winter.

Hermit Crab (Dardanus arrosor) lives in the empty shell of a snail which often bears sea anemones or sponges which serve as camouflage. As the crab grows it uses larger shells.

PHOTO: MARILYN HIATT, MPH PHOTOGRAPHY

PGL AERIAL PHOTOS

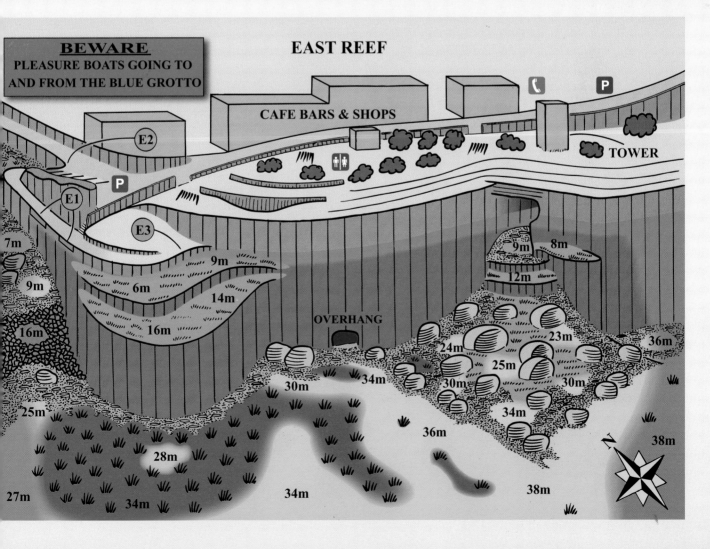

EAST REEF

BEWARE
PLEASURE BOATS GOING TO
AND FROM THE BLUE GROTTO

CAFE BARS & SHOPS

E2

E1

P

E3

TOWER

OVERHANG

7m
9m
16m
25m
27m
34m
28m
6m
9m
14m
16m
30m
34m
34m
36m
24m
30m
34m
38m
23m
25m
30m
36m
9m
8m
12m
38m

N

GHAR LAPSI

PGL AERIAL PHOTO

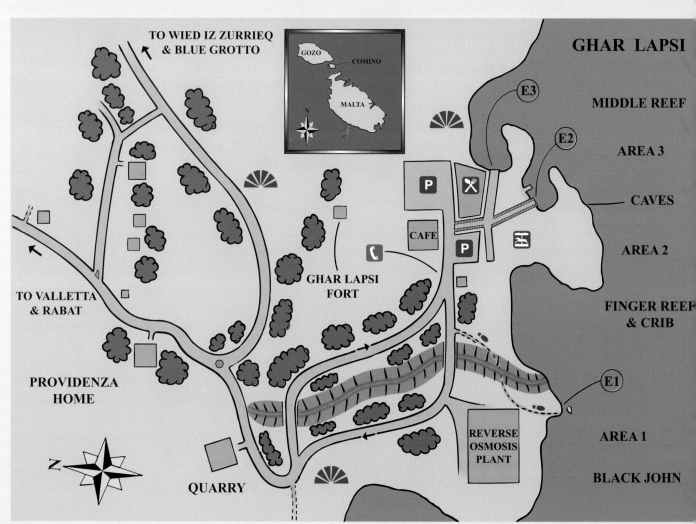

TO WIED IZ ZURRIEQ
& BLUE GROTTO

GHAR LAPSI

GOZO

COMINO

MALTA

MIDDLE REEF

E3

E2

AREA 3

P

CAVES

CAFE

AREA 2

P

TO VALLETTA
& RABAT

GHAR LAPSI
FORT

FINGER REEF
& CRIB

E1

PROVIDENZA
HOME

REVERSE
OSMOSIS
PLANT

AREA 1

N

QUARRY

BLACK JOHN

Ghar Lapsi

Ghar Lapsi is a very small hamlet which has a pretty little cove and is situated in the south of the island and is one of the few places where the sea can be entered along this area of coastline. To reach Ghar Lapsi from the north you will probably travel from Rabat/Mdina along narrow country roads for some 9km. 5km to the south is the village of Wied iz Zurrieq, famous for its Blue Grotto. Travelling along the coast road to Ghar Lapsi you will pass the Prehistoric Temples (Haga Qinn) whether you come from the north or south. When reaching the roundabout turn down the hill and past the quarry. Continue on down the hill to where the road splits in two and a one-way system is operated, where you are almost at your destination. Here you will find two car parks, ideal for dive areas 2 and 3. Next to the small car park is a steep road with steps either side leading down to the cove where your entry/exit points E1 and E2 are. Parking for dive area 1 is near the Osmosis plant, see plan.

Black John

Area 1

The dive at Black John takes you away from the popular dive sites and it is almost a certainty that you will be the only divers here. It will require a short car ride from Ghar Lapsi (see aerial photograph) as the dive site is situated at the rear of the Osmosis plant; this involves a 200 metre walk over uneven ground. Follow the rough track down to a small concrete hut then follow the pathway into a little valley, a short climb up the other side, turn left, follow the fence around the Osmosis plant going under the water outlet. Keep following the fence until you find steps cut into the rock. This leads down to a small concrete platform, which is your entry point and to the right is your exit point E1. If you look closely at the aerial photograph, you can see people standing there. Check this route before you rig. Remember it is not possible, with safety in mind, to dive this site during rough sea conditions for there is only one entry/exit point. The next nearest exit point is the cove at Ghar Lapsi, which is some 400 metres away.

There are two ways to dive this offshore reef; you can plan your dive with a maximum depth of 25m descending to the seabed directly below your entry point. Alternatively, you can surface swim to the far

The entry point at Ghar Lapsi one of the few places where the sea can be entered along this area of coastline.

side of Black John; this is the small part of the reef that is visible from the shore. This will give you an opportunity to reach depths of 38m. You must bear in mind that at times in this area there are offshore currents, in my opinion this is a dive for the more experienced diver.

From the road to the entry point is quite a difficult walk, it is strongly suggested that this route is walked before kitting up.

THE DIVE   Minimum time – 40 mins

Entry is a 2m drop to the water and below you a depth of 10m, once on the seabed move away from this area, with the reef on your left, heading east past a large rock and under an arch/overhang. Coming through the other side do a part U-turn and take a compass bearing of 200° to the main reef. On reaching the reef keep it on your left, follow it all the way round until it is heading east.

If you stay reasonably close to the reef your maximum depth will not exceed 25m, but further away from the reef depths of 30m or more are possible around the large rocks, grass and sandy areas. After some 25 minutes into your dive, depending on the time you have taken to explore and you are close to the base of the reef where you will find what appears to be a large crack which leads diagonally upwards to the top of the reef.

Once at the top of the reef head in a westerly direction along the ridge, it will take you no more than 6 minutes to reach the base of the reef at 10m that leads up to Black John itself. Now a northerly compass bearing will take you towards the coastline, first over the reef to Propeller Rock and then over the sand where the water from the Osmosis plant falls into the sea. Here there is normally an abundance of marine life. To find your exit point head west and you will pass over the large rock and overhang where your dive began, then ascend to the 6m ledge where you can do your safety stops and explore at the same time, bear round to the right for the exit point.

The alternative way to do this dive with a depth of 38m is to surface swim to the far side of Black John, continuing on until you are clear of the shallow reef. Now descend keeping clear of the boulders. Once on the seabed head in an easterly direction with the large boulders and grass on your left and the sandy area on your right, depth 38m. Keeping to this route and in approximately 9 minutes you should reach a depth of 32m. Turn to your left and facing in a northerly direction you should be able to see in front of you, a very large boulder, which has its base at 30m. Ascend to the top of this boulder and then on to the main

This jellyfish (Cotylorhiza tuberculata) is sometimes known as a fried egg, normally found along the coastline during summer and autumn. With a yellow-brown float and short tentacles ending in a small bluey-purple disc, makes it easy to recognise.

reef, now follow the ridge in a westerly direction, it should take you no more than 10 minutes to reach the base of the reef at 10m that leads up to Black John itself. **From this point of your dive to your exit, is as the same as the first alternative, E1.**

Living mainly in open water, the young of this John Dory (Zeus faber) can be seen inshore among rocks and seaweed during the summer months.

PHOTO: VICTOR FABRI, SUBWAY DIVE CENTRE

The giant tun (Tonna galea) lives on sandy seabeds, feeds on sea cucumbers and often falls prey to octopuses, can grow to 30cm.   PHOTO:COLIN STEAD

The Painted Comber (Serranus scriba) has a tapered body, slightly compressed, with a pointed head, the most common fish likely to be seen in Maltese waters .

PHOTO: JESPER KJØLLER. DYK MAGAZINE

PGL AERIAL PHOTOS

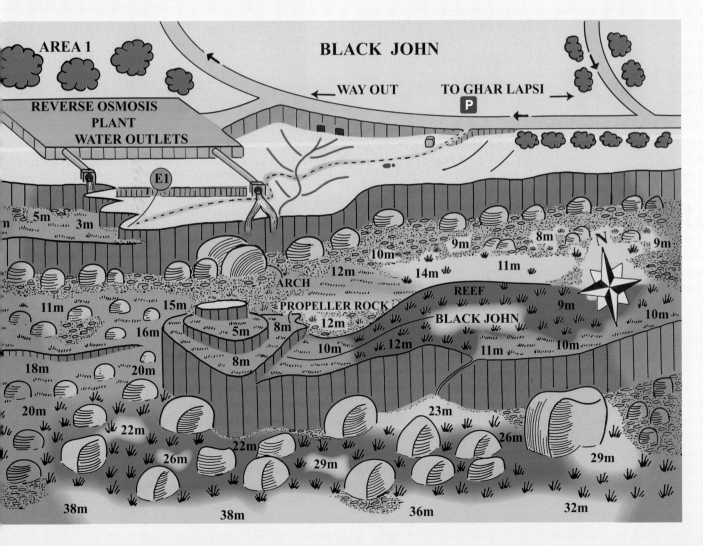

ABOVE: *Three divers just below Black John, to the south of Propeller Rock, below them the reef drops away to 36m.* RIGHT: *Diver at the entrance to the cave, with the hole in the roof, on the outer reef, Ghar Lapsi.*

The ballen wrasse (Labrus bergylta) is found living over algae covered rocky seabeds, feeds on molluscs and crustaceans.

PHOTO: JOSEPH FARRUGIA

The parrotfish (Sparisoma cretense) has strong jaws and beak-like teeth, normally swim in family groups.

PHOTO: VICTOR FABRI, SUBWAY DIVE CENTRE

ABOVE: *A diver enters the area where to his right is the rock which resembles an elephants head and trunk.* LEFT: *The seahorse (Hippocampus hippocampus) swims in a vertical position with its head directed downwards in a horse-like fashion, not easily visible.*

PHOTO: VICTOR FABRI, SUBWAY DIVE CENTRE

Finger Reef and Crib

Area 2

Before diving this area you will have to decide which route you are going to take to the cave at 19m with a hole in its roof. Route one via Finger Reef, the shorter distance of the two, or Route 2 via the Crib at 22m, if during your dive you stay in close proximity to either of these reefs this will be your maximum depth. Basically there are two main reefs, one is shaped like a finger, hence its name, the second twists and turns until it reaches the cave via the Crib. The Crib, a nativity scene, is of almost life sized figures cut from plate metal, welded to a tubular frame, placed under the water within an overhang, by the Calypso Diving Team. Around these reefs are areas of boulders, rocks, sea grass and sand. Of course within this area there are many permutations of dives giving you the opportunity to create your own dive plan.

Opposite the entry/exit point E2, within the cove, there is an entrance to a cave system, the entrance is just large enough for a diver, but there is plenty of room inside. There is a larger exit into the open sea at 8m a gulley will then lead you down on to the sand at 11m. A little further along from the first exit there is second exit to the open sea at 6m. Within the cave there are many small openings, which allow bright rays of sunlight to shine through, illuminating parts of the cave.

The Crib, which are almost life-sized figures cut from plate metal.

▌THE DIVE Minimum time – 55 mins

Your entry point E2 is immediately below the small car park at the bottom of the steep hill. Surface swim to the centre of the cove and descend, once on the bottom swim out of the cove following the reef around to your right. When out of the cove continue down over the reef heading in a westerly direction, until you reach the sand at 11m. **Alternatively** if the weather conditions permit and there is no surge in the cave it could be used for the start of the dive, or if you prefer at the end. Surface swim directly across the cove,

Divers swim across the Ghar Lapsi cove to the small pool where the small entrance to the cave system is to be found.

submerge and pass through a small hole in a rock wall, depth 1m into a little pool. The entrance to the cave is on your right, which is small, but once inside there is sufficient room for a diver to move around. Whilst descending through the cave you will see the underwater exit at 8m follow the gulley out of the cave and down onto the sand at 11m. **Here the two dives meet.** From here follow the line where the sand meets the reef in a westerly direction for approximately 2 minutes where you will see a mound covered in sea grass on your left, this is the point where the two dives separate at a depth of 12m. **See route 1 or route 2.**

Route 1. To go to the cave with the hole in the roof via Finger Reef, continue in a westerly direction over the sand into an area where there are many small boulders, the depth here is 12m. Now bear slightly to your left and the reef will start to rise beside you, here your depth will decrease to around 9m and you will be about 10 minutes into your dive. Dropping over a small ridge to a depth of approximately 11m, on your left you will see the start of what I call Finger Reef. Here it is easy to follow this reef all the way to the end, but take your time to explore the many little over-hangs filled with colourful marine life.

This Hermit crab (Dardanus arrosor) has found an empty shell in which to live and into which he retreats when threatened.

PHOTO: VICTOR FABRI, SUBWAY DIVE CENTRE

When you reach the end of the reef you will possibly be 20-25 minutes into your dive, here the depth will be 20m. From the end of the reef take a compass bearing of 60°, this will lead you in an easterly direction over the sea grass to a ridge at 16m. Drop over this ridge down to 18m, turn left and the cave entrance at 19m will be just in front of you. When entering take great care, for you may be lucky to see the groupers that are sometimes here. After you have explored the cave, leave through the hole in the roof emerging on the top of the reef at 12m. At this point you will be some 30-35 minutes into your dive and from here to your exit point E2, is a minimum time of 15 minutes. **See return route.**

Inside the cave with the hole in the roof which leads out onto the top of Finger Reef.

Route 2. To go to the cave with the hole in the roof via the Crib take a compass bearing of 210° this will lead you in a southerly direction and over the mound covered in sea grass which is surrounded by sand. For the next 7-8 minutes the area on your left will be mostly sand and on your right is mainly sea grass with two or three patches of sand.

Two divers out on the sand between the inner and outer reef, here you will normally find sting rays and flying gurnards.

Divers explore the outer reef between the Crib and Elephant Rock.

On reaching a depth of 14m, on the sand in front of you will be an area of sea grass. Continue straight on over the sea grass and within 2 minutes, at a depth of 12m you will be on top of the reef. Descend to the bottom at 16m and turn right, follow the base of the reef along for approximately 5 minutes when you should reach a depth of 22m, this is the deepest part of your dive and the Crib is in an overhang on your right hand side. Make sure that you stay close to the reef at this point or you may miss it altogether. When it is time to move on, almost immediately the reef starts to head in a northerly direction and from here it will take you around 5 minutes to reach the Double Hooks.

Cutting the corner continue over to the reef on the opposite side and from here it will take you some 5 minutes to reach the Elephant Rock – be careful for his trunk almost reaches the seabed. Once more cut the corner and continue to the reef on the other side, from here to the cave will take you no more than 4 minutes. When you have explored the cave ascend through the hole in the roof to the top of the reef at 12m. At this point you will possibly be 40-45 minutes into your dive. Of course you can at any time go up on top of the reef take a northerly compass bearing and return to the main coastline.

Return Route. From the hole in the roof of the cave follow a compass bearing of 70° until you reach a 9m drop-off to an area of small boulders at 12m. Alternatively once out of the hole head north to the ridge of Finger Reef, then in a north easterly direction follow it all the way along, then down to the area of small boulders at 12m. Now head in an easterly direction and in a very short time the main coastline will be on your left. Continue along this reef at your required depth.

Normally the entrance to the cave is marked with a small heap of stones; at this point your maximum depth should be 6m this will enable you find the reef and follow it into the cove and your exit point. If you wish you can use the route through the cave, into the cove and your exit point, E2.

PGL AERIAL PHOTOS

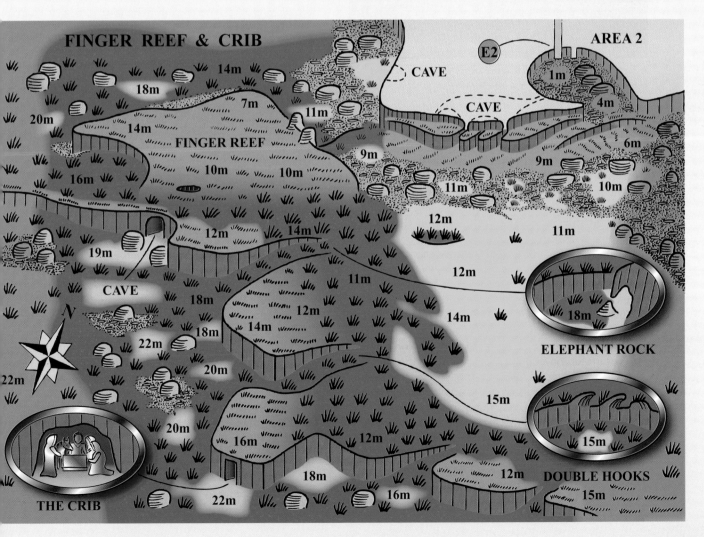

FINGER REEF & CRIB

AREA 2

CAVE

E2

1m

4m

6m

14m

18m

7m

11m

20m

14m

9m

9m

FINGER REEF

16m

10m

10m

11m

10m

12m

12m

11m

19m

12m

14m

12m

CAVE

18m

ELEPHANT ROCK

N

11m

12m

14m

18m

18m

14m

22m

20m

15m

20m

22m

16m

12m

15m

THE CRIB

18m

16m

12m

DOUBLE HOOKS

22m

15m

Middle Reef

Area 3

This site makes an interesting second dive, you have a choice of entry/exit points, normally I would use E2 but you could use E3. Within this area there are a number of reefs to explore, which are surrounded by areas of sand, sea grass and small boulders, with a maximum depth of 16m, your dive time can be variable. This dive will test your navigational skills, both with a compass and underwater pilotage, remember to take your slate and pencil.

The colour of the rainbow wrasse (Coris julis) is variable, depending on sex, age, depth and temperature. In time the females change into males, growing larger and changing colour. PHOTO: VICTOR FABRI, SUBWAY DIVE CENTRE

A family of parrot fish (Sparisoma cretense) look for food around the edges and in the posidonia (Posidonia oceanica) meadow.

Use these for your navigation and when it is time to return head in an easterly direction. When you reach the overhang Lizard Head, at the easterly end of the largest reef, continue for a short distance over the grass and you will come to a patch of sand. Follow this around to your right, locate your stone marker and take a compass bearing of 300°, which will hopefully lead you back over the small ridge and into the cove and your exit point, E1. Marine life to be found on these dives are octopus, cuttlefish, shoals of salema fish, the occasional barracudas, out on the sand eagle sting rays and get close to look at or film red mullet digging in the sand and of course many other species.

This group of fireworms (Hermodice carunculata) have found a feast to gorge on. When disturbed the worm erects its bristles which can penetrate the skin breaking off, releasing an intensely irritating toxic agent, hence the name fireworm.

THE DIVE   Minimum time – 50 mins

Your entry point E2, for this dive is situated at the bottom of the steep hill below the small car park. From the entry point E2, surface swim to the middle of the cove and descend, head out of the cove and over a small ridge, then take a compass bearing of 120° continue down onto the sand at 10m. Once here place a stone marker and continue directly over the sand to the opposite reef, then follow the line were the grass meets the sand with a compass bearing of 220°. When you have rounded the first corner, your compass bearing will be 160° you will be able to see, if the visibility is good, Middle Reef on your left-hand side with its two prominent rocks on top. This reef can be explored on your return journey. Continue on following the line where the grass meets the sand until you reach a depth of 14m. Here out on the sand, it is possible to see flying gurnards and small rays. When it is time for you to return, proceed back to the reef with the prominent rocks. Explore this reef and on its north east corner there is an area of sand, from here take a compass bearing of 50°, this will lead you to an area where there are two long reefs which run from east to west.

Situated next to the car parks are two nice restaurants, which are very popular with the Maltese and at weekends can be quite busy. During the Spring and Autumn they open at approximately 10am. Ghar Lapsi is a very pleasant place for non-divers to visit for a spot of sunbathing perhaps or a picnic; also it is a safe place for snorkelers and swimmers within the cove. Next to the small car park there is a children's playground, also public toilets. A whole day could be spent in this area maybe diving at Wied iz Zurrieq as a first dive and then on to Ghar Lapsi for a second dive, but remember that you will need to take two cylinders with you.

PGL AERIAL PHOTOS

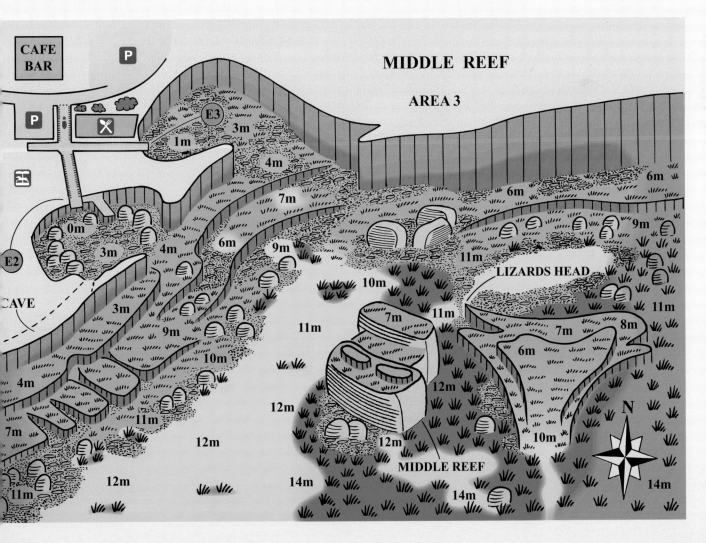

PGL AERIAL PHOT

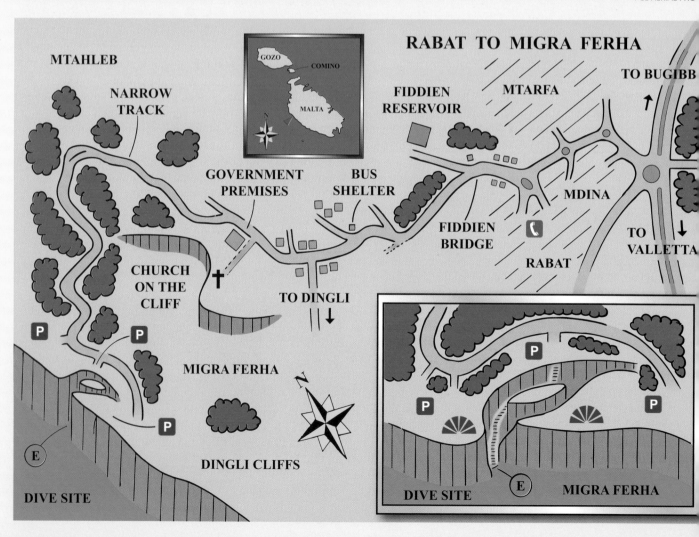

Migra Ferha

The planned route to this dive site starts by going through a valley; to the south is Mdina, known as the Silent City. This was once the ancient capital of Malta, to the north the town of Mtarfa, famous for its clock tower. This journey will take some twenty minutes to reach your destination. If you follow the route plan you will pass Fiddien Bridge, the lone bus shelter and the Government premises. Next you will then bear left on a very narrow road where some of the tarmac is missing; looking to your left over the valley you will see the Church which is built above the rock face. After a short distance the road gets better and this will lead you down to Migra Ferha. There are two car parks here; it is better to go to the first one for it is less distance to walk. Watch out for the little drop from the level of the roadway at the entrance to the car park.

This unique and unspoilt dive site should only be attempted by experienced and very fit divers, due to the fact that there are approximately 150 steps to be negotiated to reach the entry/exit point below the Dingli Cliffs, which run along this westerly coastline in each direction. Please do not upset the fishermen for they made the steps that enable us to reach sea level and they also have to replace them after heavy rain, as the gully becomes a river. Before you dive this site you must check the sea conditions, as this is your only exit for a number of kilometres. Once in the water be aware that there are some offshore currents. There are two dive area's here, to the north a large reef with depths of 16m to 9m and over the drop-off 30m plus. To the south a large area of boulders to explore, depths to 25m once you move away from the reef or the boulders, within 30 metres distance your depth will be at least 36m, from this point the bottom drops away very quickly. If you decide to dive this site take a 15 litre cylinder and make the most of one good dive. It is always a good idea, even for the very fit diver, to sit down for 20-30 minutes after your dive before attempting the climb back up the 150 steps! As this would be considered heavy exercise, the rest would give time for the slow release of nitrogen and help to prevent exercise related DCI.

Diving the Reef

THE DIVE	Minimum time – 50 mins

Once on the ledge that you will be using for your entry/exit turn to your left and you will find a nice little stepping area to assist you especially with your exit. Into the water, depth below you is 16m, when on the bottom head in a westerly direction keeping the reef on your right hand side, within 8 minutes you will reach the corner of the reef, depth 29m. From here straight out some 30 metres will give you a depth of 36m, this area is great for finding octopus and moray. Return to the corner now follow the reef in a northerly direction, the reef will still be on your right hand side.

This is possibly the only shore dive along the Dingli cliffs where there are approximately 150 steps to the sea.

A grouper (Epinephelus guaz) resting on a rock which, if you are very careful, they can normally be found. Feeds on all types of animals found among the rocks.

PHOTO: VICTOR FABRI, SUBWAY DIVE CENTRE

Within 10 minutes, you will come to an area where you will see cars littered on the bottom at 36m and deeper, from this point ascend the cliff face to a ledge at 15m, here you will also find a number of cars, they have all been pushed over the cliff top. This should be your turning point; from here you will be able to see the shoreline and the base of the cliffs, which will enable you to go to your required depth. Keeping the reef on your left, head in a southerly direction and you will find two small caves and a large over-hang, almost immediately you will have to bear round to your left, you should now be above your outward route and almost at your exit point. The return journey should not have taken more than 10-15 minutes, plus exploring time.

Diving the boulder area

█ THE DIVE   Minimum time – 50 mins

Once on the bottom follow the cliff wall in a southerly direction, almost immediately you will come to a large over-hang, this is worth a look inside, continue on the same course keeping the reef on your left. This area is littered with large boulders and between them small rocks, a haven for marine life with many places to explore.

Divers hover over the vehicles which have been pushed off the cliff top to their graveyard below, these have now become home to the local marine life.

Within 15 minutes, depending on the time spent exploring, on your left you will see a very large rock that seems to be leaning up against the cliff wall, it is also a corner where the reef changes direction, depth 25m. At this point you should turn and swim in a northerly direction, keeping the boulders on your right and the flatish area on your left staying at a depth of around 25m, remember this is a good area for finding octopus and moray.

A number plate has lodged itself on the reef. Could it be yours?

In approximately 15/20 minutes you should reach the reef wall, depth 25m, if you turn to your right follow it in an easterly direction, this will lead you into a corner below the ledge at your exit point. Alternatively you can explore the area on top of the reef before returning to your exit point. Of course you can plan your own dive and depths to cover parts of both these sites, but to fully complete both areas in one dive is really just too much and will give you no time to explore.

It is very important to remember that there are no amenities here, so bring refreshments if required. Remember you are at least a 20 minute drive away to the nearest telephone which is in Rabat, some mobile phones do not work in the Migra Ferha area. It is always a good idea to bring a non-diver with you to 'car sit' or if this is not possible, leave nothing of value in the car. If you happen to be here in the evening some beautiful sunsets can be seen over the sea.

A diver explores one of the small caves on the plateau to the north-west of the entry point at Migra Ferha.

PGL AERIAL PHOTOS

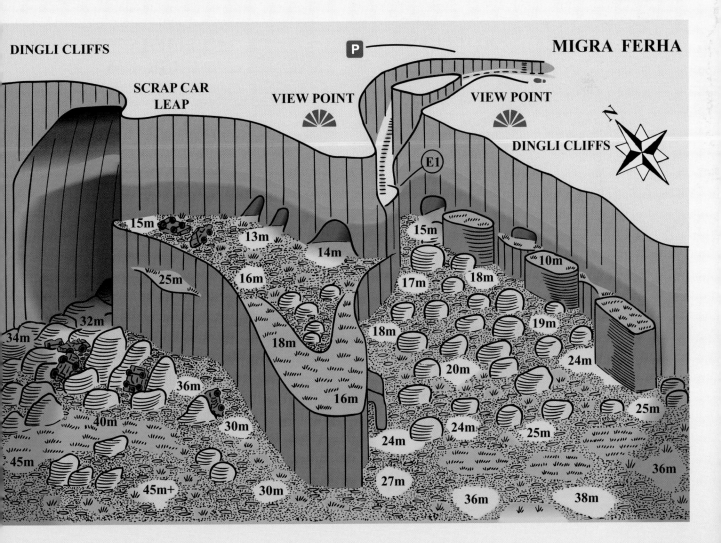

DINGLI CLIFFS

SCRAP CAR
LEAP

VIEW POINT

P

VIEW POINT

MIGRA FERHA

DINGLI CLIFFS

N

E1

15m
13m
14m
25m
16m
32m
34m
36m
40m
45m
45m+
30m
30m
18m
16m
24m
27m
15m
17m
18m
10m
19m
20m
24m
24m
25m
36m
25m
36m
38m

PGL AERIAL PHOT

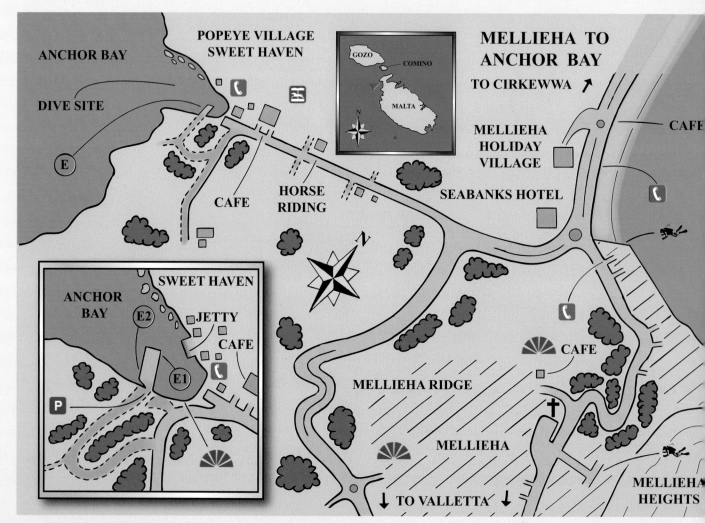

Anchor Bay

Anchor bay is a small inlet situated on the north west coast of Malta, only a short drive from Mellieha. The view from the main road going down the hill towards Mellieha Bay, before turning left to Anchor Bay, is quite breathtaking and the 'Popeye' village can be seen quite clearly from here and this is one of the few places on the island where you can see both coastlines.

This bay was made famous by the building of the timber village called Sweethaven, which was the film set for the production of the film *Popeye* with Robin Williams. A jetty was constructed to enable ships to unload materials at this isolated bay when they constructed Sweethaven, now only fishermen and divers use this jetty. The name Anchor Bay came from the anchor which was used as a mooring buoy for the barges carrying materials to construct the film set. The anchor still remains and attached to it is a long heavy chain. (see plan)

The village of Sweethaven or Popeye village was originally built for the making of the film Popeye; *it is now a very popular tourist attraction.*

Both your entry and exit points are on the jetty and will possibly require a de-kit to exit. Divers come here to complete training, for a second dive or when there are strong north to north east winds. Depth ranges are from 2m to 12m within the bay, depths of 20m can be reached, but they are some 300 metres from the jetty. Beware, for there are boats bringing parties of tourists and they land and embark from the little jetty in front of the Popeye village.

THE DIVE   Minimum time – 50 mins

The entry point used depends on your route but normally I would use the far steps E1, the depth here is 5m. Moving over the sand you will reach a bank with sea grass on the top of it. Now head about 320° but do not miss the very large anchor chain, for in

places it is covered in marine growth. Once you have found it turn left and follow it, at the end you will find a very large anchor, 8m. From here head 210° to start off with there is a small reef on your left, it helps with navigation.

Eventually you will pass an area of small rocks on your left, here leave this small reef but remain on your present compass bearing until you reach the base of the shoreline cliff face on the south side of the bay, if your depth is less than 8m turn right, if more than 11m turn left. The entrance to the cave is on the seaward side of the very large boulder, which allows no access between it and the cliff face. From your entry point to the cave, allowing for time to look around, will take you some 24 minutes.

The depth at the entrance of the cave is 10m, inside depth is 8m, once inside the cave there is a large cavern above water level in which you may surface and admire this impressive dome shaped ceiling. The area on the westerly side of the cave entrance is quite rugged and if you have the time and air, is worth exploring. When it is time to return, head 60° east keeping the cliff face on your right, from the cave to your exit point it will take you approximately 15 minutes, longer if you wish to explore. You can of course complete this dive in reverse, by going directly to the cave from your entry point.

These gilthead bream (Sparus auratus) are believed to be escapees from one of the local fish farms.

On the north shore of Anchor Bay, not far from the anchor is an area of large boulders surrounded by a sandy seabed, often to be found here is the Tun Shell.

This pretty little nudibranch (Cratena peregrina) can be found with patience, as they are so small and very difficult to find.
PHOTO: IAN FORDER, SUBWAY DIVE CENTRE

You can of course plan your own dive within the bay, but remember, the swim from the cave to your exit point E1 or E2 could possibly be completed in 15 minutes, with no time spent exploring. The nearest public telephone boxes are situated at Mellieha Bay, but in an emergency the proprietors of the Popeye Village will allow you to use their private phone in the entrance kiosk, which is manned 24 hours a day, 365 days a year either by employees or security personnel.

On to the approach road to the bay there are some riding stables where horses can be hired for visitors, obviously the 'Popeye' village itself is worth a visit. As you leave the road and go on to the track, stop at the top of the cliffs, this viewpoint is a good position to take photographs of the village and bay. There is a restaurant and gift shop next to the car park above the village. It is always a good idea to bring a non-diver with you to 'car sit' or if this is not possible, leave nothing of value in the car.

This star fish (Astrpecten spinulosus) is sometimes referred to as a sand star which can be found on medium to fine grain sand sometimes partially buried.

A small black faced blenny (Tripterygion tripteronotus) can be found among seaweed and on a seabed of mixed sand and rock.
PHOTO: SHARON METSON, H2O DIVERS

Mellieha

Perched high up on a spur, the village of Mellieha overlooks the sweeping expanse of its bay and sandy beach. It has a busy shopping centre and the steep main street is lined with a variety of shops, small bars and restaurants. Perched on the hill side in front of the church with fantastic views over the north coast of Malta with Gozo in the distance is a small family run café/bar and a children's playground, a great place to relax after a dive. In an effort to preserve both local and migratory birds, the wetland inland from Mellieha Bay has been turned into a bird sanctuary. It lies approximately 100 metres from Mellieha Bay, across the main road, and covers about six hectares and well worth a visit.

The ribbed helmet shell (Phalium granulatum) lays eggs in the posidonia meadows and on rocky bottoms, egg mass resembles large yellow sponge.
PHOTO: ALAN JAMES

PGL AERIAL PHOTOS

PGL AERIAL PHOT

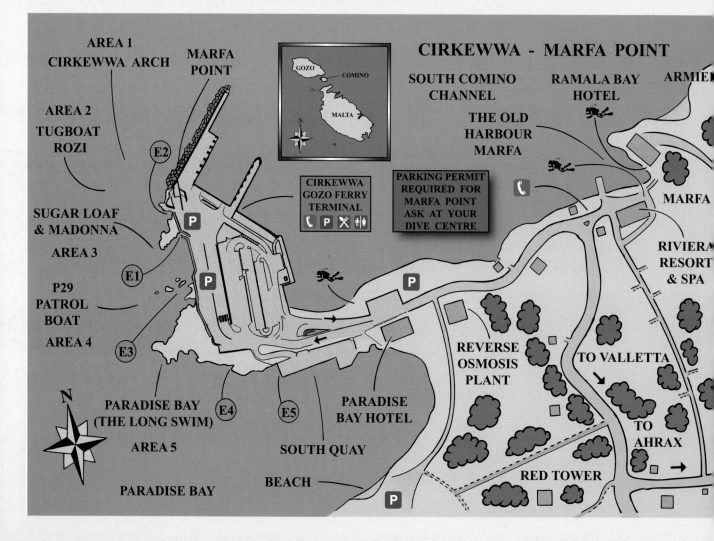

AREA 1
CIRKEWWA ARCH

MARFA POINT

CIRKEWWA - MARFA POINT

GOZO
COMINO
MALTA
N

SOUTH COMINO CHANNEL

RAMALA BAY HOTEL

ARMIE

AREA 2
TUGBOAT ROZI

E2

THE OLD HARBOUR MARFA

CIRKEWWA GOZO FERRY TERMINAL

PARKING PERMIT REQUIRED FOR MARFA POINT ASK AT YOUR DIVE CENTRE

MARFA

SUGAR LOAF & MADONNA

P

E1

AREA 3

P

RIVIERA RESORT & SPA

P29 PATROL BOAT

P

AREA 4

E3

REVERSE OSMOSIS PLANT

TO VALLETTA

N

PARADISE BAY (THE LONG SWIM)

E4

E5

PARADISE BAY HOTEL

AREA 5

SOUTH QUAY

TO AHRAX

PARADISE BAY

BEACH

P

RED TOWER

Cirkewwa (Marfa Point)

Cirkewwa is situated at the north west coast of the island and is the main terminal for the car and passenger ferries to Gozo. Most divers refer to this area as Marfa and is the most popular dive location on the island, the actual hamlet of Marfa itself is approximately 1km along the coast where there is a small harbour.

Before the terminal was built, the rocks below the lighthouse were not part of the mainland, these outcrops of rocks were known as Marfa Point. There are two quays at the Cirkewwa terminal, the north quay, which is the normal one used; the south quay is used when weather conditions dictate otherwise. The car ferries are not a problem for divers unless you leave the main dive areas and surface well out to sea. It is the small craft, fishing and pleasure boats that can be a problem; they tend to cut the corner when rounding the headland, occasionally dive boats visit this area, so beware of anchors and shot lines. Due to the fact that it is so popular it can become really busy at times. There are five dives here which of course can be interchanged to suit your qualifications and dive plan requirements, with depths down to 36m.

Groups of divers prepare to dive one of the many sites available at Cirkewwa.
PHOTO: SUE LEMON

Cirkewwa terminal (Marfa Point) south quay in the foreground, north quay with a ferry moored alongside, the islands of Comino, Cominotto with Gozo in the background.

PGL AERIAL PHOTOS

Cirkewwa Arch
Area 1

This unusual arch some 12m below the surface and 8m above the sea bed has a compass bearing from the lighthouse directly over the reef of 320°. Your route is not direct but will take you along the side of the reef, which can be used, for navigation; the approximate distance for this route is 180 metres. Most of the sea bed area of this dive site is covered in sea grass with large boulders and small areas of sand. On your outward journey you will find a small cave, which can be explored, while returning along the shallow depths of the reef, where the marine growth is short, there are many nooks and crannies which make good hiding places for marine life.

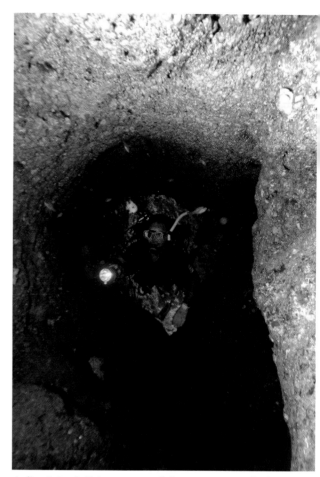

A diver's torch lights up one of the many caves which can be found in this area, illuminating the corals to their true colours.

The Arch at Cirkewwa is a really good place for some unusual photography.

█ THE DIVE   Minimum time – 40 mins

Entry point E2 is just below the lighthouse. From the entry point surface swim around to the end of the reef, once on the north west side of the lighthouse descend to 6-7m, now swim in an easterly direction past a large reef/boulder when the next reef appears in front of you, descend bearing to your left continue down to a depth of 14m, here the bottom is covered in sea grass and the main reef will be on your right

hand side. Continue along the reef until you come to an area of sand, be sure not to miss the little cut out in the reef, for on the left-hand side of this cut out is the entrance to the cave. Once you have entered the cave leave by the first exit on your left, as the other exit is too small for divers, continue to follow the reef on your right. Within a short distance the reef bears sharply to the right, at this point you can either follow the reef to the Arch or take a compass bearing of 350°

Take your time and explore this area while admiring the breath taking view of the reef formation. If you are lucky, under the Arch there are sometimes large shoals of amberjacks, especially if there is a slight current, if you are really careful you can get very close to them, which makes a great photographic opportunity. When on the seabed below the Arch take care not to stir up the sand, moving under the Arch towards the reef wall at the far end, where there are a number of hiding places for groupers and moray eels.

On your return route follow the reef until you are above the cave; if there are divers inside the bubbles form a curtain, again another chance for an unusual photograph. After you have passed the cave bear right past the first boulder/ reef then cross over to the main reef, you will now be below the lighthouse where you can exit at E2 or if the sea is choppy and you have the air then continue to Susie's pool E1, at your chosen depth.

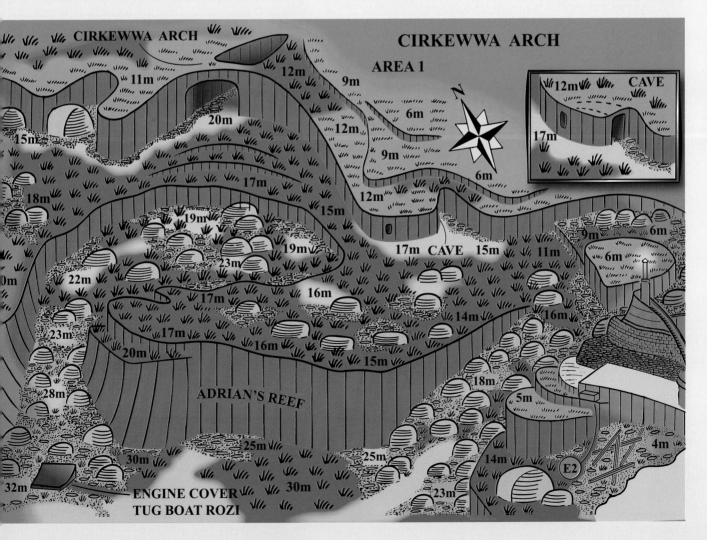

CIRKEWWA ARCH

CIRKEWWA ARCH

AREA 1

CAVE

ADRIAN'S REEF

ENGINE COVER
TUG BOAT ROZI

CAVE

E2

Cirkewwa diver attractions

The Tugboat *Rozi*

The tugboat Rossgarth *working in Grand Harbour, later sold to Tug Malta and re-named* Rozi.

PHOTO: BY KIND PERMISSION OF BETTINA ROHBRECHT, HAMBURG

The Rozi *in Grand Harbour which is where she spent almost 20 years of her working life, later she was scuttled at Cirkewwa in 1992 originally as an attraction for a passenger submarine.*

PHOTO: COURTESY OF TUG MALTA

This 30m tugboat named *Rozi*, built in Bristol, England in 1958 by Charles Hill & Sons Ltd, for Johnston Warren Lines Ltd, of Liverpool and launched as *Rossmore*. She was renamed *Rossgarth* in 1969 and in 1972 was sold to Mifsud Brothers (Malta Ship Towage) Ltd, Malta, retaining her name. In the same year she sailed from Liverpool for Malta where in 1973 she was registered. She was sold to Tug Malta in 1981 and renamed *Rozi* and was sold to Captain Morgan Cruises, Malta who scuttled her as an artificial reef off Cirkewwa in 1992 as an attraction for a tourist submarine. Approximately 130 metres west of the lighthouse at a depth of 34m she sits upright on a sandy seabed. There was a time when tourists enjoyed seeing divers on the *Rozi*, but the submarine has long since gone. During the intervening years thousands of divers from all over the world have enjoyed diving on her, and seeing the marine life that have made the *Rozi* their home.

ABOVE: *Many fish are attracted to the* Rozi *as a safe haven.*
LEFT: *A diver admires the bows of the* Rozi.
BELOW: *A large anchor situated not far from the* Rozi.

P29 Patrol Boat

The arrival of the P29 to Malta from Germany on the 29th August 1997.

The patrol boat *P29* formerly Boltenhagen, which now lies at a maximum depth of 38m off Cirkewwa, Malta's most popular dive location, started life in former East Germany. The *P29* is a Kondor class boat designed and built on the Peenewerft, Wolgast in East Germany in the 1960's 52 metres in length weighing 360 tons. It was primarily a minesweeper, though several variants also existed, possibly engaged in fisheries protection, border control or formed part of the German Democratic Republic logistical fleet.

In August 1997, after a three week voyage from Germany, the Armed Forces of Malta's Maritime Squadron took delivery of their third Kondor vessel, the *P29*. When the ship arrived in Malta it was greeted by the family and friends of the crew. The Kondor vessels were the first war ships the AFM ever commissioned, and it was thanks to them that the Maritime Squadron was able to participate in naval exercises with other European fleets.

From 1997 until 2004, when she was decommissioned, the *P29* patrolled the coastal waters of the Maltese Islands, fulfilling her duties with search and rescue operations, fisheries protection duties and exercises: of

The stern of the P29 where the empty second reel can be seen attached to the deck the first one is hovering over the concrete block.

course the naval exercises took her further a field into International waters of the Mediterranean. In 2000 and 2001 the Kondors supported the prestigious Royal Malta Yacht Club's Middle Sea Race off Lampedusa.

In September 2005 the *P29* was sold to the Malta Tourism Authority to be scuttled as an attraction for divers. She was cleaned and made environmentally safe and was finally scuttled on the 14th August 2007 off Cirkewwa.

ABOVE: *A diver hovers above the bows of the P29 at 32m, here the seabed is 38m.* BELOW: *The upper structure and port side of the P29.*

The Tugboat *Rozi*
Area 2

▌THE DIVE   Minimum time – 50 mins

There are a number of permutations for this dive; your entry point E2 is from the south side of the lighthouse. Your dive plan will either be to surface swim to the end of the reef, and then down to the first level at 14m, pass directly over the rocky valley to the reef on the other side, depth 15m. Follow the edge of the reef for about 70 metres, on your left down on the bottom you will see a path of sand shaped like a banana which separates the sea grass. The *Rozi*'s bows lie just to the

Don't sit on this toilet as someone is using it for a home!.

right of this path; dive time to the wreck is approximately 6 minutes.

The alternative is a surface swim out to the *Rozi*, on a compass bearing of 300° using the same entry point E2. You will have to take great care and keep an eye out for small boats cutting the corner. Also the currents that occur here from time to time are inclined to push you off course without you realising it. I think the best plan is to descend to a minimum depth where you can use the reef for navigation. For your return journey you have three choices, most divers plan to return to Susie's Pool E1, but of course you can exit at E2.

Return route 1. Mid-way port side of the wreck follow a compass bearing of 150°, to the anchor, which is 50 metres away at a depth of 32m. From this point continue on a compass bearing of 120°, this will lead you back on to the reef, when you have reached it, ascend to your required depth then head in a southerly direction keeping the main reef on your left. Once you have reached the swim-through cave at 11m and either passed through it or taken the short trip round, then continue to follow the reef wall. Within approximately 2 minutes at a depth of 11m you will find a ledge that will lead you up into the training area and Susie's Pool.

Return route 2. Leave the stern of the *Rozi* behind you and following a compass bearing of approximately 60° until you reach the top of the reef, at approximately 17m. At this point turn right; continue along the edge of the reef until you reach the rocky valley cross over to the other side. Here the reef rises to the surface, near

A view from inside the bridge on the Rozi *looking towards the anchor.*   PHOTO: JESPER KJØLLER, DYK MAGAZINE

E2, bearing in mind to reach this point from the wreck, will take you some 5-6 minutes. Once you have reached your required depth bear to the right, keeping the main reef on your left and you will pass the small arches in the reef; continue on to the swim-through cave. Follow the reef at 5m to exit at the stony path or at 11m to find the ledge and overhang that will lead you into the training area and exit at Susie's Pool E1.

Return route 3. This I consider to be my favourite return route. Leave the bows of the *Rozi* passing over the engine cover, which lies on the sand, and follow a compass bearing of 30°. Continue in this direction following the gently sloping reef to higher ground. At a depth of around 20m you will find a small drop-off on your right, follow its edge until you have a reef in front of you, continue to the top of this reef, depth 11m. Taking a southerly compass bearing will lead you directly over the Arch and on to a reef where you can select your own depth; the minimum time from the wreck to this point will take you 6 minutes. Follow the reef all the way to your exit point E2, on the south side of the lighthouse.

A diver swims underneath the stern; although the prop is long gone the rudder still remains.

PGL AERIAL PHOTOS

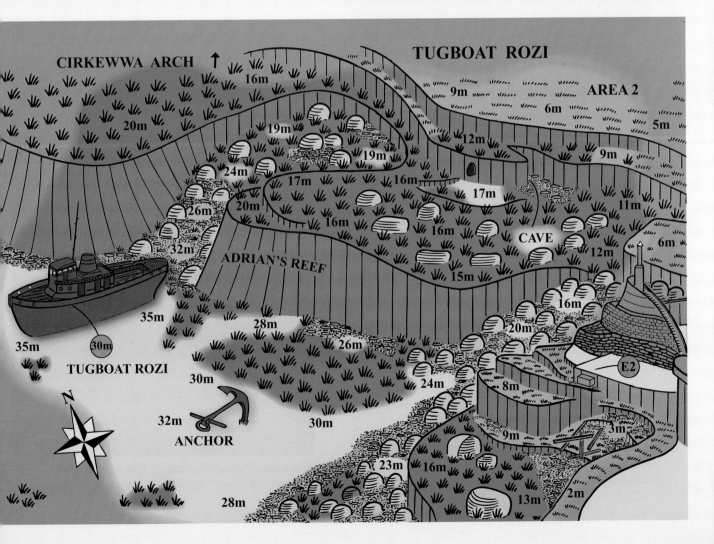

CIRKEWWA ARCH

TUGBOAT ROZI

AREA 2

16m

9m

6m

5m

20m

19m

12m

9m

24m

19m

17m

11m

17m

16m

20m

16m

CAVE

6m

26m

16m

16m

12m

32m

ADRIAN'S REEF

15m

16m

35m

20m

E2

35m

28m

8m

30m

TUGBOAT ROZI

26m

30m

35m

30m

24m

3m

32m

9m

ANCHOR

30m

23m

16m

13m

2m

28m

Sugar Loaf – Madonnna Statue

Area 3

This dive area has many permutations and variations and you can navigate your way around by using the reef, generally it runs from north to south. Most divers who come to Cirkewwa (Marfa Point) normally dive this site first. A visit to the Madonna Statue, then on to Sugar Loaf, which is a huge rock detached from the main reef and rising some 8m from the seabed. Once out of the training area and over the drop off you will find the seabed reasonably flat but with many boulders littering the bottom; also the many large and small overhangs within the reef to explore, make this a good dive site.

This huge boulder called Sugar Loaf is surrounded on one side by smaller rocks, where groupers are often found.

When it is time to return, ascend the reef to your required depth and head south, keeping the coastline reef on your left, you will come to the swim-through cave at 11m, once you have gone through or round to the other side, continue along the reef, over the Madonna cave. Within this area there are many small crevices and little over-hangs to explore. Once at the ledge at 11m, move to your right and you will find a very large over-hang, sometimes hiding right at the back on a small ledge you may see a grouper. The roof of this over hang is covered with brightly coloured small soft coral, this maybe a good opportunity for photographs. Moving from the ledge area there are depths of 6m and 3m for stops if required, through the training area and exit at the Susie's pool E1.

The Madonna statue sits serenely in a small cave and is visited by many divers.

▌THE DIVE   Minimum time – 40 mins

Entry for this area would normally be made at Susie's Pool E1, once under water head in a westerly direction along the stony path to the drop-off, over and down on to the bottom. Now turn right in a northerly direction and in a very short distance, in a corner you will find a small fissure at a depth of 18m. Here you will find the Madonna statue, which is also the home for many cardinal fish. Follow the reef down over the large boulders, round the corner, watch out for groupers lying on the rocks, between the main reef and Sugar Loaf, and remember they are very shy, so you have to move slowly. The large rock on your left is called Sugar loaf.

A young diver progressing through his training takes his first dive near the edge of this drop off above the Madonna.

SUGAR LOAF & MADONNA

AREA 3

LIGHTHOUSE

N

SUSIES POOL

TRAINING AREA

STONEY PATH

ARCH

HANNAH'S REEF

THE LEDGE

MADONNA

SWIM THROUGH

SUGAR LOAF

OLD MANS NOSE

E1 · E2 · E3

1m · 2m · 1m · 0m · 0m
3m · 3m · 3m
3m · 0m · 3m · 2m · 4m · 6m · 3m · 5m
0m · 5m · 6m · 11m
3m · 0m · 9m · 2m · 7m
5m · 6m
12m · 18m · 20m · 9m · 0m · 4m
11m · 20m · 9m · 7m
15m · 20m
15m · 25m
19m · 26m · 20m
24m · 20m · 26m · 24m
28m · 28m · 27m · 29m

P29 Patrol Boat
Area 4

▌THE DIVE   Minimum time – 45 mins

Route 1

Enter the water at Susie's Pool E1, surface swim out between the two rocks, now head in a westerly direction above stony path to the drop off and descend. From here the distance is 100 metres to the stern of the *P29*. Take a compass bearing of 270° and if the visibility is good you will be able to see the reef on your right hand side until Sugar Loaf comes into view. In front of you and to the south of Sugar Loaf, on a sandy seabed will be a concrete block almost buried, at this moment in time there is a plaque on the far side. You are now half way there, if the visibility is not so good leave the drop off and drop down over the boulders, rocks and sea grass until you reach the sand; if you are taking a bearing of 270° you should find the concrete block and plaque. Continue with the same compass bearing of 270°. From the drop off to the *P29* should take you no more than 4-5 minutes.

On this concrete block is a plaque in memory of the British diver Frank Pembridge. It is the halfway mark to the P29 *if using Route 1.*

Route 2

Entry point E3 Paradise steps. I suggest that you surface swim to the 9m ledge above the Old Mans Nose, you must go around the last rock to reach the ledge which is on the north side of the reef if you intend to use the compass bearing I have given. Now descend and from the Old Mans Nose and take a compass bearing of 310° if, and when you see the sand you will note that on

The bridge and main mast, the top of which is 18m below the surface.

your left there is a wide angled corner in the reef where it changes direction and on your right an area of sea grass running out into the sand in the shape of a finger pointing towards the wreck. Your route should be half way between these two points. The distance from the ledge to the side of the *P29* is 100 metres, the same distance as route 1 and should take no longer than 4-5 minutes.

Note: If the visibility is not too good and you are intending to swim mid water, beware of the currents which sometimes occur in this area, only a slight current will drift you off course and consequently you will miss the wreck.

Return route

When it is time to leave the wreck a compass bearing of 90° will take you back to the concrete block and Sugar Loaf whereas a bearing of 130° will take you back to the reef below the Old Mans Nose. Of course you can take any compass bearing between the two which will lead you back onto the main reef and your exit point.

FRANK PEMBRIDGE first stared diving when he was on active service in Malaya. He saw an article in a magazine called *Popular Science* on how to make your own aqualung, this was completed, it worked and Frank was the first one to try it out. He began diving in Malta in 1957 with a man called Vince, in 1985 he was invited to Malta by Charles Cassar to assist in a Life Saving Course, apart from this Frank, who at the time was the National Diving Officer of the SAA, organised many other courses over the following years. Since 1990 he was a frequent visitor to the Maltese Islands, then annually with his dive club from 1994. Sadly Frank passed away on the 5th October 2006.

PGL AERIAL PHOTOS

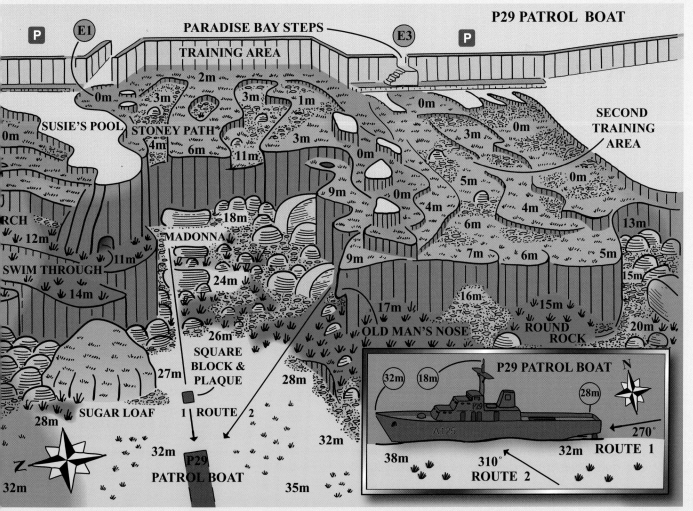

P29 PATROL BOAT

PARADISE BAY STEPS

TRAINING AREA

SUSIE'S POOL

STONEY PATH

SECOND TRAINING AREA

MADONNA

SWIM THROUGH

SUGAR LOAF

SQUARE BLOCK & PLAQUE

ROUTE 2

P29 PATROL BOAT

OLD MAN'S NOSE

ROUND ROCK

P29 PATROL BOAT

A.125

ROUTE 1

ROUTE 2

270°

310°

Paradise Bay

Area 5

The long swim is the nickname given to this site by myself, but in reality it can be completed, taking a leisurely swim, in less than 40 minutes. During this dive there are many different types of under-water scenery to observe and places to explore. There are two entry points; one on the western end of South Quay E5, and another a few metres along the reef in a little cove, E4 entry point, if using E5 remove all the equipment that you require for your dive, put your suit on, then take the car and park it near your exit point E3, then return to your buddies on foot.

Red scorpionfish (Scorpaena scrofa) is the largest of the Mediterranean scorpionfish easily recognised by the large number of appendices around the head.

PHOTO: IAN FORDER, SUBWAY DIVE CENTRE

▌THE DIVE   Minimum time – 50 mins

From each entry point your direction is the same; the only difference is the depth, 5m at the quay and 9m at the entrance to the little cove. When you are under water just follow the reef in a westerly direction keeping it on your right hand side. After a short distance you have a choice to stay on the ledge at 10m or go down to the next level at 15-18m. If you decide to stay at 10m after some 6-8 minutes you will find a curve in the reef, inside this area is an arch, good for photography. If you went to the lower reef it will take you 10-12 minutes or one minute from the arch to the large boulder right up against the main reef, it is possible to swim under it but the entrance is hidden by smaller boulders. Once through the other side **you can take one of two routes:** the first one with a maximum depth of 32m, the second has a maximum depth of 20m. The first option is to follow a compass bearing of 270° down to an area of large boulders, with a maximum depth on the sand of 32m. Once you have run out of bottom time or you just want to move on, take an easterly compass bearing, heading back up the reef, taking your time to explore, when a depth of 20m is reached you should be between Valley Way and Round Rock.

Alternatively, continue round the reef keeping it on your right, where the seabed rises to 16m, here you will find Chris's Rock; this smallish rock resting on stones makes a great hiding place for marine life, we once found a nice cuttlefish here. From here move on along the base of the reef to a depth of 19m which is the start of Valley Way a narrow route between the main reef and boulders. In this area there are many hiding places for marine life such as morays, groupers, octopuses and large scorpion fish. When you reach 11m, bear left between two rocks, once through these looking down and slightly to your left you will see a stony seabed at 19m and the very large overhang at the base of Round Rock, explore this area and then ascend Round Rock onto the ridge at 9m and head into the second training area and E3.

Cirkewwa is quite an interesting place to sit and watch the ferries going to and fro from Malta to Gozo. The islands of Gozo and Comino can be seen quite clearly from here and an excellent place to take some souvenir photographs of the area. There is a restaurant and bar where hot and cold snacks can be purchased with tables to sit at and relax in the sun.

Saddled bream (Oblada melanura) mostly found in small groups moving along the reefs at shallow depths looking for food.   PHOTO: VICTOR FABRI SUBWAY DIVE CENTRE

Divers surveying the boulder area on the western side of this dive site.

PGL AERIAL PHOTOS

PARADISE BAY

(THE LONG SWIM)

AREA 5

ROUND ROCK

VALLEY WAY

BEN'S ARCH

NOTE:
PARKING PERMIT
IS REQUIRED, ASK
AT YOUR DIVE
CENTRE

SOUTH QUAY

CHRIS'S ROCK

TUNNEL ROCK

PARADISE BAY

N

E3
E4
E5

PGL AERIAL PHOT

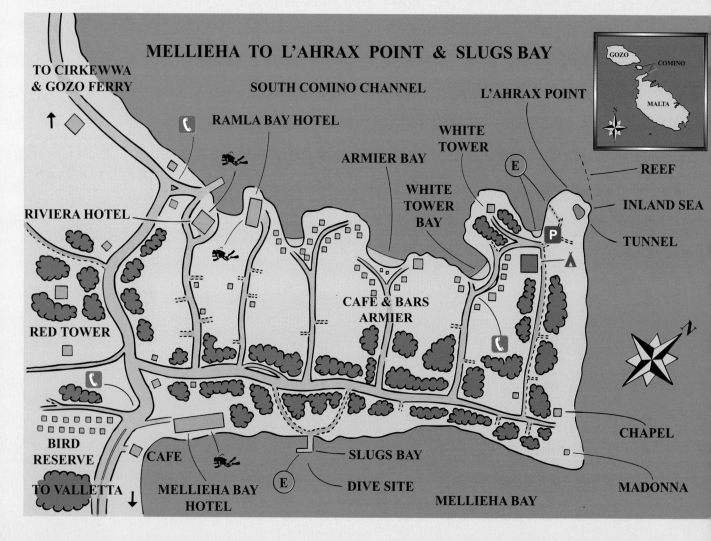

MELLIEHA TO L'AHRAX POINT & SLUGS BAY

TO CIRKEWWA
& GOZO FERRY

SOUTH COMINO CHANNEL

L'AHRAX POINT

RAMLA BAY HOTEL

WHITE
TOWER

GOZO COMINO

MALTA

ARMIER BAY

REEF

RIVIERA HOTEL

WHITE
TOWER
BAY

INLAND SEA

TUNNEL

CAFE & BARS
ARMIER

RED TOWER

BIRD
RESERVE

CAFE

CHAPEL

TO VALLETTA

MELLIEHA BAY
HOTEL

SLUGS BAY

DIVE SITE

MELLIEHA BAY

MADONNA

L'Ahrax Point

To reach Ahrax Point follow the road from Mellieha to Cirkewwa past Mellieha Bay and the sandy beach continue up the hill on the other side, at the top of the hill turn right, but be careful as it is a bad junction to cross. From here to your dive site is approximately 2.5km and will take you some 10 minutes. Follow this road for about 2km then the road ahead narrows, at this point you have two choices one; turn left down to White Tower Bay, in Maltese `Ramla tat –Torri`, which is a summer village for the Maltese people. Bear right and follow the bay around, and on the other side turn right again, at the next junction turn right, this will lead you to the camp site or two; continue down the narrow road and take the first left. The track is quite rough but it leads directly to the camp site and your entry point is opposite the main building, there was a time when you were able to continue further round to the other side of the bay to where the track ends, a short distance from here is a concrete pad but someone has constructed a wall, illegally, across the entrance of the track whilst this wall remains you will be unable to use entry point E2.

Entry point for this out of the way dive location of L'Ahrax which is short distance from the camping site.

Green wrasse (Labrus viridis) found among coastal rocks and seaweed feeding on small crustaceans, molluscs and small fish.   PHOTO: JOSEPH FARRUGIA

This 'away from the madding crowd' dive site is situated on the most northerly point of Malta, and is definitely worth a visit especially when the visibility is good, a little more difficult to navigate in bad visibility. If you decide to dive here remember that all amenities are some distance away. There are a number of ways to dive this site but it could be divided into two main areas. The north reef, which is reasonably level with a maximum depth of 10m, once over the edge you have a drop off down to 23m, away from the reef depths of 30m plus can be reached. The second area is the South Reef Tunnel and Inland Sea, maximum depth on the reef is 12m, over the ledge depths of 22m can be reached; the tunnel is reasonably shallow at 8m. The best time to dive this site is a.m. with the sun directly on the reef, later in the day the reef will be in the shade and all the bright colours will have disappeared. The coast line is very rugged here which makes it almost impossible to exit and even more difficult to walk on with diving equipment. There is a small area, which is suitable for an emergency exit if required. {see plan}. You can follow one of my two dive plans or you can plan your own to reach the reef. Many dive centers boat dive this site.

Cardinal fish (Apogon imberbis) in one of their favourite places in a small crevice and hanging like a curtain are squid (Loligo vulgaris) eggs, which hatch in June or July.

RIGHT: *The sea rose (Peyssononnelia squamaria) is red seaweed with a small fan of partially superimposed horizontal laminae. Grows on rocks and poorly illuminated rocky seabeds and cover the floor of this tunnel.* MAIN PICTURE: *Ahrax point tunnel to inland sea.*

The large boulders, which litter the seabed below the North Reef at L'Ahrax.

L'Ahrax Point – North Reef

The dive (1)

▌ THE DIVE   Minimum time – 50 mins

Use entry point E1 and once in the water surface swim following the coastline, keeping it on your right to the sandy gullies, depth 3-4m now descend and take a compass bearing of 350°. Most of the seabed will be covered in sea grass, after about 11 minutes you will reach an area of small jagged rocks, where the marine growth is short. The stones are in a circle and for some reason it reminds me of a mini Stone Henge. Now take

A beautiful shoal of barracuda (Sphyraena sphyraena) which can be seen throughout the year in open water, at the surface or in deep water.   PHOTO: GAVIN GALEA, MELDIVES DIVE CENTRE

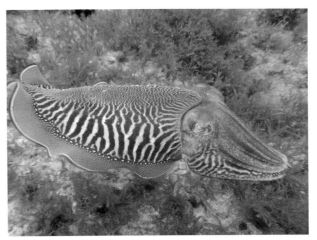

A cuttlefish (Sepia officinalis) has variable colouring due to its exceptional mimetic talents.

PHOTO: SHARON METSON, H2O DIVERS

a compass bearing of 30° continuing over the sea grass to an area of short marine growth just before you reach the drop off. This distance will possibly take you a further 6 minutes.

If you decide to go over and once on the bottom your depth will be around 23m or deeper if you move away from the reef, head in a southerly direction keeping the main reef on your right. Running along beside the reef are some very large boulders, the sea bed is covered with sea grass and sandy patches, don't forget to keep an eye in the blue for any dentex or barracuda passing by. When it is time to return ascend to the top of the reef, continue to follow the edge until you meet the main coastline reef at 6m, bear right, from here it is almost 250 meters to your exit point, this could take you as long as 15-20 minutes. If you have the air take your time and explore this shallow reef. On your way back you will pass a small quarry with a depth of 10m with a little cove at the rear and inside there is a small arch. Continue to follow the reef all the way round until you reach the sandy gullies from here when it becomes shallow, if you wish you could surface and swim to your exit point E1.

This spiny lobster (Palinurus elephas) hides in crevices and among rocks on the bottom.

PHOTO: VICTOR FABRI, SUBWAY DIVE CENTRE

South Reef Tunnel and Inland Sea

The dive (2)

▌THE DIVE   Minimum time – 50 mins

Using entry/exit point E1 from here surface swim following the coastline all the way round until it meets the main reef you can of course descend at any time you wish to, this distance of approximately 250 meters will possibly take you some 20 minutes. At this point you will need to descend unless you have already done so, here the depth will be approximately 6m, keeping the coastline reef to your right and head in a southerly direction for about 6 minutes you will come to a distinct corner where the coastline reef now runs in a southwesterly direction, continue to follow its line. The average depth in this area will be 12m. Within 2 minutes you will be able to see up on your left a rock shaped like an eagle's head, the entrance to the tunnel, which leads to the Inland Sea, is on your right.

You will be unable to see straight through the tunnel, as there is a slight bend in it, the depth inside is 8m. The floor of the tunnel is covered in small rocks and they are in turn covered in red seaweed, these hard petal like flowers remind me of roses. When you leave the tunnel return to the distinct corner, now head in a north westerly direction until you reach the drop off, you should pass a lone rock right on the edge of the drop off. Now follow the ridge along in a northerly direction until it turns and head west, continue to where the reef meets the coastline, it is quite easy to follow as it is shaped like the letter D. From this point your return route is the same as dive number one.

A locust lobster (Scyllarides latus) has a squashed, rectangular body wider at the front than the rear. Does not swim , but walks on the bottom.

PHOTO: GAVIN GALEA, MELDIVES DIVE CENTRE

Facilities like a telephone and café are available when the camp site is open, otherwise there are no amenities within this area, the nearest telephone and café are some distance away (see plan) A reminder that you are diving a site away from it all, that means emergency services as well, so you must check the sea conditions. Although it is harder, I think it is more enjoyable to dive this site from the shore rather than a boat.

A free swimming octopus (Octopus vulgaris) seems to have found a friend and has attached itself to the divers arm for closer investigation!

The grey triggerfish (Balistes carolinensis) lives among rocks and seaweed near shore feeding on small organisms, as its mouth does not open widely. Rapidly loses its blue colour when taken out of the water.

PHOTO: KEVIN DEBATTISTA, SUBWAY DIVE CENTRE

PGL AERIAL PHOTOS

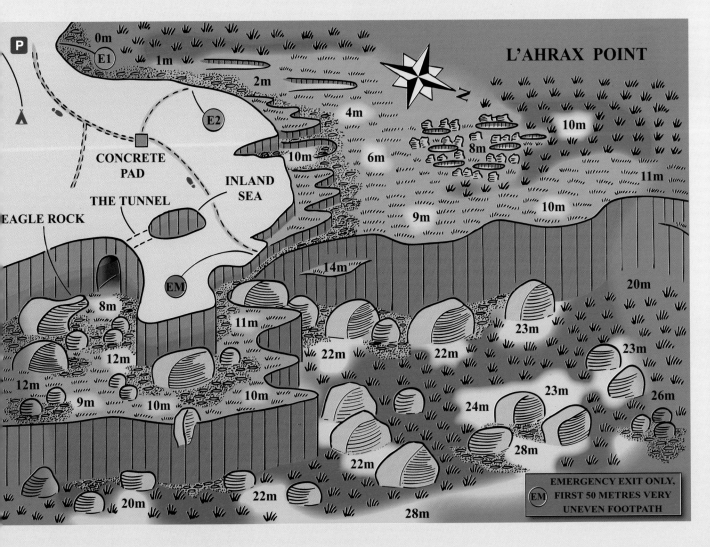

L'AHRAX POINT

P

0m
E1
1m
2m
4m
10m
E2
CONCRETE PAD
10m
6m
8m
10m
11m
INLAND SEA
THE TUNNEL
9m
10m
EAGLE ROCK
14m
EM
8m
11m
20m
12m
22m
22m
23m
23m
12m
9m
10m
10m
24m
23m
26m
20m
22m
22m
28m
28m

EMERGENCY EXIT ONLY,
EM FIRST 50 METRES VERY
UNEVEN FOOTPATH

Slugs Bay

The name of this dive site does not do justice to this peaceful, pretty area on the north side of Mellieha Bay, with its arch, jetty and secluded cove and is only disturbed by walkers during the spring months admiring the many colourful wild flowers. Entry for this dive can be made from the rocks or the jetty; I would normally use entry point E1 and exit at E2.

To reach Slugs Bay the directions are the same as for Ahrax Point, but after turning right at the top of the hill continue for just under 1km. When you have passed the turning to Armier, continue round a slight bend and then on your right hand side you will find an entrance to a track, which will lead you down to Slugs Bay. Normally a 4x4 will be required for the 400 metre drive, some people do take cars to the parking area above the cove, but due to the weight of diving equipment, passengers are advised to walk.

Common jellyfish (Pelagia noctiluca) the most familiar of the species found in Maltese waters. Very abundant some times, collecting in large numbers in bays.

PHOTO: ALEXANDER ARISTARKHOV, SUBWAY DIVE CENTRE

The dive area consists of rocks, sea grass and areas of sand with a maximum depth of 12m. To the east of the dive site, in an area of small shingle/sand, fossilized sharks teeth have been found, remember that in Malta it is illegal to remove certain items from under the water. This is not a very popular dive site, due to the conditions of the track, especially after heavy rainfall, but if you have a 4x4 that's great. It is a site used mainly when sea conditions do not permit diving elsewhere on the island, the bay is protected from the north northwesterly seas.

THE DIVE
Minimum time – 50 mins

This dive site is good for training new divers or to test your skills in navigation. The way I normally dive this area is to enter the water from the outer part of the jetty, entry point E1. Once on the bottom head out over the sea grass and sandy areas with a compass bearing of 140° for approximately 5 minutes, now turning left and a compass bearing of 50° for a further

A white tufted worm (Protula tubularia) has a cylindrical limestone tube with an erect terminal section.

PHOTO: VICTOR FABRI, SUBWAY DIVE CENTRE

8-10 minutes. Here you will find a small reef, where the seabed is covered in shingle: this is the area where shark teeth have been found. Now follow the reef all the way round to your left until you have a compass bearing of 270°, this will lead you towards the arch. When it is time to return, head back to the sandy area, with a compass bearing of 180° after a short distance, bear to your right up and over the little reef on to the area of sea grass. For the next 3 minutes or so use a compass bearing of 230° then a bearing of 270° would be required in order to take you towards the jetty or into the cove and your exit point E2. Maybe it would be a good idea to plan your own dive here and discover how good you are with the compass.

One or two points to remember are that there are no facilities here at all and the emergency services are some distance away at Mellieha. When walking on the jetty extra care must be taken if it is wet or your shoes are wet, as it can be **extremely slippery.**

Spinous spider crab (Maja squinado) can be found on rocky, algae rich seabeds.
PHOTO: SEAN HILL, MEDIADIVE

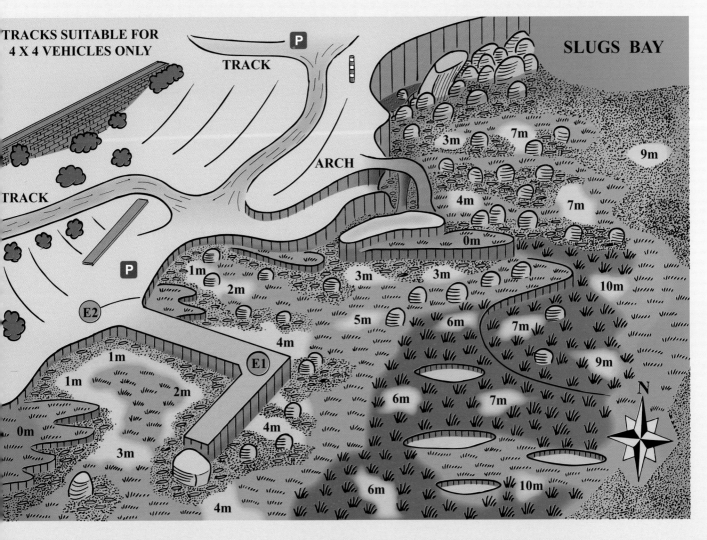

PGL AERIAL PHOTO

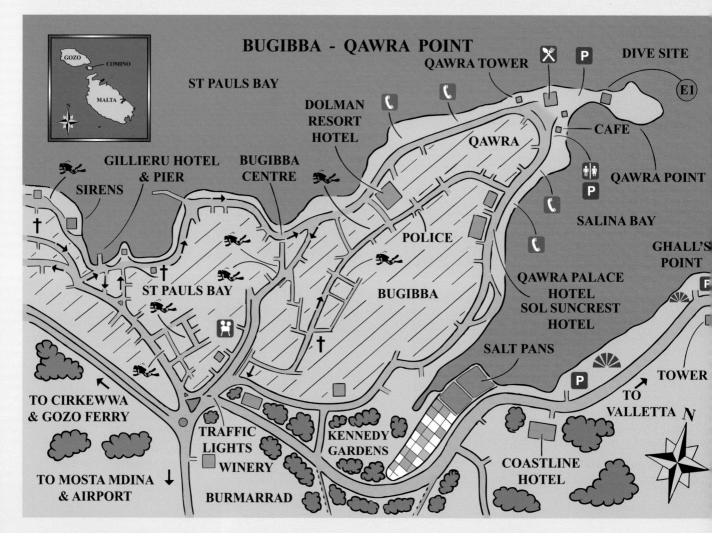

BUGIBBA - QAWRA POINT

GOZO
COMINO
MALTA
N

ST PAULS BAY

QAWRA TOWER

DIVE SITE

E1

DOLMAN
RESORT
HOTEL

QAWRA

CAFE

GILLIERU HOTEL
& PIER

BUGIBBA
CENTRE

QAWRA POINT

SIRENS

SALINA BAY

POLICE

GHALL'S
POINT

ST PAULS BAY

BUGIBBA

QAWRA PALACE
HOTEL
SOL SUNCREST
HOTEL

SALT PANS

TOWER

TO CIRKEWWA
& GOZO FERRY

TO
VALLETTA

N

TRAFFIC
LIGHTS

KENNEDY
GARDENS

TO MOSTA MDINA
& AIRPORT

WINERY

BURMARRAD

COASTLINE
HOTEL

Qawra Point

This dive site is situated very close to the busy resort of Bugibba / St. Pauls Bay which is half way between Mellieha and Sliema, on a peninsular of land on the north coast called Qawra Point. From Sliema take the coast road and when you have passed the Coastline Hotel at Salina Bay, then in approximately 2km take the next turning right. At the T-junction turn right and follow the road all the way to Qawra Point. From Mellieha, at the end of the St. Paul's Bay by-pass, is a large roundabout, follow the signs to Valletta, after the traffic lights take the first left, at the T- junction turn right and follow the road all the way round to Qawra Point. When looking at the coastline of the northern side of Qawra Point it could be described as a straight coastline running east to west with two points and a small bay on the headland.

There are a number of ways that you could plan your dive here and I have selected three. Just off the north shore opposite the pool and your entry point, is a large level area with average depths of 8m, further out the seabed gently slopes off to 36m. This large inshore area is an excellent place to finish your dive, a second dive, or visit the cave, here you will often find thousands of glass fish. Once through the cave you will find yourself

Divers outside the Fra Ben cave doing a familiarization equipment dive. PHOTO: ALEXANDER ARISTARKHOV, SUBWAY DIVE CENTRE

in a small inland sea, in which you can surface and snorkel around a central rock. The last two dives suggested are deeper, 30m plus, and are suitable for experienced divers only. Sometimes due to northerly winds it is not possible to dive this site as the entry/exit point is surrounded by jagged rocks and therefore requires calm sea conditions.

THE DIVE (1)   Minimum time – 40 mins

The first dive is suitable for all grades of divers. Once you have entered the water head in a northerly direction, this will take you over an area covered by short marine growth, sea grass and many small gullies, with an average of depth of 6m to the first point on the headland. Once you have rounded the corner head into the small bay keeping the reef on your right hand side, this will lead you to the cave and small inland sea, be careful not to miss the entrance, for if the sun is casting a shadow it will be difficult to see. When

leaving this area, and you have enough air, turn right and head in a northerly direction, just before the end of the bay you will find an area with rough rocks and boulders they are covered in coral and marine life and if you have camera a good opportunity for macro photography. Remember you are now 15 to 20 minutes away from your entry point. When it is time to head back follow the reef in a south westerly direction not exceeding a depth of 8 to 9m. This will take you into the area by the pool, now head south to shallower ground and your exit point. It is possible to complete this dive with a maximum depth of 6 to 7m.

TOP: *The sun shines through this large blow hole within the Fra Ben cave.*   PHOTO: ALEXANDER. SUBWAY DIVE CENTRE
ABOVE: *Irregular starfish (Coscinasteria tenuispina) with 6-12 different length arms, body covered with prickly plates and spines.*

Peacock's tail (Padina pavonica) is a brown algae, light brown and whitish, with darker horizontal stripes. Shaped rather like a peacock's tail, hence the name.

An ear shaped shell the Lamellated haliotis (Haliotis lamellose) has a row of holes for the sensory filaments of the mantle. On the rock to the right is a small nudibranch (Thuridalla hopei) just visible.

THE DIVE (2)   Minimum time – 50 mins

The second dive will take you to 30m plus. From the entry point surface swim out for 8 to 10 minutes on a compass bearing of 330° you can of course go under water but you will pass over mostly sea grass and use valuable dive time. Now descend to the sea bed if your depth is 28m or less follow the reef to the bottom, if your depth is 32m or more head south back to the base of the reef. Follow the line where the reef meets the sand in an easterly direction, your depth will gradually increase to 36m, this should take you approximately 10 minutes. Here you will see a number small jagged rocks dotted around in the sand. This is a good time to start heading back, remember it will take you around 10 minutes to reach a depth of 9m at a slow ascent. The majority of seabed you will pass over is covered with sea grass with small sunken areas of sand.

The time and distance travelled on the bottom reef will dictate where you end up, you will be of course looking for the larger areas of sand at a depth of 19m and the small arch (see plan) Continue on, turning east when you reach the reef, depth 15m, this will take you on to another area of sand, cross the sand to the other side still keeping the reef on your right. In a small corner of the reef there is a plaque in memory of four Maltese divers who lost their lives in a tragic accident. Continue up over the drop off where you will find a small ledge, keeping this on your right, it will lead you towards the cave. Take your time to explore both the cave and the small inland sea. When it is time to return, head out of the cave, now keeping the reef on your left, once round the point head in a south westerly direction towards the pool and your exit point, if you have left some marker stones, it will be easier to find.

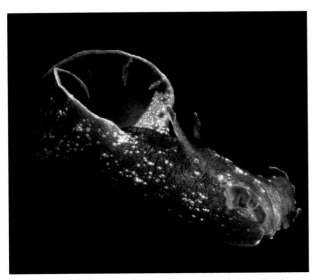

The sea hare (Aplysia depilans) has a thin shell completely covered by its mantle, found on rocky, algae rich seabeds.

Golden zoanthid (Parazoanthus axinellae) lives on rocky bottoms and on other organisms: e.g. sponges, colonies can cover broad surfaces.

Having a great time!

1 – *Entry point at Susie's Pool.*   2 – *Group of divers at Dwejra.*
3 – *Diving Dingli Cliffs.*
4 – *Off to dive HMS Stubborn.*   5 – *Just dived the X127 Lighter.*
6 – *The Blue Hole Dwejra.*   7 – *Group of divers over the Rozi.*
8 – *Even the Project Manager dives!*
9 – *Divers around the bridge of the P29.*

THE DIVE (3)   Minimum time – 60 mins

In my opinion this deep and long dive should be undertaken with a 15 litre cylinder and an independent air source. From your entry, surface swim to the furthest point of headland, this will take 10 to 15 minutes. From this headland surface swim out in a northerly direction for approximately 5 minutes, of course you can go under the water but bear in mind that you will lose valuable dive time. Descend to the bottom of the reef, with a depth of about 30m, on this rocky part of the reef you will find a large old heavy fishing net, at this point the reef drops away again onto a sandy seabed at 40m.

If your surface swim was too far and you are unable to see the reef on your descent, head in a southerly

Top middle: The Greek bating sponge (Spongia officinalis) has been fished for, for centuries in the Mediterranean.
Left: This is the commercial 'bath sponge' Spongia officinalis forms massive, rounded growths, with a rough spiky surface.
Right An encrusting red sponge Crambe crambe grows on rock between 5 and 30m, forming thick irregular sheets.

direction. Now follow the main reef in an easterly direction, black and yellow sponges litter this area of the dive site. Within a few minutes on your right you will find a sandy gap in the reef some 30 metres wide and running in a southerly direction here turn right and follow the westerly side of the gap to its end.

Now ascend the reef up to the sea grass, here your depth will be 22m bearing in mind from this point it

Asinella polypoides this sponge's colonies look like a small trees with cylindrical branches.

Divers returning to shallower waters over the sea grass find a shell which was probably left over from target practice as there was a range in this area.

will take you some 10 to 15 minutes to reach a depth of 9m and further 25 minutes to your exit point. Continue on south south-westerly direction over the sea grass slowly ascending, once you have reached a depth of 9m or less head in a westerly direction, staying at this depth keeping the shallower water on your left. If you keep your depth between 6 and 9m eventually this will lead you into the area by the pool and your exit point.

Please note that Qawra Point often gets quite busy with boat traffic which are inclined to come close to the shore when rounding the headland, especially in summer periods and at weekends.

On the south side of the point is a very pleasant place for those non-divers to just sit and watch the world go by, sun bathe, swim or maybe snorkel. There is a restaurant and an excellent café' not far from your parking place. Once again this is a popular area for the local people and can become quite busy at weekends.

St. Paul's Shipwreck

St. Paul's islands can clearly be seen from Qawra point and the history of the shipwreck is as follows;

According to the Acts of Apostles, St. Paul and St. Luke were on their way to Rome to be tried as political rebels when their ship foundered on the rocks of Malta. The actual site of the shipwreck is generally thought to have been one of the islets to the north of St. Paul's Bay. The islanders welcomed the Apostles and for an entire winter they sheltered in a cave at Rabat. It was from here that St. Paul preached the Gospel, converting the Roman governor, Publius, who became the first Bishop of Malta.

A huge statue of St. Paul today distinguishes the islet. The islets are uninhabited but you can hire a boat to have a closer look at the statue. Once a year the Maltese sail over in fishing boats to celebrate open-air mass by the statue.

PGL AERIAL PHOTOS

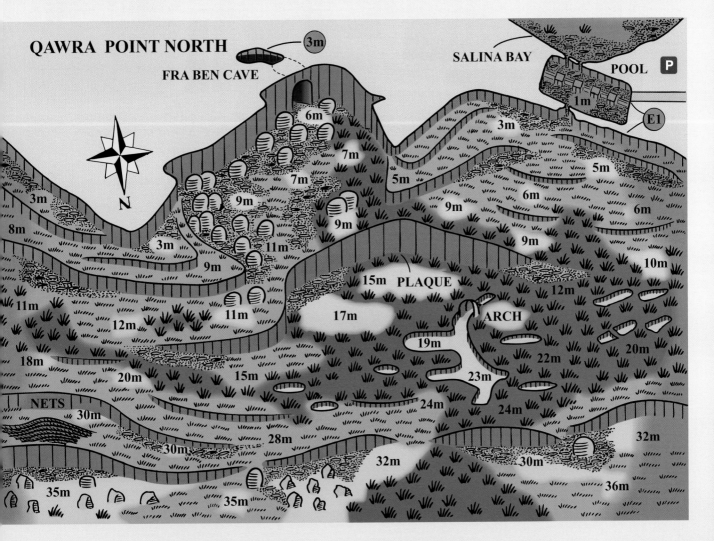

QAWRA POINT NORTH

FRA BEN CAVE

3m

SALINA BAY

POOL

P

6m

1m

E1

3m

7m

5m

5m

7m

6m

5m

9m

6m

9m

9m

9m

3m

11m

10m

3m

8m

N

9m

15m PLAQUE

12m

11m

11m

17m

ARCH

11m

12m

19m

22m

20m

18m

20m

15m

23m

24m

24m

NETS

30m

30m

28m

32m

32m

30m

35m

35m

36m

Below the boat ...

1 – *Diver with a torpedo over the winch on the* Um el Faroud. *2 – Divers returning to the boat. 3 –Spot the diver! 4 – P29 motif on the rear of the chimney. 5 – Diver on the staircase of the* Karwela. *6 – The tugboat* Rozi *enjoyed by numerous divers. 7 – The Blue Dome Cathedral Cave.*
8 – Divers below the Arch at Cirkewwa.

PGL AERIAL PHOTOS

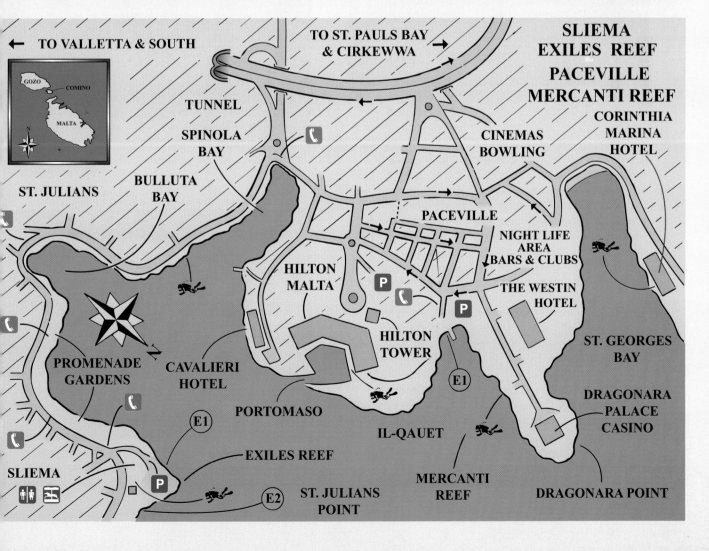

TO VALLETTA & SOUTH

TO ST. PAULS BAY & CIRKEWWA

SLIEMA
EXILES REEF
PACEVILLE
MERCANTI REEF
CORINTHIA MARINA HOTEL

TUNNEL

SPINOLA BAY

ST. JULIANS

BULLUTA BAY

CINEMAS BOWLING

PACEVILLE

NIGHT LIFE AREA BARS & CLUBS

HILTON MALTA

THE WESTIN HOTEL

HILTON TOWER

ST. GEORGES BAY

PROMENADE GARDENS

CAVALIERI HOTEL

PORTOMASO

IL-QAUET

DRAGONARA PALACE CASINO

E1

E1

SLIEMA

EXILES REEF

E2

ST. JULIANS POINT

MERCANTI REEF

DRAGONARA POINT

GOZO
COMINO
MALTA

Paceville – Mercanti Reef

Situated on the north coast near Dragonara Point and not too far from St Julians, this is a different type of dive site with its entry point almost in the heart of Malta's main night life centre. To find this site head towards St Julians, there you will see the Hilton tower. The entry point and parking are to the north side of this building, follow the details on the local map but watch out for the narrow one way streets and do not park unless you are sure it is okay to do so.

THE DIVE
Minimum time – 50 mins

Most of the boat traffic will pass by on the outside of the reef so should not be a problem. From your entry point you have just over a 250 metre surface swim, less if you are able to use the beach front on Dragonara Point as this route is shorter, it will take you almost 20 minutes to reach the marker post from E1.When you reach the reef, descend, unless you have already done so, below the marker post is a small shallow valley of stones which run out in the direction of your route

An offshore reef with many overhangs and places of interest to explore.

back to your exit point Now head north until you reach a large area of flat rock with gullies running out in a westerly direction, after exploring this area, turn round head back in a southerly direction past the marker post. Now follow the reef in a southerly direction keeping it on your left hand side for some 6 minutes, in front of you will be a large rock/boulder, it looks a bit like a blackberry, now you have a choice;

One: you can continue all the way along the reef round the little horseshoe and the pointed end with a small hole in the reef, this looks like an animal sitting up with its front leg supporting its head, along the back of the reef it is much flatter after passing the 6 humps you will now be 20 minutes into your dive and 40 minutes away from your exit point, turn and retrace your steps to the small stony valley below the marker post, maximum depth so far is 10m. From here your return journey will take you approximately 20 minutes with a maximum depth of 12m on a compass bearing of 250°.

Two: go on the inside between the reef and Blackberry rock, now take a bearing of 200-210° to the southern end of the inshore reef exploring the rugged east side before returning to the end, then head in a northerly direction so that the inner reef is on your left and when the visibility is good you will see the main reef on your right. Follow this to the end of the valley here, if you have taken the time to explore, you could be 40 minutes into your dive. Your return route is the same 250 metres; 20 minutes with a compass bearing of 250° this will test your navigational skills. There are far too many small overhangs fissures and places to explore to be indicated on this small map, this is an excellent dive and should not be rushed. The marine life here is plentiful, so take your camera.

The Hilton tower is the tallest building in Malta; it has a wine bar on level 22 with fantastic views from all sides, to visit this bar it is advisable to book. Within this area there are many types of bars, discos, night clubs and restaurants so why not make it an evening to remember.

A striped seabream (Lithognathus mormyrus) feeds on small invertebrates which it drives out by digging in the sediment.
PHOTO: VICTOR FABRI, SUBWAY DIVE CENTRE

(Hypselodoris valenciennesi) Nudibranch gastropod mollusc, with a body similar to a snail's, very elongated and with undulated edges. PHOTO: IAN FORDER, SUBWAY DIVE CENTRE

PGL AERIAL PHOTOS

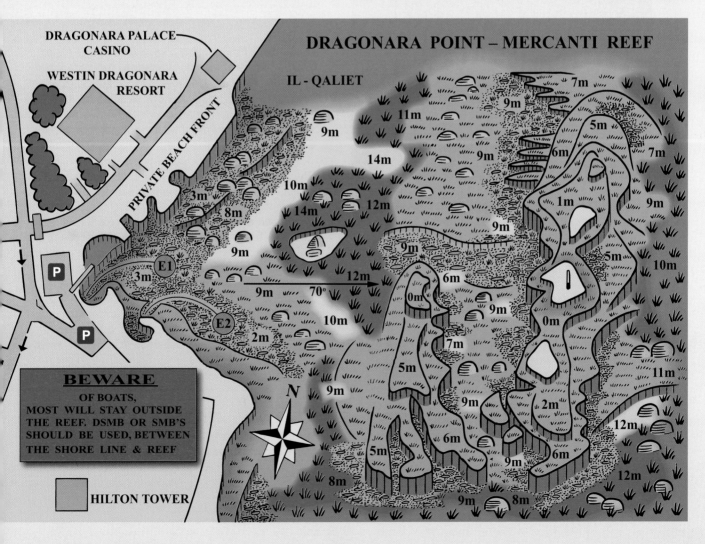

Exiles St. Julians Point – Sliema

This dive site is situated approximately half way between the main centres of St. Julians and Sliema. From St. Julians follow the coast road until you pass the water polo pool then as the road turns sharply to the right the Barracuda restaurant is directly in front of you. From here it is approximately 500 metres before you turn left down a narrow road that leads to a car park and your dive site, another landmark is the St. Julians Tower. From Sliema front continue along Tower Road, which is the coastal road, past the Fortizza restaurant travel for about 1km where the St Julians Tower will be on your right. Here there is a sharp left-hand bend with a centre barrier, immediately after this you will have to turn right down the narrow road to the car park and dive site.

This nice little dive site is situated on the outskirts of Sliema; normally diving only takes place here when it is not possible to dive elsewhere, due to rough sea conditions. There are other reasons to dive this pretty gentle sloping reef, the less experienced diver will enjoy this dive site, it is also an excellent place for training especially in navigational skills, or you quite simply want a change. The entry/exit point here is not difficult, with a gentle sloping reef down to the sand at 13m, which will take you about 5 minutes. Depths of up to 20m can be reached at the end of the reef. This is a very interesting reef to explore with many small gullies and overhangs, also an abundance of marine life.

Hiding in the sand the star-gazer (Uranoscopus scaber) snatches passing tiny shrimps and other morsels.

PHOTO: GAVIN GALEA, MELDIVES DIVE CENTRE

The triggerfish (Balistes carolinensis) is becoming a more common sight in the Maltese waters.

PHOTO: KEVIN DEBATTISTA, SUBWAY DIVE CENTRE

THE DIVE
Minimum time – 40 mins

Once in and under the water, take a compass bearing of 300° follow this gentle sloping reef all the way down to where the reef meets the sand at 13m. Here you will need to turn right, heading in a northerly direction, following the line where the reef meets the sand. If you continue in this direction exploring as you go you should reach a depth of 20m in approximately 20 minutes into your dive. Around the depth of 20m the reef begins to level out and more boulders appear on your right hand side, here you have two choices:

One: you can return heading in a southerly direction, up and over the reef towards the double point in the reef, most of the seabed is covered in sea grass. At a depth of 9m it gradually changes to short marine growth with many gullies and small reefs with numerous hiding places for the inhabitants. The rocks and reefs are covered in coral with fire worms and starfish looking for their next meal, octopus and moray also roam these reefs.

The second choice: turn to your right and head in a direction of 130-140° and within 7 minutes you will be at a depth of 7m, most of the seabed to here would have been covered in sea grass, but like the other route home it changes to areas of short marine growth and gullies. These increase in size if you venture away from your route and head out in an easterly direction where depths of 14m or more can be reached, always returning to a depth of 6-9m and following your course. If your dive time has now reached 40 minutes, head south to shallower waters and your exit point E2 where there is a small pool area which will allow you to exit the water easily, it would help if you checked out E2 before you rig.

Exiles bar/café is a nice place to rest after your dive and fill in your logbook, but it is not normally open during the winter months. All other facilities are a short distance away.

PGL AERIAL PHOTOS

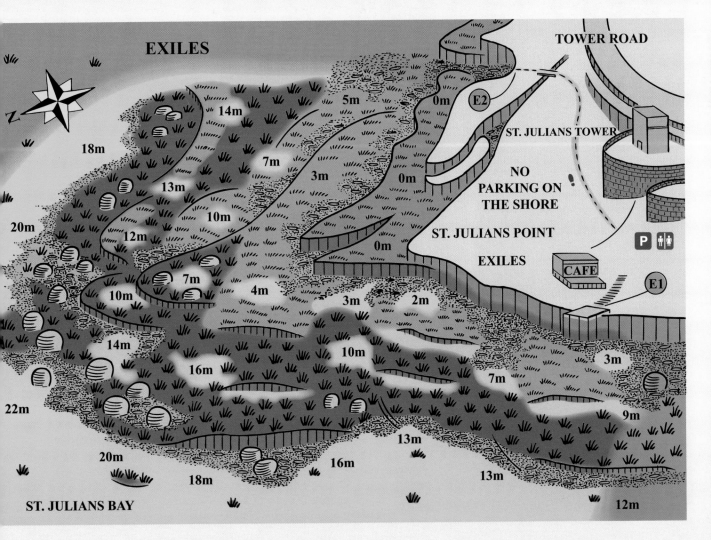

Secrets below the surface

1 – A shoal of salema fish (Sarpa sarpa) at Reqqa Point.
2 – A shoal of two- banded sea bream (Diplodus vulgaris) PHOTO: COLIN STEAD. 3 – Looking to the surface.. 4 – Snorkel diver.
5 – Peacock worm (Sabella pavonina) PHOTO: SEAN HILL, MEDIADIVE.
6 – Double Arch Reef. 7 – A nudibranch (Hypselodoris tricolour) PHOTO: SHARON METSON, H2O DIVERS. 8 – Looking for the ghost of the Count of Monte Christo! 9 – The sailing ship Charlotte Louise, built in Scotland in 1942, featured in a number of films including the Count of Monte Chritso, in the film she was known as 'Jeune Ame'lie'.

PGL AERIAL PHOTOS

TO VALLETTA

GZIRA   MARINE STREET

MANOEL ISLAND
X127 LIGHTER

SLIEMA FORTIZZA REEF
CORAL GARDENS

THE STRAND   FORTIZZA 🍴 🅿 📞

FORTIZZA REEF

PRELUNA
HOTEL

E1

E2

SLIEMA
CENTRE 📞
🅿

HARBOUR
COMINO ISLAND
CRUISES

E3

CAFE
BAR

YACHT
MARINA

ENTRY
PERMIT
REQUIRED
=
MANOEL ISLAND
FORT
MANOEL

🅿

SLIEMA
CREEK

SLIEMA
CENTRE
TIGNE
SEA
FRONT

CORAL GARDENS

GOZO   COMINO

MALTA

FORTINA SPA
HOTEL

🅿

HEAD OFFICE
CAPTAIN
MORGAN
CRUISES

E1

X127 LIGHTER
(CORALITA)

ROYAL MALTA
YACHT CLUB

THE NEW
TIGNE
CENTRE

LAZZARETTO
CREEK

TIGNE FORT

MARSAMXETT HARBOUR

Fernandes
CAPTAIN
MORGAN

Fortizza Reef & Coral Gardens – Sliema

This dive site is only a few minutes away from the bustling centre of Sliema, with its shops, cafes, bars and seafront promenades, so maybe if your partner is not diving he or she could go shopping or just sit enjoy a drink and watch the world go by. When coming from St Julians drive along the coast road with the sea on your left, when you pass the St Julians Tower; continue along Tower Road for a further 800 metres. Immediately after the Fortizza restaurant, which will be on your left and before the zebra crossing, turn left into the car park. From the other direction, almost opposite the Preluna Hotel on the left, just after the zebra crossing turn right into the car park. Sometimes you may have to wait for a space to park.

Normally both of these sites are used for a second dive or when sea conditions do not allow diving at the more popular sites. When you have rigged go down the narrow road to the lower level, you will be above the polo pool, cross over to the far corner and down on to the sun terrace, bear left and go to the furthest corner

The two dive sites here have many wide gullies, tunnels, arches and overhangs to explore.

where you will find steps leading onto the rocks and the little horseshoe cove which is entry/exit point E1. Once upon a time we had to walk past the front of the Fortizza restaurant along the street. The first time I did this I felt most strange walking along the street in full diving kit! Just past the restaurant there is an entrance into the Preluna Beach Club, sun terrace and swimming pool, there is a dive centre here and if you are using this route permission must be obtained before you get rigged.

This dive site is good for practising your navigational skills, either with a compass or by pilotage, with a tunnel, arch and a short cave to find. This dive site has a maximum depth of 16m, if you continue further out it gently gets deeper. There are many places of interest to explore on this reef with a surprising amount of marine life, given the locality and due to the reef being reasonably shallow makes it an excellent place for photography when the visibility is good.

THE DIVE
Minimum time – 45 mins

The entry point for this dive site is E1, which is in front of the Preluna Beach Club pool. Once in the water you will find an area shaped like a bowl, swim straight out of this area and drop over a 3m wall and down to 6m keep close to the reef on your left. Stop at the end of this reef, depth around 8m, your compass bearing to Mushroom Rock is 35° and approximately 60 metres in distance; this should not take more than 3-4 minutes. First of all you will swim over sea grass then short marine growth, and then you should see what is called Mushroom Rock, which from certain angles looks just like a giant mushroom. Drop over a little reef just to the left of this rock, when on the bottom bear left and on your right will be the tunnel. Go through the tunnel, on emerging the other side keep going forward taking a compass bearing of 60° you will pass three distinct rocks on the left reef. After the third one, bear left into an open area covered in sea grass, in front of you there will be another reef, here there is small cave which leads on to the top of the reef. Return to the third rock and continue with a compass bearing of 60° there are two more bowl areas to explore, if you reach the furthest one, your depth will be 18m you are some 15 minutes from Mushroom Rock and a further 5-6 minutes to your exit point E1.

Your return route is to follow the opposite side of the valley back to Mushroom Rock and then use the same route back to E1 or if you have the time and air continue round the shore line to exit E2 or E3 Of course you can plan your own dive but it would be wise to include Mushroom Rock, as this is a good pilotage point for navigation especially for your return journey.

This shark sucker (Echeneis naucrates) is the only one I have ever seen in Maltese waters.

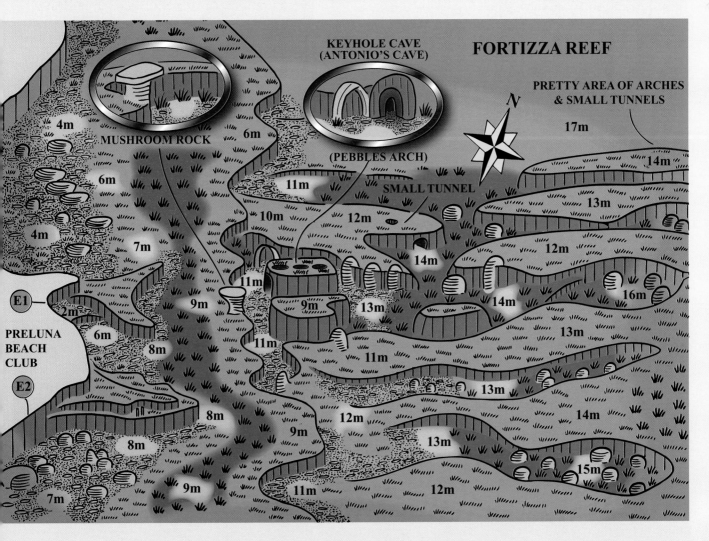

KEYHOLE CAVE
(ANTONIO'S CAVE)

FORTIZZA REEF

PRETTY AREA OF ARCHES
& SMALL TUNNELS

17m

MUSHROOM ROCK

(PEBBLES ARCH)

SMALL TUNNEL

PRELUNA
BEACH
CLUB

E1

E2

Coral Gardens

When you have rigged follow the narrow road down to the lower level above the polo pool cross over and down onto the sun terrace, head towards the opposite side where there are rocks, below you is your entry point E2.

Navigating this dive is much easier when the visibility is good, otherwise if it is new to you maybe you should consider taking a dive guide with you, as you may miss so much of this extraordinary dive, with a maximum depth of 17m if you explore further to the East Reef. In good visibility a camera here is a must.

THE DIVE   Minimum time – 55 mins

With the sun shining the reflections from under the water make an unusual photograph.

PHOTO: MARILYN HIATT. MPH PHOTOGRAPHY

From your entry point E2 follow the small reef on your left in a north westerly direction to its furthest point, depth will be 7m. From here take a compass bearing of 60° over the sea grass, within 2-3 minutes you will reach Wedge Rock and its distinct little cove. Go down into this narrow valley where you are going to turn right, note, if you had turned left it would have led you to Mushroom Rock. Keeping the reef on your right hand side continue to the three little tunnels, once you have checked them out cross over to the other side and turn down the valley with a depth of 13m, on your right are the Coral Gardens, your direction is north easterly.

There are many small mushroom shaped rocks covered in coral and surrounded by sea grass on this plateau. From the end of this valley take a compass bearing of 150° or southerly, this will lead over the reef at 11m and maybe you will find the white battery. Before you enter the Limestone Reef please explore this area with extra care and good buoyancy as you admire this unique underwater landscape, around the area of pinnacle rocks the depth is 14m, this could be the deepest part of your dive,. Now, head in a westerly direction into Boulder Canyon and from the narrow exit bear to the right across the bottom of Scorpionfish Valley. Head north keeping the reef on your left, pass the double swim through to Wedge Rock. Take a bearing of 240° which will take you over to your

starting reef and E2 but you could possibly continue round to E3 if you have the time and air. Of course there are many dive permutations for this area; I have chosen probably the most popular one.

A note to the reader

It has taken millions of years for the canyon system to form. Fragile caves and windows have formed and in turn provided unique ecosystems within themselves. Please avoid the temptation of swimming through the windows in the reef limestone, you would surely damage them! The caves and swim throughs are also fragile so watch your buoyancy and fins.

Gerrard De Waal

You must be aware that many small yachts and motor boats travel along this coastline, some passing directly over the reef.

If you intend to use E2 or E3 as an exit in your dive plan, first check that the ladders are in place.

These shallow limestone reefs have been shaped by the sea over many years.

Ornate wrasse (Thalassoma pavo) this one is a male with the distinct blue markings.

PGL AERIAL PHOTOS

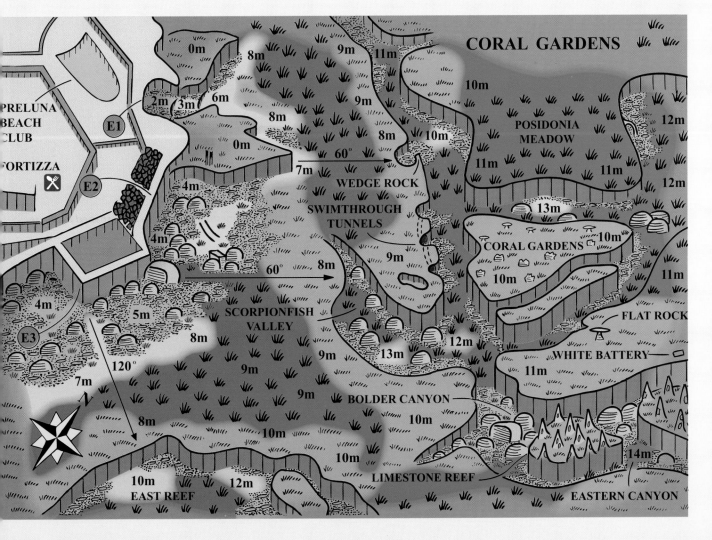

The *X127* Water Lighter (*Coralita*)

In February 1915 Walter Pollock of James Pollock and Sons was sent for by Lord Fisher on behalf of the Admiralty. Walter Pollock was asked to design and oversee the construction of 200 motor landing craft (support vessels) built for the 1915 Dardanelles landings in the Gallipoli campaign during World War I these were designated 'X Lighters'.

The hull construction was based on the Thames river barges with a 60% parallel bottom and a spoon shaped bow with a drop down ramp, this would enable them to deal with the steep shelving beaches and soon gained the nickname 'Black Beatles'. Each one weighed 135 tons, and was 35 meters in length with a beam of 6.5 metres and had accommodation for 12 men.

X Lighters were built in 30 ship yards in England and Scotland. *X127* was built by Goole Shipbuilding and Repairs Co. Beverly, Yorkshire, and she was fitted with a Campbell 80 BHP engine with twin props.

The *X127* was converted to carry water and fitted with a Tangye water pump engine to pump the water out of the hull to reservoirs on shore.

These vessels were towed the 3,000 miles from Immingham on the river Humber via Plymouth to the large natural harbour of Mudros on the Agean island of Lemnos, this took approximately 25 days. At Cape Hellas on the Gallipoli peninsular two reservoirs were built, the

British diver Dave Mallard (centre front) has just completed four years research on the X Water Lighter and invited four Maltese diving colleagues to accompany him to crack a bottle of champagne on the wreck to celebrate the fact. Front left: Antonio Anastasi, Maltaaqua; Patrick Milton, Divewise. Top left: Rupert Mifsud,Buddies; Darrel Borg Cardona, Aquatica: and Martin Vella, Malta Marine Foundation. 4th December 2004. PHOTO: BY KIND PERMISSION OF DAVE MALLARD. ISLE OF WIGHT

Water Lighters could transfer water from the ships to the beach then pumped it to the reservoirs.

The *X127* involved with the successful withdrawal of troops and horses after what some would say was one of the bloodiest battles in World War I. From 1920 many

The wreck of the World War I X Lighter 127 now lies below the surface of what was the submarine base HMS Talbot, *Marsamxett Harbour, in the background St Lukes Hospital.*
PHOTO: DAVE MALLARD, ISLE OF WIGHT

Two of the Lighters under construction on the River Tyne in Newcastle in 1915.
PHOTO: TYNE & WEAR ARCHIVE SERVICES NEWCASTLE-UPON-TYNE

LEFT: *A number of landing craft (Lighters) on west beach, Suvla, Gallipoli, Turkey in January 1916.* OPPOSITE: *A Water Lighter, probably the X127, taking part in the successful evacuation of the troops from Gallipoli, Turkey in 1916.*
PHOTOS: DAVE MALLARD, ISLE OF WIGHT

of the 200 Lighters were sold to private companies, shipping agents and the governments of Greece, Egypt, France and Spain, 16 Lighters went to Malta, *X127* was one of these. At first she continued her duties as a water carrier, then she was converted to a fuel oil Lighter carrying shale oil for the tenth Submarine Flotilla, HMS Talbot, Manoel Island Marsaxmet Harbour, Malta.

On Friday 6th March 1942 the submarine base was attacked by dive bombers and during a second attack the submarines *P36* and *P39* were damaged by near misses and the fuel Lighter *X127* caught fire, listed and shortly afterwards sunk. She remains in the same position today laying upright on a 20 degree slope, the bow at 5m and the stern at 22m. Listed by Lloyds as Wreck No. 37379

The extensive research for this wreck has been painstakingly undertaken by David Mallard of the Isle of Wight. For over twenty years I and many others have know this wreck as the *Coralita*. It was in March 2003 when David decided to start his research into this wreck and a year later it seemed possible that it was the Lighter *X131*, he discovered a photograph of the fishing trawler *Coral* together with the *X131* in dry dock number 3, Grand Harbour, both vessels had been damaged by an air raid on 21st April 1942.

The name *Coralita* may have originated from this trawler but David found no evidence to support this, so it remains a mystery. Further research ruled out the *X131*, and in November 2006 David found the vital information proving that in fact, what everyone has always known as the *Coralita*, is actually the Lighter *X127*.

The launching of two of the X Lighters on the River Tyne in Newcastle in 1915.

PHOTO:TYNE & WEAR ARCHIVE SERVICES, NEWCASTLE-UPON-TYNE

THE DIVE

Once in the water, surface swim along in front of the arches, now descend and head in a westerly direction at a depth of 10-12m staying at this depth until you reach the wreck. Starting at the spoon shaped bow, on the forward deck are footholds for the horses, a fitting for the mast and on each side fairleads and towing bollards. Moving down the starboard side passing over the chain locker, on your right on the small upper structure are two hatches, inside is one of the two Tangye water pumps, just look, in the deck there is a hole where something has been removed.

The entry point for the X127 *Lighter. Bear in mind that the exit point is to your left.*

The next four hatches on your right, are for the water tanks, above the tanks is the gun platform, although a gun was never fitted. Further down is the steering pedestal and the compass plate, around the front of this is what remains of the bullet proof screen. Next is the living accommodation, the scuttle entrance with a ladder and the large skylight above the accommodation for light and ventilation.

Moving down to the stern you will pass the engine room, from here you will be able to see the quadrant rudder, it is 90° out of true from the plan; this probably happened when the blast from the bomb pushed the rudder round, pulling the pedestal over, unfortunately the rudder and props are covered with silt.

The steering chains run along the deck on both sides of the engine room. You will also see the flag pole fitting, rear fairleads and towing bollards, looking in the engine room doorway (door missing) you can see the twin cylinders of the Campbell engine with the flywheel in front, the weight of the engine is 5.5 tons. Fitted to the engine room walls are four sixty gallon water tanks and in the roof a skylight also the remains of the engine silencer.

On the port side of the engine room are the brackets for the spare anchor. Moving up and along the portside deck, to the left hand side is the visible bomb damage, showing the damaged hull plating with bent and twisted metal frames. To the right hand side is the twisted remains of the davits that would have held the dinghy. Continue along the wreck where you will find further damage possibly caused by the submarine P39 being pushed up against the Lighter, when the three bombs were dropped alongside.

Moving away from the bow in an easterly direction explore this man made reef looking out for cuttlefish and octopus which frequent this area, whilst making your way to your exit.

All of the compartments on the wreck have silt inside, some more than others, so please do not try to enter, just look. Remember this is a busy harbour, so keep to the wreck and do not continue in a westerly direction past the wreck, and on your return stay reasonably close to the wall/coastline.

The ladder leading down into the pump compartment where there are two Tangye engines.

The two open hatches lead to the Tangye engine pump compartment.

The main towing bollards situated fore and aft on this wreck.

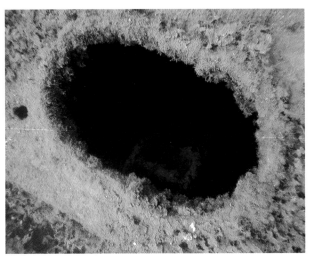

The hatch and ladder to the water tanks, of which there are four

KEY TO DIAGRAM (RIGHT)

A	Crew quarters	J	Steering pedestal
B	Engine room	K	Gun platform
C	Rudder	L	2 water tank
D	Rudder quadrant		hatches
E	Engine room	M	Main water tanks
	doorway	N	2 water tank
F	Engine room		hatches
	skylight	O	Tangye engine
G	Engine exhaust		hatches
H	Scuttle to	P	Exhaust and air
	accommodation		intake
I	Accommodation	Q	Horse footholds
	skylight	R	Landing ramp

PGL AERIAL PHOTOS

X127 WATER LIGHTER (CORALITA)

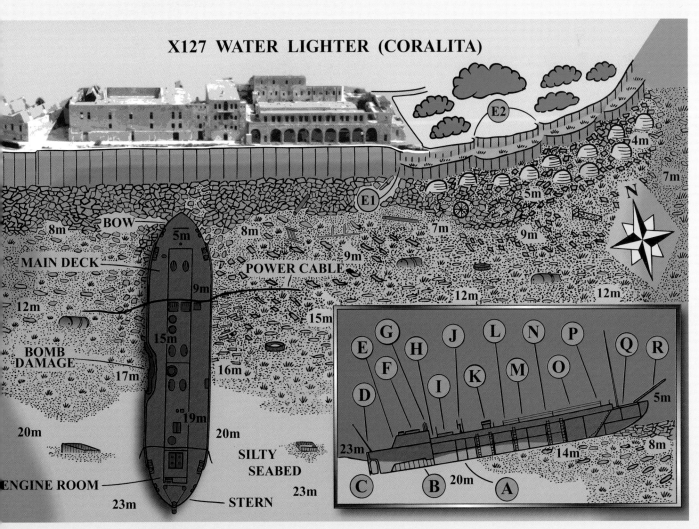

PGL AERIAL PHOTO

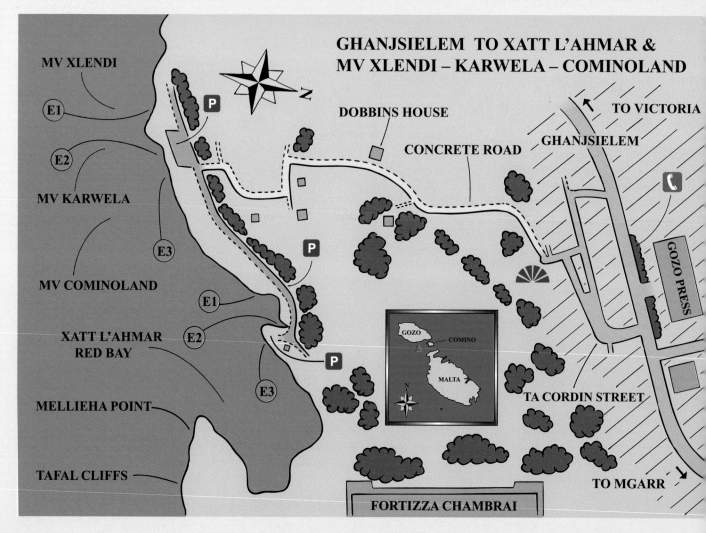

GHANJSIELEM TO XATT L'AHMAR &
MV XLENDI – KARWELA – COMINOLAND

MV XLENDI

E1

E2

MV KARWELA

E3

MV COMINOLAND

E1

XATT L'AHMAR
RED BAY

E2

MELLIEHA POINT

E3

TAFAL CLIFFS

DOBBINS HOUSE

CONCRETE ROAD

TO VICTORIA

GHANJSIELEM

GOZO PRESS

GOZO   COMINO

MALTA

TA CORDIN STREET

TO MGARR

FORTIZZA CHAMBRAI

Xatt L'Ahmar (Red Bay)

To reach this dive site you must first find the village of Ghanjsielem, which is situated on the main road between Victoria and Mgarr, once in this village turn off the main road opposite the Gozo Press. From this point the dive site is approximately 800 metres. Follow the route plan to the viewpoint maybe stopping to have a look at the view over to Comino and Malta with the boats going to and fro, a good point for photographs. From here you can see the single track which winds down the hillside to the sea, you should be aware that although most of the road is made of concrete there is a short distance of track near Dobbins stable where conditions can be difficult after heavy rain. When you arrive at the coastal track turn left for Xatt L' Ahmar and right for the wrecks.

Wrecks of MV *Xlendi*, MV *Karwela* and MV *Cominoland*

Wreck – MV *Xlendi*

MV Xlendi *on her last journey being towed out of Grand Harbour on the 12th November 1999.* PHOTO: CHARLIE SCICLUNA

It was on the 12th November 1999 at 2.15pm, after about 3 hours getting her into position, the Gozo ferry boat MV *Xlendi* was scuttled off the south coast of Gozo as an artificial reef and for the use of divers. This double ended Ro Ro car passenger ferry was built in

The last sight of the MV Xlendi *as she slips slowly beneath the waves to create Gozo's first artificial reef.*

PHOTOGRAPH GRAHAM BLACKWELL

Denmark by Helsingar Ship Builders with a gross weight of 1123 tons and a length of 77 metres. Unfortunately on the way down she struck part of the reef and landed upside down on a sandy bottom at 42m at a slight angle, resting partly on the funnel and the upper structure, with the hull upturned at 24m. After a few days the funnel and part of the upper structure collapsed and she went totally in an upside-down position, she still lies on a sandy bottom at 42m, but her hull is now 36m in depth. This is still an excellent dive, with the reef so close you can first dive the Xlendi and then go on to the reef to complete your dive. Remember that if your dive plan requires stops, the emergency services are some distance away, so keep an eye on your depth and time while on the wreck.

MV Karwela *in Marsamxett Harbour during her last working days.* PHOTO: GEORGE ZAMMIT BRIFFA, CAPTAIN MORGAN CRUISES

MV Cominoland *in Marsamxett Harbour during her last working days.*

PHOTO: GEORGE ZAMMIT BRIFFA, CAPTAIN MORGAN CRUISES

Being a Ro-Ro ferry therefore has a propeller at each end of the vessel, a diver surveys one of them on the upturned hull

▌THE DIVE   Minimum time – 45 mins

Check your entry and exit points, for if you decide to use the westerly entry point E1, to exit from here is not possible, you will have to exit from the easterly entry/exit points, E2 or E3. The route to your entry/exit points starts at the westerly end of the car park, from here walk towards the little headland almost directly in

A diver hovers by one of the MV Xlendi's *rudders*

front of you. Which ever entry point you use surface swim round to the west side of the little headland and here the compass bearing to the Xlendi is 200° and approximately 60 metres in distance.

Enter the water at this point E1, but remember your exit is on the other side of the little headland, E2. I normally surface swim for a short time following the compass bearing towards the Xlendi, just before losing sight of the reef below me I descend. Staying above the

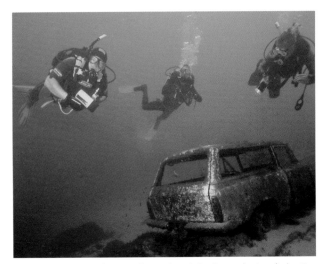

Three divers visit the car that missed the boat, but only just!

reef, but just keeping it in sight, will guide you down to the upturned hull; this should take you no more than 4 minutes. Follow your dive plan whilst on the wreck but I suggest you leave the hull at the western end as the sandy slope leading to the reef above is much closer. Follow it up to your required depth, when this is reached, turn right, and follow it in an easterly direction when the reef drops away close to the headland, continue on into a large area of shallower waters now you are not far from your exit points, E2 or E3. Of course you can spend as much time as your air will allow on this reef.

The marine life in this area is very good with a good chance of finding octopus also cuttlefish, I once saw three cuttlefish all grouped together.

The cuttlefish (Sepia officinalis) are normally found swimming in the shallower waters of this dive location

PHOTO: VICTOR FABRI. SUBWAY SCUBA, DIVE CENTRE

PGL AERIAL PHOTOS

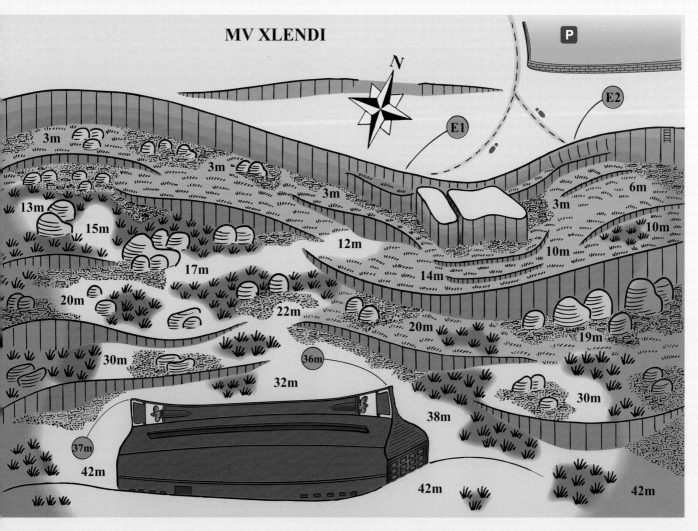

MV XLENDI

N

P

E1
E2

3m
3m
3m
6m
3m
13m
15m
10m
12m
10m
17m
14m
20m
22m
20m
19m
30m
36m
32m
30m
38m
37m
42m
42m
42m
42m

The Scuttling of the MV *Karwela* and MV *Cominoland*

On the 12th August 2006 at 0100 hrs the MV *Karwella* and MV *Cominoland* were towed out of Marsa and through Grand Harbour, Valletta to Gozo. It took over seven hours to scuttle these two wrecks; the *Karwela* was finally sunk at 16-00 hrs followed by the *Cominoland* 25 minutes later. So with their air filled blue buoyancy tanks they sank below the waves and now they both sit upright on the sandy seabed at 42m, some 60 metres apart and in my opinion due to their depths they are separate dives. Both wrecks had been made environmentally safe by Cassar Ship Repairers of Marsa, Malta.

MV *Karwela*

The MV *Karwela* was built in West Germany in 1957 by Jos. L. Meyer of Pepenburg. This passenger ferry with a steel hull weighing 497 tons and 48 metres in length and a beam of 8 metres was first registered in West Germany as the Nordpaloma. She came to Malta in December 1986 and in May 1992 she was purchased and registered by Captain Morgan Cruises. Sliema, Malta.

THE DIVE   Minimum time – 40 mins

Your entry point will be E2 or E3 now surface swim to the east side of the little headland, from here follow the underwater reef out with a compass bearing of 160° to the drop off, when you can see this drop off, descend to 9m. Now follow the ridge in an easterly direction until you reach the Finger, on the far side there is a crack running all the way down the reef. From this point take a compass bearing of 150° slowly

A diver at the bows of the MV Karwela *secures his delayed surface marker buoy*

descending to her depth, the distance from the Finger to the MV *Karwela* is 40 metres, you will approach her side on. Now you can explore the wreck, when it is time to leave, head in a northerly direction, once on top of the reef take your time to explore the areas of boulders and gullies whilst doing your safety stops. Now follow the reef in a north westerly direction to your exit point either E2 or E3.

ABOVE: *The propeller and the rudder below the stern of the MV* Karwela. RIGHT: *Resting on a sandy seabed at a depth of 42m is the MV* Karwela.

PHOTOS: JESPER KJØLLER, DYK MAGHAZINE

RIGHT: *MV* Karwela *off the south coast of Gozo just before she was scuttled on 12th August 2006.*
BELOW: *MV* Karwela *(Jylland Cruises) in Marsamxett Harbour, in the background St Luke's hospital in the early 1990's*
PHOTO: GEORGE ZAMMIT BRIFFA, CAPTAIN MORGAN CRUISES.

RIGHT: *MV* Karwela *sinks slowly beneath the surface watched by many spectators*
PHOTO: BRIAN AZZOPARDI, ATLANTIS DIVE CENTRE

ABOVE: *MV* Cominoland *(Jylland Cruises) leaving Marsamxett Harbour, in the background St Elmo Bay.*
PHOTO: GEORGE ZAMMIT BRIFFA, CAPTAIN MORGAN CRUISES
RIGHT: *MV* Cominoland *just west of Xatt l'Ahmar (Red Bay) just before the scuttling on 12th August, 2006.*

129

MV *Cominoland*

Built in England in 1942 by Philip & Son Ltd of Dartmouth and named *Minor Eagle*. This 295 ton passenger ship 34 metres in length and with an 8 metre beam, was first registered in Malta in May 1992, when it had been purchased by Captain Morgan Cruises. Sliema, Malta and she was re-named *Cominoland*.

◼ THE DIVE Minimum time – 45 mins

Using entry points E2 or E3 and once in the water surface swim out heading in a south-easterly direction. While you are still able to see the seabed descend and continue on your course until you come to the edge of the drop off. Follow it along in an easterly direction past the Altar stone to the area of boulders where you will find an old fishing net, here you need to descend and moving forward with a compass bearing of 150°, the wreck will be side on to your course.

ABOVE: *A diver approaches the bridge of the MV* Cominoland.
PHOTO: JESPER KJØLLER, DYK MAGHAZINE

Taking this route you should be on the wreck within 8 minutes. After you have explored the wreck and it is time to return to the reef and higher ground; you have two choices one: from the wreck head north towards the reef, once there stay on your course until you reach your safety stop depth, now turn and head in a westerly direction. A depth of 6m or less will lead you to your exit points E2 and E3.

Second choice: If you wish to return to your exit point via a different route and you have the air then try this, but only if the visibility is good and there are no currents. Leave the bows of the MV *Cominoland* head in a westerly direction 270° slowly ascending whilst moving forward, after you have passed over the MV *Karwelas*' bows, take a bearing of 330° to the top of the Finger, 9m. The distance you have travelled will be 100 metres and will possibly take you 10 minutes to reach a depth of 9m. Now head north into a large shallow area of small gullies and short marine growth, where you can explore and complete your safety stops close to the exit points, E2 and E3.

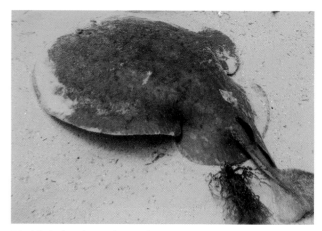

Marbled electric ray (Torpedo marmorata) they often rest on the wrecks, normally found on sandy seabeds partly buried. This fish can give quite a powerful electric shock.
PHOTO: COLIN STEAD

These three wrecks are deep dives and should only be attempted by divers who have experience in deco diving.

The bows and the fore deck of the MV Cominoland.

PGL AERIAL PHOTOS

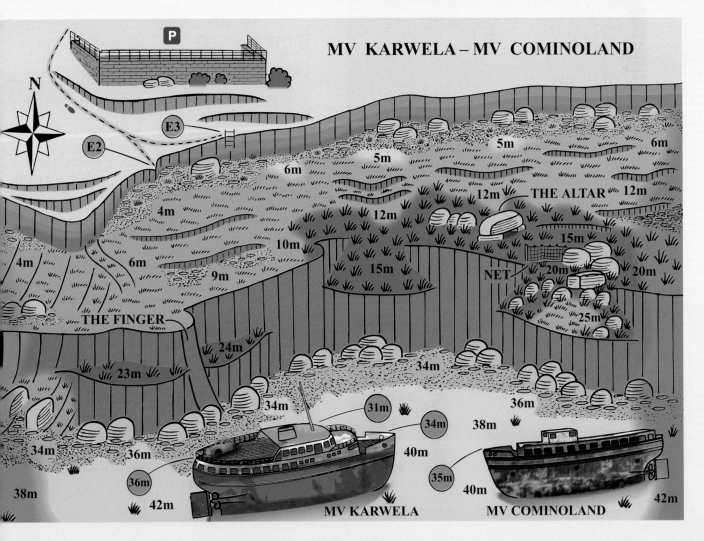

MV KARWELA – MV COMINOLAND

Xatt L'Ahmar (Red Bay)

There are three entry/exit points at this dive site also there are a number of ways to dive this area, I have selected just two.

THE DIVE (1)   Minimum time – 45 mins

Using entry point E2, surface swim taking a compass bearing of 200° before you lose sight of the seabed, descend to 6-9m and continue on the same course. You should reach a depth of 20m within 6 minutes, which is at the top of the slope covered in sea grass and boulders and drops down to 30m plus. Descend down the eastern side of the slope to the bottom depth 34m.

Now follow the base of the reef in an easterly direction, the reef now becomes a cliff face. Along this route, visit the cave, the lone rock at 40m and the overhang, continue for a further 3-4 minutes your dive time now should be 20 minutes.

A diver admires the colours of the hard and soft corals just inside the entrance to a cave.

Now ascend the cliff face to its ridge at 24m and head north over the sea grass on to the short marine growth, at 6m you should see the headland and a large rock which rises to the surface, if not turn left and

Brown meagre (Sciaena umbra) Lives in pairs or small groups among rocks, at cave entrances, under ledges and at drop offs.   PHOTO: COLIN STEAD

Mediterranean moray (Muraena Helena) whose bite can be dangerous hides mostly in holes and fissures.

PHOTO: JOSEPH FARRUGIA

follow the coastline to it. From the large rock take a north westerly bearing to exit point E3, at a leisurely swim this will take about 15 minutes.

THE DIVE (2)   Minimum time – 50 mins

From entry/exit point E3 on a south westerly bearing surface swim across the bay to the headland on the other side, this will only take a few minutes. Pass over the large rock at the end of the headland and descend on to the short marine growth at 9m then head south to the edge of the drop off 24m, turn right and continue along the edge in a westerly direction until at 20m the drop off becomes a slope covered in sea grass and boulders, your dive time should now be around 10 minutes. Descend the slope on the eastern side down to 30-34m now at the foot of the slope turn left and head in an easterly direction. If you follow the line at the bottom of the drop off, not missing the cave, then out to the lone rock at 40m and back to the overhang. Continue on for another 3-4 minutes your dive time at this point will possibly be 25 minutes. Ascend the cliff face to 24m now head in a northerly direction to the large rock at 6m at the end of the headland. Return across the bay taking a north westerly bearing to exit point E3. At any time you may wish change your dive plan and head for shallow water, take a northerly bearing, this will lead you directly into the bay.

Just another small reminder that the emergency services are some distance away. Also there are no facilities or refreshments so it maybe a good idea to bring some along with you.

PGL AERIAL PHOTOS

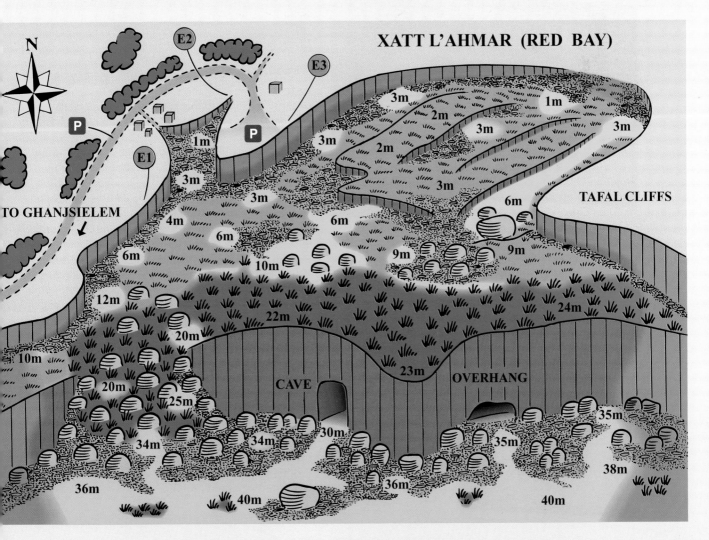

XATT L'AHMAR (RED BAY)

N

E2
E3
P
E1
P

1m

3m
1m
2m
3m
3m
3m
2m
3m

TO GHANJSIELEM

3m
3m
6m
6m

4m
6m
9m
TAFAL CLIFFS

6m
6m
10m
9m

12m
22m
24m

20m
20m

10m
23m
OVERHANG

20m
CAVE
25m

34m
34m
30m
35m

36m
36m
35m
38m

40m
40m

Shore marine life & reefs

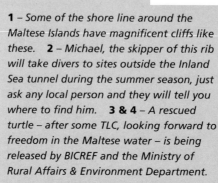

1 – *Some of the shore line around the Maltese Islands have magnificent cliffs like these.* **2** – *Michael, the skipper of this rib will take divers to sites outside the Inland Sea tunnel during the summer season, just ask any local person and they will tell you where to find him.* **3 & 4** – *A rescued turtle – after some TLC, looking forward to freedom in the Maltese water – is being released by BICREF and the Ministry of Rural Affairs & Environment Department.*

PHOTOS BY KIND PERMISSION OF THE DEPARTMENT O INFORMATION **5** – *The octopus (Octopus vulgaris) as can be seen here, has excelle. camouflage. The female lays numerous eggs which it tends until they hatch.* PHOTO: MARILYN HIATT, MPH PHOTOGRAPHY **6** – *An unhappy grouper (Epinephelus guaza) after being disturbed.* PHOTO: VICTO FABRI, SUBWAY DIVE CENTRE **7** – *There are m spectacular reefs to be found in the wate of the Maltese Islands.*

PGL AERIAL PHOTOS

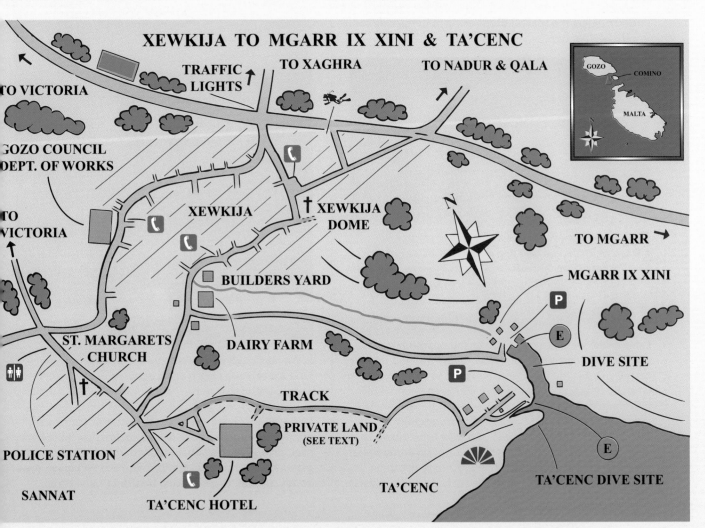

Ta'Cenc

There are a number of routes to this dive site but possibly the best one is from the traffic lights at Xewkija, which lies on the main road halfway between Victoria and Mgarr. If you are travelling from Victoria, turn right, from Mgarr turn left. Follow the signs to Sannat, which is about a 1.5km drive, then a further 4km to your dive site. Once in Sannat drive into the centre past the police station and toilets, bearing left at the Church, at the top of the hill bear left, sign posted Ta'Cenc and Dolman Cliffs. After a short distance, leaving the residential area behind, the road becomes a track; from here it is about 1.5km. Follow this track until the road changes to a tarmac surface, by this time you will be travelling downhill and the sea will be in front of you. Continue along this road until you reach a sharp bend to the left next to a bungalow, once round it take the first turning right, this will lead you down to a headland and turning circle.

Please do not park in the turning circle or your car will be towed away, there is a small area for parking just before the turning circle. When you have parked the car walk down to the turning circle, turn right and face the south, here you will find steps leading down to your entry/exit point. This dive site is normally used when sea conditions are not so good elsewhere on Gozo. The little cove or inlet is sheltered from most sea conditions, so why not visit this dive site when sea conditions are good elsewhere. You will enjoy this unusual dive site and it is quite possible you could be the only divers here. Your only entry/exit point is at the bottom of the steps. Once under the water and round the headland, check for currents before going too far.

Moving away from the main reef and the area of large boulders the seabed drops away quite quickly to depths of 40m plus.

The common torpedo ray (Torpedo torpedo) electrocutes animals which get too near and feeds on them, delivers an electric shock when touched. PHOTO: ALAN JAMES

THE DIVE   Minimum time – 45 mins

Once in the water surface swim to the opposite side of the inlet and descend to 6m, now follow the reef face all the way round the point until you start to head in a westerly direction. I suggest here you keep your maximum depth to 10m until you reach the large overhang in the corner (see aerial photograph) Take time to explore this semi cave, your dive time should be 12 minutes. Now descend deeper straight down over the boulders to your chosen depth, the average depth on the line where the sand meets the reef and the boulders,

is 32m. Once you have chosen your depth head in an easterly direction, within this area there are many very large boulders, you can use them as stepping stones. At any time you wish to return to the main reef head north west and go to your chosen depth, then follow the main reef keeping it on your left hand side all the way round into the little inlet and exit point E1, where you can explore and complete any safety stops required. Of course you can plan your own dive, which could include a visit the cave at 16m to the north side of the inlet.

Below here down approximately 99 steps is the entry point for the dive. Fesse Rock is at the entrance to the bay which is a very popular boat dive.

This land is private and owned by the Ta'Cenc hotel, during the summer peak period permission must be sought to dive this site. Please do not block the road or park in the turning circle otherwise we will loose the goodwill extended to divers by the Ta'Cenc Hotel.

PGL AERIAL PHOTOS

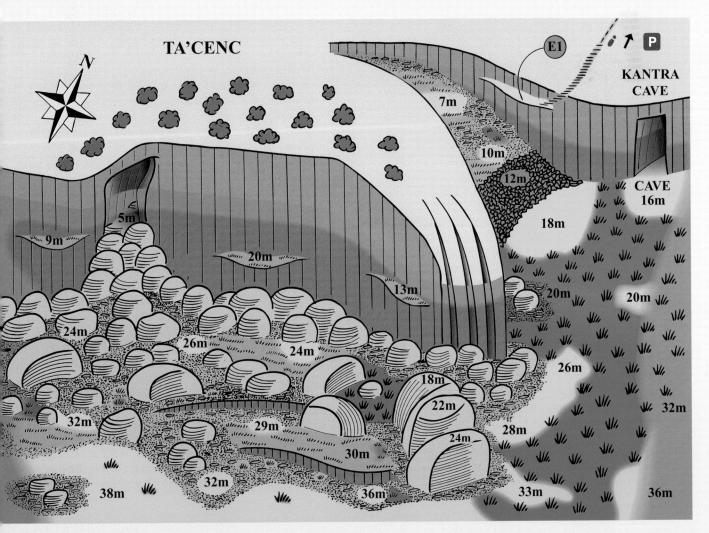

Mgarr ix Xini

There are two routes to this dive site; either route will take you through Xewkija, the route to Sannat centre is the same as the directions for Ta'Cenc. From the traffic lights to your dive site the distance is approximately 6km. From Sannat centre, bear left at the church and at the top of the hill just before a fork in the road and the telephone box, turn sharp left. Be careful you can easily miss this turning; there is a signpost to Mgarr ix Xini. Follow this road down to the farm buildings at the bottom of the hill; turn right, this is a single-track road with passing places.

Alternatively drive directly to the Xewkija dome church, either from the traffic lights or the small roundabout, on the road that leads to Mgarr. The distance for this route is approximately 4km. The only problem is that the road from here to the farm buildings is through the residential area and is not easy to follow, but is sign posted to Mgarr ix Xini and Ta Cenc. Once at the farm buildings you have to turn left along the single-track road, which will lead you right down through the valley to the little hamlet of Mgarr ix Xini and your dive site.

A small young nudibranch believed to be an Onchidoris muricata.   PHOTO: SHARON METSON. H2O DIVERS

Not easily visible the cute little seahorse (Hippocampus hippocampus) likes to attach itself to the Posidonia leaves swaying in the currents.

PHOTO: SHARON METSON. H2O DIVERS

This out of the way pretty little inlet is the perfect place for a night dive, but also used for a second dive or when sea conditions elsewhere are not so good. With a gentle sloping bottom and an easy channel to navigate, for all intents and purposes the inlet runs from north to south. The bottom is mostly sand with some sea grass but this changes to mostly sea grass the deeper and further you go. Remember that there are no places to exit the water other than the exit points shown on the plan.

THE DIVE   Minimum time – 50 mins

Once rigged walk to the right hand side of the bay along the little jetty to the steps at the end, this is where I would enter the water. My dive plan would be to surface swim along the west wall of the channel until the depth below me is about 5m. This is the area where the small boulders end and the sandy area begins. Once on the bottom I would head in a southerly direction following the line where the rock face/coastline meets the sand. The depth gently descends to 10m; here there is a cave with a 3m entrance, which narrows at the rear, your time to this point will be approximately 15-20 minutes.

To reach the second cave from here will take you a further 10 minutes and down to a depth of 16m. This is quite a large cave, which can be safely entered for it does not go back too far. At this point you are within three to four minutes of the entry/exit point E1 at Ta'Cenc which you could use in an emergency. Now take a compass bearing of 60° to cross over the inlet, this will take you about 3 minutes, your return journey from here to E2 is approximately 25 minutes.

During the summer this site is a good place to find and maybe photograph seahorses. If you cover the full route it could take you up to 60 minutes but of course you can make your turning point to suit your own dive plan.

At Ta'Cenc and Mgarr ix Xini when making your dive plans please remember that the emergency facilities are some distance away should they be required.

It is sometimes possible during the summer and some weekends to obtain refreshments at both of these dive locations, if in any doubt it may be a good idea to bring your own.

PGL AERIAL PHOTOS

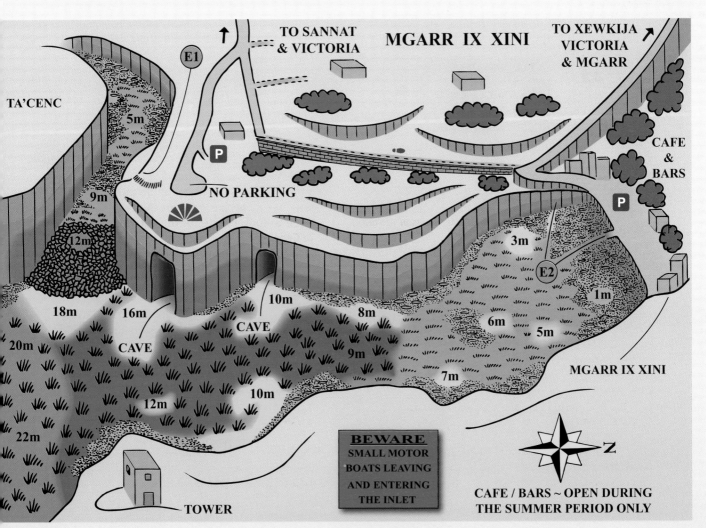

TO SANNAT & VICTORIA

MGARR IX XINI

TO XEWKIJA VICTORIA & MGARR

E1

TA'CENC

5m

9m

12m

18m   16m

CAVE

20m

22m

12m

10m

CAVE

8m

9m

10m

TOWER

BEWARE
SMALL MOTOR
BOATS LEAVING
AND ENTERING
THE INLET

P

NO PARKING

CAFE & BARS

P

3m

E2

1m

6m

5m

7m

MGARR IX XINI

N

CAFE / BARS ~ OPEN DURING
THE SUMMER PERIOD ONLY

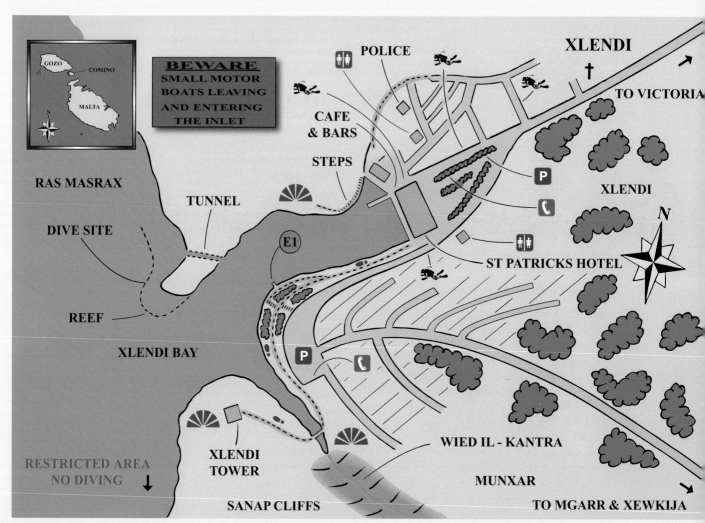

Xlendi

This quaint little village of Xlendi is situated on the southwest coast of Gozo with its large sandy inlet and excellent facilities. There is really only one route to Xlendi and that is from Victoria, a distance of approximately 3km. When driving through the residential area of Victoria be careful not to miss the sign posts for Xlendi, as the streets are narrow with many turnings. Once you head out of the built up area of Victoria the road winds down through a small fertile valley. As you enter Xlendi fork left, past the car park continue up the hill, at the top, the road widens out and here on the right hand side is where you park, you will find the entrance to the path and steps which lead down to your entry/exit point E1. From this vantage point you will have a full view of Xlendi Bay, its reef, the entry point and the sea front promenade.

The actual dive site is around the headland on the opposite side of the bay, with a 70-metre long tunnel which runs through the headland with a maximum depth of 8m, for which you will require a torch. The main reef just off the headland forms part of the dive plan.

THE DIVE   Minimum time – 50 mins

It is best to rig where you have parked the car and then walk down to the entry point E1, which is next to a concrete diving platform with some metal steps for your entry/exit. Please do remember that these steps

The Xlendi tunnel gives the photographer an ideal opportunity for some unusual photographs.   PHOTO: CHRIS GRAY

are normally removed during the winter months. It is not quite deep enough close to the shore for a stride entry, so do be careful for entry is not easy. To locate the entrance of the tunnel which is below the surface, look for the steep cliffs on the other side of the bay, running down is a formation of rock which looks like a spine, directly below this is the entrance or take a compass bearing of 330° from your entry point; the swim across the narrow bay will take 3-4 minutes. The depth at the entrance to the tunnel is 5m, with a ledge rising to 3m just inside, within a few metres there is a large rock in the centre which you will pass on the left, at this point it is quite dark and you will need a torch.

The Narval shrimp (Plesionika narval) is elegant-looking with a smooth carapace and a long lacy rostrum bending slightly upwards. Pale red with red and gold stripes.

PHOTO: AUGUST JANKER, ATLANTIS DIVE CENTRE

Once you have passed this point the depth increases to 8m and from here normally you can see the exit. From this point in the roof of the tunnel are cracks which allows the light to shine through, with this light and the light from the exit this makes a unique opportunity for some unusual photographs.

The red Scorpionfish (Scorpaena scrofa) is easily recognised by the large number of fringed appendices around the head, mouth and sides.   PHOTO: VICTOR FABRI, SUBWAY DIVE CENTRE

Cuttlefish (sepia officinalis) lays large round blackish eggs in March which it attaches to seaweed in shallow water, eggs hatch during April-May.
PHOTO: VICTOR FABRI, SUBWAY DIVE CENTRE

Salema fish (Sarpa sarpa) and an Ornate wrasse (Thalassoma pavo) are all feeding on the reef.
PHOTO: GAVIN GALEA, MELDIVES DIVE CENTRE

Once through the tunnel and on the other side you will find that this is a good area for looking for morays and octopus. When it is time to move on, head in a southerly direction, keeping the reef on your left, when the inner reef direction turns to the east and there is an area of sea grass in front of you, providing the visibility is good; from here you will see the outer reef. If this is not possible take a compass bearing of 180° and continue over the sea grass until you come to the outer reef follow the reef all the way round, keeping it on your left, this route will lead you back into the bay. You can of course follow the inner reef round which is a much shorter route and has a maximum depth of 12m, unlike the outer reef which has a maximum depth of 25m. Once you are heading in a northerly direction and you reach depths of 8-9m you are in the area where you started the dive and the exit point.

Xlendi village is quite a busy little place with some small shops to visit which sell locally made crafts. It is also a very pleasant pastime to sit at one of the restaurants or bars on the waters edge with a lovely view of the bay and soak up the atmosphere of the place. You will find that the restaurants give good value many serving the fresh local dishes also the delicious Gozo wines. If you fancy a climb, on one side of the bay there is a footpath to a viewpoint and if you are feeling really fit you can climb to the top, an excellent position

to take some souvenir photographs. On the other hand you could take a stroll along the promenade by the water and sit and soak up the sun on one of the many seats provided. This is a very peaceful and picturesque bay to spend some time and just relax.

Striped red mullet (Mullus surmuletus) whose long barbells are used to disturb sand to reveal the small animals on which it preys.
PHOTO: VICTOR FABRI. SUBWAY DIVE CENTRE

The photographer was lucky to catch this chance meeting of a Flying gurnard (Dactylopterus volitans) and a Common torpedo ray.
PHOTO: GAVIN GALEA, MELDIVES DIVE CENTRE

(Maia squinado) the spiny spider crab camouflages itself with small pieces of seaweed which it places on its back using its pincers.
PHOTO: KEVIN DEBATTISTA, SUBWAY DIVE CENTRE

PGL AERIAL PHOTOS

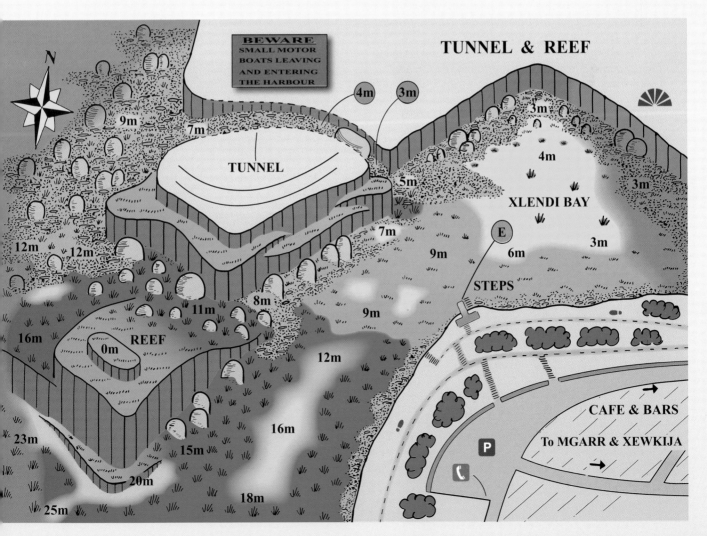

BEWARE
SMALL MOTOR
BOATS LEAVING
AND ENTERING
THE HARBOUR

TUNNEL & REEF

N

9m

7m

4m

3m

3m

TUNNEL

4m

XLENDI BAY

5m

3m

12m

12m

7m

9m

6m

3m

E

STEPS

8m

11m

9m

16m

REEF

0m

12m

16m

23m

15m

CAFE & BARS

20m

18m

To MGARR & XEWKIJA

25m

P

PGL AERIAL PHOTO

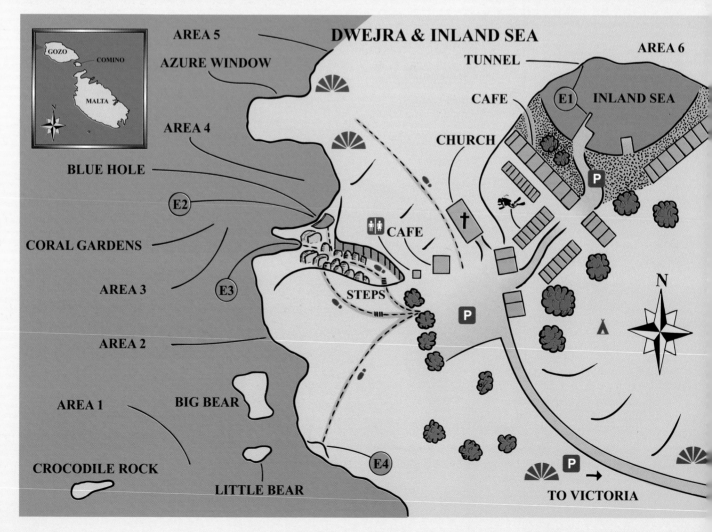

Dwejra

This proposed World Heritage site at Dwejra Point with its unique coastline has been the backdrop on many film sets. Its outstanding landmarks above the surface and its beauty below, has given pleasure and enjoyment to thousands – tourists and divers alike. The area of Dwejra is normally referred to by divers as the Inland Sea, Azure Window or the Blue Hole, in fact Dwejra is a small hamlet approximately 5km from Victoria and is situated on the west coast of Gozo. A short distance away overlooking Dwejra is the village of St. Lawrenz.

To find Dwejra, drive out of Victoria heading in a westerly direction, sign posted to Gharb, after about 3km turn left and follow the signs to Dwejra. Next, turn left at the church once out of the residential area at the top of the hill you will be overlooking Fungus Rock and Dwejra Bay. When you are almost at the bottom of the hill, on your right you will get your first view of the Inland Sea and the Tunnel. At the bottom of the hill there is a large car park.

The small bar/café at Dwejra is a pleasant place to sit after a dive.

The Inland Sea

The Inland Sea is a small expanse of shallow water with a maximum depth of 2m linked to the sea outside by the tunnel through the rock. The tunnel is approximately 80 metres in length and inside the seabed drops from 3m at the entrance to 26m at the exit. Both the Inland Sea and the tunnel are routes for small pleasure boats.

The Azure Window is a column of rock 80 metres in circumference and rising 20 metres out of the sea which supports a bridge of rock from the headland forming an arch/window. This is very picturesque on a beautiful day, but look for the post card which shows the full force of the sea.

The Blue Hole is round and 16m to the seabed where there is a large window which allows you to venture out into the spectacular underwater world of Dwejra Point. On the opposite side to the window there is a cave.

All these wonders have been created by waves and rough seas over thousands of years, only time and the sea will change these massive structures.

The Blue Hole is possibly the most popular dive site in this area of Dwejra. It is approximately 20 metres in diameter and 16m in depth.

Dwejra Point attracts more divers than any other dive site on Gozo and most of the divers that travel from Malta visit here first. With its normally excellent visibility and a number of unique dive sites, it is no wonder it is so popular. For the dives, I have listed six areas or dive sites for your consideration, but of course you can mix and match your dive plan. There are many species of fish, types of marine plants and coral to be seen in these areas. Watch out for groupers lying on rocks and under the over-hangs, the quieter and less movement you make the less likely you are to disturb them. Don't forget to keep an eye out in the blue, for this is where you are likely to see the larger fish such as dentex and shoals of barracuda.

I strongly suggest that you check out all entry/exit points before you kit up. Whilst walking in these areas please be careful especially with your kit on and after it has been raining when your route can be extremely slippery.

It can be seen from the photograph how this outcrop of rock got its name, Crocodile Rock.

Little Bear to Crocodile Rock
Area 1

To find the entry/exit point E4, for this dive is not easy, you first have to navigate your way to a small ledge opposite the rock called Little Bear, which has a compass bearing of 220° from the café in the car park. This is not a straight path but a twisty route over the rocks and holes. E4 is not visible until you are immediately above it and this is the only place along this part of the coastline that you can enter/exit the water. (see aerial photograph)

This is an excellent dive with a reef which runs from Little Bear to Crocodile Rock and continues to the north point of Dwejra Bay. The average depth on the reef is around 8m, with drop-offs from 25m to 36m, depending on your location. Swim away from the rock face and the depth will quickly increase to 50m plus. During a dive along this ridge I had a visit from a lone barracuda who came right up along side me, we made eye contact and within a minute he was gone, I felt I had had a visit from an alien.

A diver exploring the reef below Crocodile Rock.

▌THE DIVE   Minimum time – 50 mins

Enter the water, E4, when on the bottom move over to the right hand side of Little Bear, then drop over the edge of the reef, bottom depth about 25m. Face the reef and on your left will be the entrance to Rogers Cave, when you have had a look follow the reef in a south westerly direction, allow around 30 minutes to reach Crocodile Rock. This of course depends on how long you spend at Rogers Cave and exploring areas below the drop off. Normally, when you are below Crocodile Rock you will be able to see the reef rising to

the surface, another indication that you are below Crocodile Rock is that the line of the reef changes to a southerly direction. When it is time for you to return ascend to the top of the reef to retrace your steps at a shallower depth along the ridge to Little Bear, an excellent area for photographs, then on to your exit point, E4. Don't forget to look out into the blue for that elusive alien (barracuda) and other large fish that may pass by.

The pretty little nudibranch (Hypselodoris elegans).

PHOTO: COLIN STEAD

A fireworm (Hermodice carunculata) is having a feast on a jelly fish (Aurelia aurita).   PHOTO: VICTOR FABRI, SUBWAY DIVE CENTRE

This is not a welcoming gesture from the Grouper (Epinephelus guaza) having his space invaded!

PHOTO: VICTOR FABRI, SUBWAY DIVE CENTRE

PGL AERIAL PHOTOS

LITTLE BEAR TO CROCODILE ROCK

AREA 1
CROCODILE ROCK

Big Bear & Coral Gardens
Area 2

For this dive site I would use entry/exit point, E3. From the main car park to E3, head in a westerly direction towards the sea, down a few steps and bear to the right; continue down some timber steps into the gully. Follow the gully all the way down to the bottom, take your time as in places it is not an easy route. Once you reach sea level pass through a narrow gap between the cliff face and a large boulder, bear round to your left and E3 will be in front of you. Here you have a nice reef with a drop-off to 30m away from the reef and like many areas here it slopes away quite quickly to 50m plus. Big Bear rock is the largest of the three rocks in this area, once under the water it can be explored all the way round. To the south of this reef are a number of large boulders surrounded by areas of sand and small rocks; on the north side is Rogers Cave. On the east side is a valley of rocks and boulders that cover the seabed.

This rock gets its name from the shape of a bear's head, which can be recognised from certain places as you drive down the hill to Dwejra.

be possible to mistakenly enter the cave, as the entrance is very wide. Remember my request; please do not enter this cave. Once past the cave take a south westerly bearing over the large rocks down to the lower reef at 30m. When you have explored this area and it is time to head for higher ground continue up the slope in an easterly direction this will take you to the cliff face of Big Bear and Rogers Cave, your dive time will be approximately 35 minutes. Ascend to the ledge at 8m above Rogers Cave and cross over to the coastline reef, now turn left and head in a northerly direction down the inside of Big Bear. As you now possibly will be staying above 9m once you have passed over the top of Coral Cave, ascend to 6m here you will see a distinct 'U' shape in the top of the reef, this is your route back into Coral Gardens. The depth of this entrance is 6m, once further in; the depth will decrease to 5m and to your exit, E3.

A Request from the Author

There is another cave in this area {see plan} it is called Coral Cave. At this point I am going to make a request and also give a warning! Would you please be kind enough to refrain from entering this cave. There are two reasons; sadly in 1999 two divers tragically lost their lives within this cave for it is very large and difficult to navigate when the silt has been stirred up. The second reason is the damage being caused to the coral in the cave, not only by divers' equipment, but also the air bubbles. This cave is possibly going to be a restricted area by law, but until such time your co-operation would be greatly appreciated.

This clearly shows the 'V' entry to the Coral Gardens.

▌THE DIVE   Minimum time – 45 mins

Be careful at this entry point for the water is very shallow at first, so you have to paddle. Once in the water surface swim out to the middle of the reef where the depth will be around 3m, now swim towards the open sea in a southerly direction and out of the 'U' shaped opening, now descend to the sea bed you will have a drop of approximately 25m. Turn left and follow the reef you will pass in front of Coral Cave, this is not normally a problem but if the visibility is poor it would

Brown comber (Serranus hepatus) found all year round in small shoals on all types of seabed, close to the shore in summer and further out in winter, capable of self-fertilisation.

PGL AERIAL PHOTOS

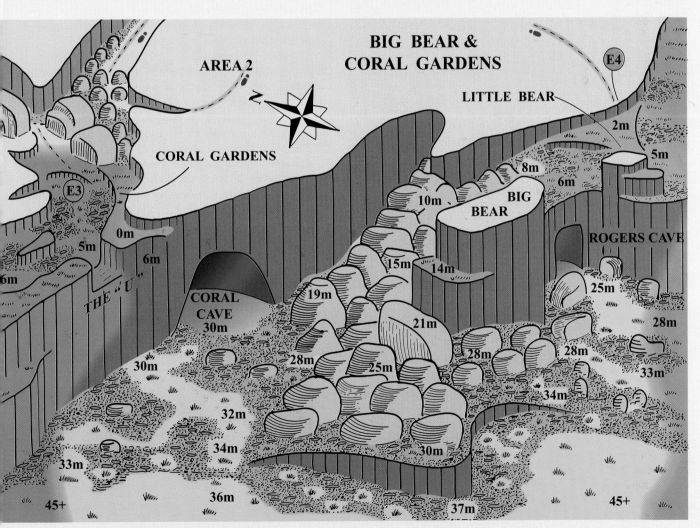

BIG BEAR &
CORAL GARDENS

AREA 2

LITTLE BEAR

E4

2m

CORAL GARDENS

5m

8m

6m

E3

10m

BIG
BEAR

ROGERS CAVE

0m

5m

6m

15m

14m

25m

6m

THE "U"

19m

28m

CORAL
CAVE
30m

21m

33m

30m

28m

25m

28m

28m

34m

32m

30m

34m

33m

36m

37m

45+

45+

The Blue Hole & Coral Gardens

Area 3

For this dive site I would use entry/exit point E3. From the main car park to E3, head in a westerly direction towards the sea, down a few steps and bear to the right; continue down some timber steps into the gully. Follow the gully all the way down to the bottom take care, as it is quite un-even and with steps cut into the rock, which are difficult to negotiate. Once you reach sea level entry point E2, to the Blue Hole will be on your right and on your left will be two large boulders, go round these and you will find your shallow entry point, E3. This dive allows you to explore the outer underwater reef, which takes you further away from the shore than any other dive here.

A very well camouflaged nudibranch (Hypselodoris messinensis) PHOTO: SHARON METSON, H2O DIVERS

▌ THE DIVE   Minimum time – 50 mins

Once in the water swim away from the shallows and descend towards the open sea, your depth here will be 2m and 6m when you come to the 'U' shaped opening. From this opening the drop off to the seabed is approximately 25m. At this point your minimum time to the Blue Hole is around 15-20 minutes. Once on the seabed, or your chosen depth, turn and head in a northerly direction keeping the reef on your right, when you reach the end of the reef follow it round, once you have turned the corner you will be heading in an easterly direction, from here it will only take you a very short time to reach the 'crack' as local divers refer to it. At the bottom of this 'crack' the depth is 27m, now enter this large fissure making sure your depth is below 14m, ascend slowly up into Coral Gardens where your depth will be 7m, now bear to your right and follow the gully to the 'V' opening. Your dive time at this point could be 25 minutes depending on your depth and time taken exploring around the headland. Turn right and with the reef on your right hand side follow it all the way round to the Window and the Blue Hole, this will take some 20 minutes. I suggest that you now keep a maximum depth of 8-9m. Once inside the Blue Hole, whilst completing safety stops if required, admire your surroundings or just diver watch before you exit E2.

A Grouper (Epinephelus guaza) in the Blue Hole. Lives on rocky bottoms with plenty of crevices, feeds on all types of animals found among the rocks. PHOTO: VICTOR FABRI, SUBWAY DIVE CENTRE

The dive starts in Coral Gardens and ends at the Blue Hole, if you check out the aerial photograph you will clearly see your entry and exit points, Blue Hole E2 and Coral Gardens E3, both the 'U' and 'V' openings and the top of the 'crack', but of course you can plan your own dive. There is from the 'U' opening, a 25m drop-off onto the seabed, with the average depth around the reef face of 30m, but if you move away the seabed quickly drops to depths of 50m plus.

Painted comber (Serranus scriba) is seen mostly in shallow waters all year round. PHOTO: JESPER KJØLLER, DYK MAGAZINE

PGL AERIAL PHOTOS

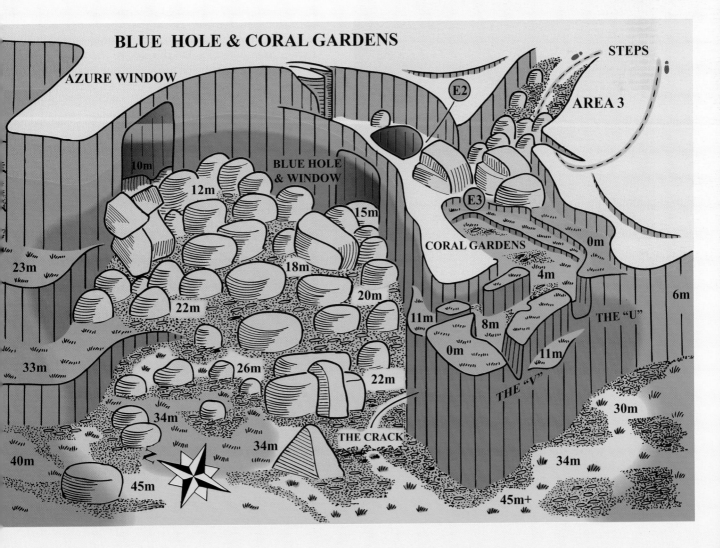

The Blue Hole & Azure Window

Area 4

For this dive site I would use entry/exit point E2. From the main car park to E2, head in a westerly direction towards the sea, down a few steps and bear to the right; continue down some timber steps into the gully. Follow the gully all the way down to the bottom, take your time as in places it is not an easy route. Once you reach sea level pass through a narrow gap between the cliff face and a large boulder, bear round to your right and E2. The Blue Hole is possibly the most popular dive site of the six areas I have covered, quite unique, but in my opinion, not the best. On this dive you will enter the Blue Hole, circumnavigate the column of the Azure Window and a visit to the cave is worth while, a torch will be required.

During a severe winter storm huge pieces of rock fell from the Azure Window adding to the underwater landscape.

Two divers admiring the beauty of the Blue Hole and Window.

▌THE DIVE   Minimum time – 40 mins

Once in the water descend you will pass the top of the window at 7m on your way down to the sea bed at 16m. Looking out of the window the cave will be directly behind you. When going out through the window you can go **one of two ways** to the Azure Window, take a compass bearing of 300° and swim over the many boulders and rocks until you reach the southwest corner of the column. **Alternatively,** you can turn left, follow the reef around until you reach the 'crack', from here take a northerly course, keeping your depth around 25m with the boulders on your right and the open sea on your left until you reach the southwest corner of the column.

The column will help with your navigation, for the outer and inner walls run almost north to south and the side walls, east to west. The total distance to circumnavigate this column under water is approximately 250 metres. On the far side of the pillar there are two main ledges, below these it drops away to depths of 50m plus. On this side of the Azure Window is the best place to catch a glimpse of those giant groupers, remember that they are very shy so approach gently. When you reach the area below the arch, rocks cover the bottom and boulders, keeping the reef now on your left will lead you back to the Window and Blue Hole. Once inside and if you have sufficient bottom time and air left, take time to explore the cave. The deepest part of the cave is at the entrance, which is 16m, once inside it slightly curves to the left, rising to a depth of 13m at the back. When it is time to go to your exit point, E2, slowly ascend within the Blue Hole.

Nudibranch (Peltodoris atromaculata) distinctive brown and white, feeds on sponges

PGL AERIAL PHOTOS

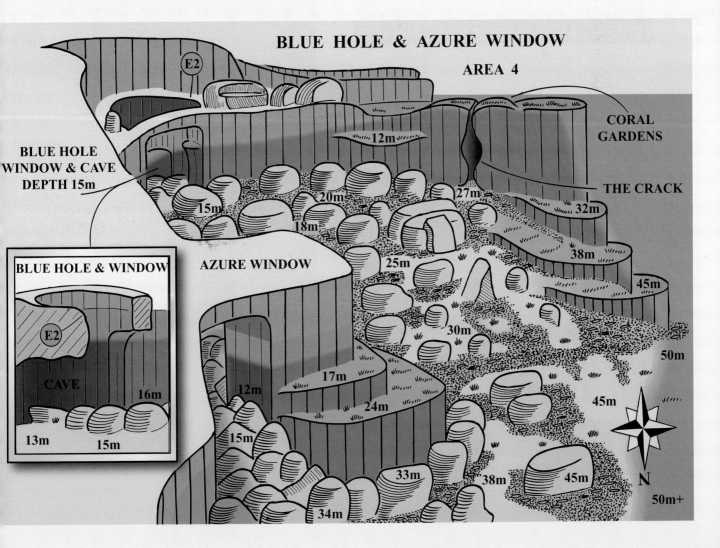

BLUE HOLE & AZURE WINDOW

AREA 4

E2

CORAL GARDENS

BLUE HOLE
WINDOW & CAVE
DEPTH 15m

12m

THE CRACK

27m

32m

15m

20m

18m

38m

BLUE HOLE & WINDOW

AZURE WINDOW

25m

45m

E2

30m

50m

CAVE

16m

17m

45m

12m

24m

13m   15m

15m

45m

33m

38m   45m

34m

N

50m+

Inland Sea to The Blue Hole
Area 5

This dive plan will guide you from the Inland Sea E1 to the Blue Hole E2, via the tunnel and the Azure Window. A route of approximately 400 metres with a time of 50 minutes, there are no exit points along this route. Your only help is the pleasure boats, if they are running, which travel with tourists through the tunnel to the Azure Window. Once out of the tunnel stay at your required depth and keep to the coastline reef, the sides of which drop away to 50m plus in places. This dive should only be attempted in calm sea conditions and is only recommended for experienced divers.

Beware of the small motor boats carrying tourists during your dive through the tunnel, it is most important that you keep to the sides, especially if you have to surface or you are in shallow water.

One of favourite places to relax after a dive is the small bar/café at the waters edge of the Inland Sea.

▌THE DIVE   Minimum time – 50 mins

Your entry point E1 is by the slipway at the Inland Sea, you then surface swim to the left of the entrance of the tunnel. For this dive a torch is recommended. Once under water your depth will be 3-4m, this will quickly

Dive boats which are normally for hire during the summer periods-just ask for Michael.

increase to 9m and then to 16m; a further drop to 25m and the last part of the tunnel is reasonably flat with a maximum depth at the exit of 26m. Your compass bearing through the tunnel is approximately 330° and a distance of roughly 80 metres. When you are through the tunnel turn left and keep the reef on your left-hand side at all times. The first part of the reef will take you in a westerly direction, but after a few minutes it will change to a southerly direction. The following times and depths are where the described pilotage points can be found; after 12 minutes 24m a rock wedged in-between a fissure of two rocks. 14 minutes 21m, a rock shaped like a pointing finger. 16 minutes 18m, a triple ledge close together. 20 minutes 18m and halfway with an 18m ledge and two boulders below. After around 22 minutes you will find a little cove where the seabed is covered with boulders and you might think that this is the Azure Window, but cross over to the other side (see aerial photograph) and continue to follow the outside of the reef round, 26 minutes, 19m and a whitish rock on a ledge. In approximately 30 minutes, you should be under the arch; from here it is no more than 3 minutes to the window of the Blue Hole and your exit point E2. This is only a guide; you can of course vary your depth and time to suit you and your dive plan.

The grouper (Epinephelus guaza) lives in crevices, holes and caves on rocky bottoms.   ALAN JAMES

The common squid (Loligo vulgaris) lays numerous eggs in clusters attached to seaweed or rocks which hatch in.
PHOTO: VICTOR FABRI, SUBWAY DIVE CENTRE

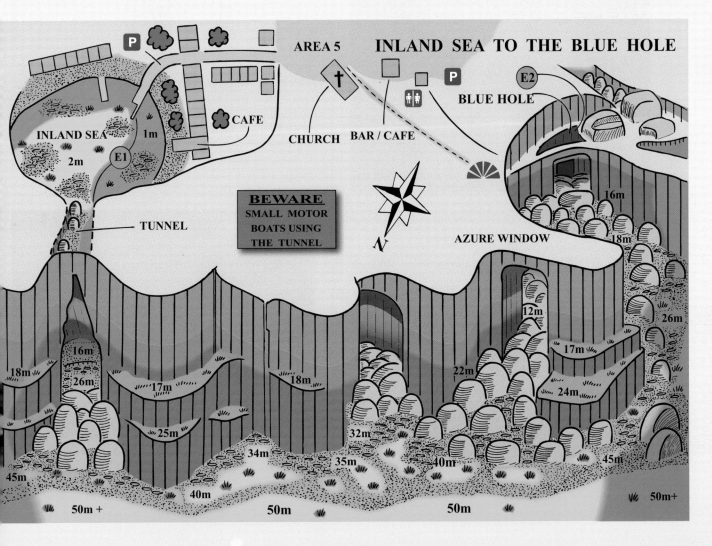

AREA 5

INLAND SEA TO THE BLUE HOLE

E2

BLUE HOLE

INLAND SEA

1m

CAFE

CHURCH

BAR / CAFE

2m

E1

BEWARE
SMALL MOTOR
BOATS USING
THE TUNNEL

TUNNEL

N

AZURE WINDOW

16m

18m

16m

26m

12m

26m

18m

17m

18m

17m

22m

24m

25m

32m

34m

35m

40m

45m

45m

50m +

40m

50m

50m

50m+

Inland Sea & Tunnel

Area 6

This unique dive with its 80-metre tunnel with depths from 3m to 26m and large enough to accommodate a double decker bus with space to spare, makes an exciting dive. Remember the tunnel is the only route to your exit point E1, the next nearest exit point south is 400 metres and to the north half way round the island. You will need a torch. Once out of the tunnel your selected dive plan will determine which way you want to go. Both reefs, apart from some ledges, fall away quite quickly to depths of 50m plus. Just because it is calm at the entrance of the tunnel the outer sea conditions must be checked before diving.

See note on previous dive referring to small boats using the tunnel.

A diver on the seaward side of the tunnel entrance leading to the Inland Sea. PHOTO: ALEXANDER ARISTARKHOV, SUBWAY DIVE CENTRE

| **THE DIVE** | **Minimum time – 40 mins** |

Your entry and exit point E1, is by the slipway near the Inland Sea car park. Surface swim to the left-hand side of the entrance to the tunnel and descend; here the depth is only 3m, so keep to the side until you are safely in deeper water. If you have to surface within the tunnel keep to the sides. The tunnel slopes down to 26m to its exit over a distance of approximately 80 metres. Once outside the tunnel, continue over the boulders to your required depth, bearing in mind, the sandy area below you is 50m once you have reached your chosen depth. The compass bearings from the exit of this tunnel are; if you turn left they start westerly

and then southerly, if you turn right they are north to northeast. Your dive plan will dictate which way you turn, if you decide to turn right and head toward the northern side of the tunnel entrance, please note on your return to the tunnel there is an entrance to a cave which can be confused with the tunnel, but it is much smaller, so just double check. Hopefully you have brought your torch so you can take your time exploring the tunnel on your return. Please remember when you reach the Inland Sea entrance and you are over the boulders, your depth can be 3m or less, therefore you must keep to the sides.

Gold star coral (Astroides calycularis) forms colonies under shady rock ledges or in caves, the polyps are bright orange.

All the normal facilities are here; there is a café at the top car park and another overlooking the Inland Sea. They are reasonably priced and after your dive it is nice to sit, take refreshments and fill in your logbook. This area is very popular with the tourists as well as divers, but there is a lot to see and do, so it does not seem to get too crowded. When parking your vehicle by the Inland Sea keep to the area of large pebbles for it has been known that vehicles get stuck where the smaller stones are. There is a telephone box at Dwejra but if needed the next nearest one is at Gharb in the square, which is situated in front of the church.

The Forkbeard (Phycis phycis) is an attractive and quite solitary fish, easily recognisable from the barbell on the lower jaw. PHOTO: VICTOR FABRI, SUBWAY DIVE CENTRE

PGL AERIAL PHOTOS

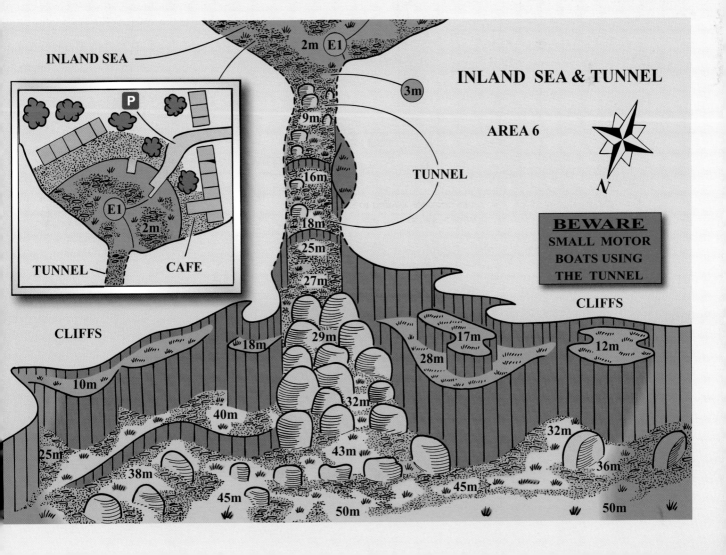

INLAND SEA

2m E1

3m

9m

16m

18m

25m

27m

INLAND SEA & TUNNEL

AREA 6

TUNNEL

N

BEWARE
SMALL MOTOR
BOATS USING
THE TUNNEL

CLIFFS

CLIFFS

18m

29m

17m

28m

12m

10m

32m

40m

25m

38m

43m

32m

36m

45m

45m

50m

50m

P

E1

2m

TUNNEL   CAFE

PGL AERIAL PHOTO

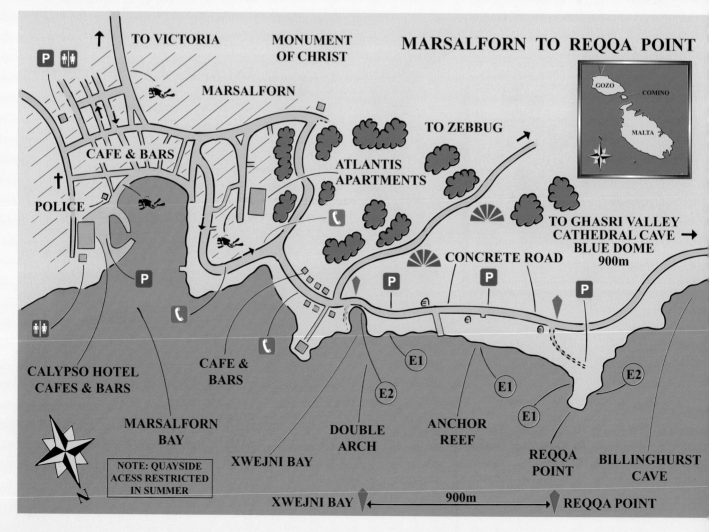

Marsalforn

The three dive sites of the Double Arch, Anchor Reef and Reqqa Point are situated on the north coast of Gozo, not far from the seaside resort of Marsalforn. When driving out of Marsalforn, the bay should be on your right hand side, the opposite side to the Calypso Hotel. Follow the coast road keeping the sea on your right, just as you drive through the last area of residential buildings on each side of the road, then in front of you and on your right will be Xwejni Bay with its slipway, this is where the concrete road starts. The distance from Marsalforn centre to Xwejni Bay slipway is approximately 1.8km Xwejni Bay has a distinct landmark on the east side, in the form of a large sand stone rock, which has been moulded into an unusual shape by the sea and wind.

Marsalforn offers many places to sit relax and enjoy some refreshment after your dive

To reach your entry points for two of these dives it will be necessary for you to negotiate the salt pans, great care should be taken when doing this as they are still being worked today and if the little shop in the sandstone cliff is open you will be able to promote the cottage industry by purchasing a small bag of sea salt.

The bay with local name of the washing machine – if seen in rough weather you will understand why it has been given this name. In the above photograph a dive boat can be seen over the Double Arch.

Double Arch

There are a number of dive sites around the world with single arches, but this site with its double arch is quite unique. It is some 200 metres off shore and can take up to 20 minutes to reach and you must allow 25 minutes for your return. Do check your entry point E1, this is known by local divers as the washing machine. If you

A black sea bream (Spondylisoma cantharus) lives on rocky or sandy seabeds close to Neptune grass.

PHOTO: ALAN PORTER, NDS DIVE CENTRE

are here when the sea is rough or there is a large swell, you will understand why it has been given this name. An excellent dive when the visibility and weather conditions are good and well recommended. This dive is only suitable for experienced divers who are skilled in navigation and should only be attempted when there are no currents and calm sea conditions

The average depth below the arch is 36m, to the west side is a reef and the arch forms a bridge between it and the main reef. The reef has a maximum depth of 17m but is surrounded by depths of 30m plus, often haunted by shoals of barracuda coming up from the deep and swimming over the reef then descending on the other side.

The greater weever (Trachinus draco) is found in the shallows half buried in sand, it has a venomous dorsal fin.

PHOTO: VICTOR FABRI, SUBWAY DIVE CENTRE

▌THE DIVE   Minimum time – 55 mins

For this dive may I suggest that you follow my dive plan, normally I would enter and exit at the washing machine E1, but of course you can exit at Xwejni Bay E2, but I do not use this as an entry point for the Double Arch. At entry point E1 just below the surface where you enter the water, are two large vertical round holes, which have been created by the sea. Once you have entered the water surface swim out just past the two points of land, about 8-10 minutes, depth here will be about 9m, this is where I descend. Once on the bottom I take a north bearing on the compass and head for the first reef, this will take about 8 minutes. Before moving off and during your swim, check for any currents. The sea bed is covered in sea grass and slopes gently down to the ridge of the first drop off where the depth is 15m, at this point you should find a double bowl area, below this area at 24m there is a broken anchor. From the centre of the two bowls take a northerly compass bearing and cross the deeper area towards the double arch, the approximate distance is 40 meters.

Caloria elegans a small nudibranch posing for a photograph.
PHOTO: IAN FORDER, SUBWAY DIVE CENTRE

compass bearing which will take you back to the arch, pass over it and follow the ridge of the reef all the way round until you come back to the double bowl, at 15m, this should take approximately 6-8 minutes. From this point take a southerly bearing on your compass, it will take you about 8-10 minutes to reach a depth of 9m and a little longer to reach the main coastline reef. If your navigation has been good you will find the point of land between Xwejni Bay and the Washing Machine. At this point you will have to decide which exit point you are going to use, turn left for E2 and right for E1 although this may be decided for you, for sometimes when returning there seems to be a slight current at this point coming from the west. If this is the case, exit at Xwejni Bay, E2.

The unique Double Arch at Xwejni Bay.

Once you have had a good look around the arch and maybe taken some photographs, go up on the reef to the west of the arch. This reef is reasonably small in area and you will have no problem in going round the top of it in less than 5 minutes, remember unless you surface you are at least 25 minutes away from a depth of 9m. When you decide to return take an easterly

The head of the tube worm (Serpula vermicularis) has tentacles around it for feeding, any passing shadow or contact causes instant retraction into the tube.

PHOTO: VICTOR FABRI, SUBWAY DIVE CENTRE

PGL AERIAL PHOTOS

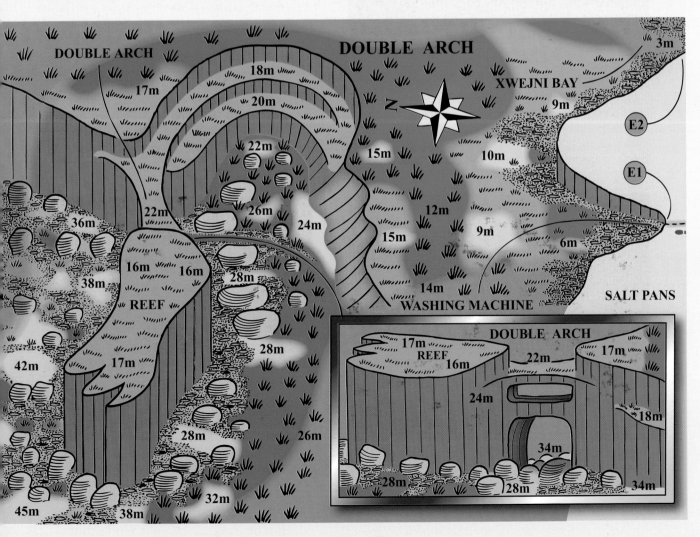

Anchor Reef

From Xwejni Bay slipway drive along the concrete road for 500 metres towards Reqqa Point, on the right hand side will be a single rock opposite a track leading to a cave dwelling, a further 100 metres on, on the right over the wall is the start if a track which used to lead to the salt pans (see aerial photograph).

A diver enjoying the underwater scenery on the south point of Anchor Reef.

Anchor reef has long been the name of this dive site and I have been informed on good authority that there used to be an anchor here. The tales then become a little hazy; one, some visiting divers from a country not too far away, raised the anchor and took it ashore, only to be arrested by the local constabulary, I can only presume that they have been released by now! Two; maybe the anchor which is in two parts near the Double Arch originally came from here? I have been told by a very good source that it was in the museum in Victoria, but they were unable to trace it, so I am afraid it must still remain a mystery!

This interesting dive is only just a short part of the reef which runs from Reqqa Point in the west, with steep slopes which are littered with boulders and rocks, to the Double Arch in the east where the reef has much more dramatic drop offs. The average depth here is 50m plus. Quite often I have seen large groupers just resting on the rocks in this area. Remember you only have one entry/exit point the next closest are some distance away at Xwejni Bay or Reqqa Point.

▌ THE DIVE   Minimum time – 45 mins

Take care when going to entry point E1 and especially down the small steps which have been cut out by fisherman. Once in the water descend to around 9m, below you the reef drops away quite sharply, to your left is the start of a 9m ledge, to your right there are a number of ledges ranging from 9m down to 25m. Looking down and to your right you will see a flatish platform at 24m all these are good indications that your exit point is above you. Now descend to your chosen depth, once this is reached head in an easterly direction, after about 12-15 minutes and at a depth of 33m the reef changes from a steep slope to a sheer cliff, continue in the same direction at your chosen depth and around 25-30 minutes into your dive the reef direction will change from a 60° bearing to 120°. Now I suggest you ascend to the top of the reef at 12m and make this your turning point, follow the reef edge in a westerly direction back towards your exit point. Within 50 metres either side of your exit point are two areas of rugged rocks and small boulders to explore, often this area is frequented by large shoals of salema fish which come here to feed. This is an excellent area to complete your safety stops.

Tompot blenny (Parablennius gattorugine) is usually found sitting on the rocky seabeds.

PHOTO: SHARON METSON, H2O DIVERS

The white spotted Octopus (Octopus macropus) is very similar to the common Octopus, but has longer arms and is reddish with white blotches.

ALAN JAMES

PGL AERIAL PHOTOS

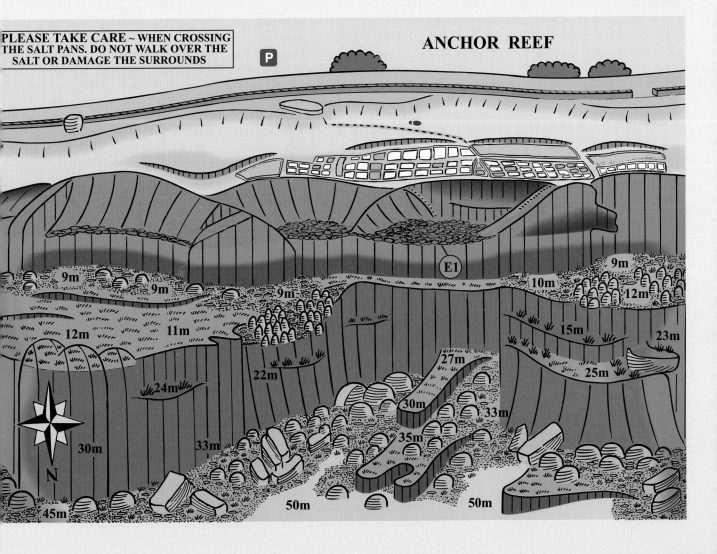

PLEASE TAKE CARE ~ WHEN CROSSING
THE SALT PANS. DO NOT WALK OVER THE
SALT OR DAMAGE THE SURROUNDS

ANCHOR REEF

Reqqa Point

The easterly entry/exit for the reef off Reqqa Point.

From Xwejni Bay slipway drive along the concrete road for approximately 900 metres, here you will find a track which leads down onto the hard sand stone, follow this to your parking space (see aerial photograph). This to me is a very special dive site normally with excellent visibility, a unique plateau at 17m below the surface with its surrounding depths of 50m plus. There is also an abundance of marine life here, which is very good for photography; all this makes it an excellent dive site, possibly the best on the Maltese Islands, maybe my favourite. There are two entry points, E1 and E2, take care when walking to them for the ground is very uneven and the rocks are extremely jagged. E1 at Reqqa Point has a little platform; an exit from here would require a deep-water exit routine. E2 to the west side can be used for entry and exit providing the sea conditions are good. A note of caution, after a storm even though the sea looks calm Reqqa Point can be prone to swell from the North West.

▌THE DIVE   Minimum time – 50 mins

The decision of which entry point to use may depend on the weather, but if conditions are good my favourite dive plan would be to enter from the westerly entry point, E2. Once in the water surface swim to your left around the little point, then continue for some 30 metres, from here you should have a descent of 35m to the bottom. This gives me a buzz, just slowly drifting down the rock face.

Once on the bottom and if your plan is to go to 50m, leave the cliff face behind you and head on to the sand. If it is just a bounce dive then turn to your right and use the three large boulders as stepping stones this will lead you up to the flat topped pinnacle at the end of the reef, depth 17m. To return to the main coastline and your exit point E2 take a southerly compass bearing or just follow the reef. If your dive plan is to use entry point E1, once in the water and you descend to the seabed to 20m, to navigate all the way to the flat topped pinnacle you can use the reef. You will of course, depending on your experience select your maximum depth, bearing in mind that if you stay at 20m or less, this will be a mid-water swim. From the flat topped pinnacle to the main coastline take a southerly compass bearing, or just follow the reef, either will lead you to exit point E2.

When you are below your exit point E2, at the end of both these dives and you have sufficient air remaining, you can continue along the cliff face at your required depth in a southerly direction, remembering that you will have to use exit point E2. Normally at 6m you can see the bottom at 50m, which means you often have visibility of 40m plus; out in the blue a chance of seeing the larger fish which often frequent this area. In my opinion this is an excellent way to end this particular dive.

It is only a short drive back into the village of Marsalforn where you can find a large selection of very attractive restaurants, cafes and bars, mostly situated around the bay. Fresh fish is almost always on the menus and together with the lovely crispy bread made in Gozo, is a real feast.

The nearest telephone is in Obajjar Bay which is next to Xwejni Bay on the road back to Marsalforn.

The shoal Salema fish (Sarpa sarpa) seen here at Reqqa Point, are perfectly synchronised in their behaviour.

A diver below the pinnacle at Reqqa Point.

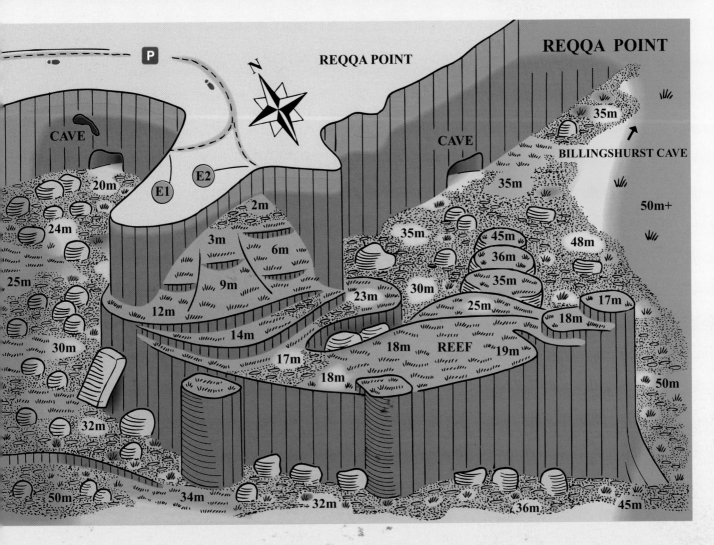

REQQA POINT

REQQA POINT

CAVE

P

N

CAVE

35m

BILLINGSHURST CAVE

20m

E1   E2

2m

35m

50m+

24m

3m   6m

35m

45m

48m

25m

9m

30m

36m

12m

23m

35m

30m

14m

25m

17m

18m

32m

17m

18m   REEF   19m

18m

50m

50m   34m   32m   36m   45m

A shoal of amberjacks (Serola dumerili) above Reqqa Point.

MAIN PICTURE:
Diver above the pinnacle at Reqqa Point where the reef drops away to 50m plus.

Snakelock anemones (Anemonia sulcata) easily identified by its long tentacles which are only partly retractable.

PGL AERIAL PHOTOS

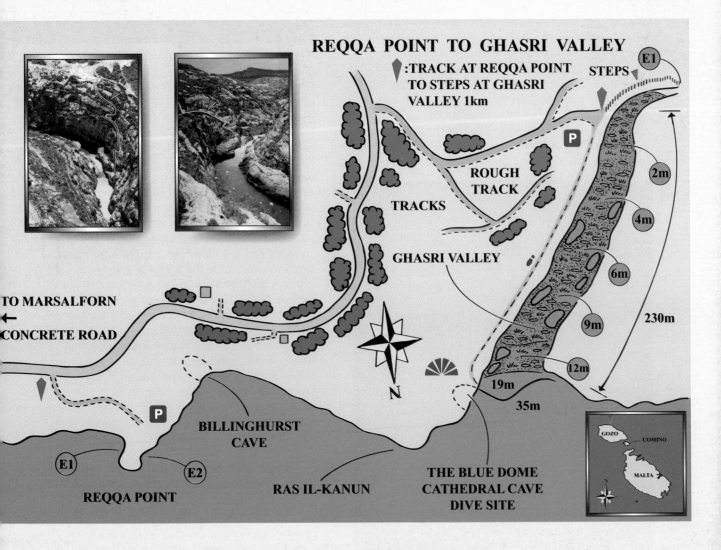

REQQA POINT TO GHASRI VALLEY

:TRACK AT REQQA POINT
TO STEPS AT GHASRI
VALLEY 1km

STEPS

E1

P

ROUGH
TRACK

TRACKS

GHASRI VALLEY

2m

4m

6m

9m

230m

12m

19m

35m

N

TO MARSALFORN

CONCRETE ROAD

P

BILLINGHURST
CAVE

E1

E2

REQQA POINT

RAS IL-KANUN

THE BLUE DOME
CATHEDRAL CAVE
DIVE SITE

GOZO   COMINO

MALTA

Ghasri Valley

This dive site is situated on the north coast of Gozo, 3.6km west of the seaside village of Marsalforn. To find this site take the coast road from Marsalforn to Xwejni Bay, from the slipway continue along concrete road towards Reqqa Point, from here travel for a further 600 metres, now turn right down a track and fork left, follow this track almost to the end and turn right into the parking place (see local map)

The Blue Dome – Cathedral Cave

This really is a different type of dive well away from the crowds, with its ninety nine steps, 250 metre narrow gorge and shallow waters which lead out into the open sea, together with the magic of the vivid blue colours on the surface in the Dome, it has to be seen to be believed. Please do not attempt this dive if there is a swell. Of course I can tell you that most people undertake this dive from a boat, but I am not most people, although on the odd occasion I have used one. It is very important to do a buddy check at this dive site, just to make sure you do not forget something, the last time I dived here I arrived at the entry point minus my fins!

THE DIVE   Minimum time – 50 mins

Once you have negotiated the steps to E1 you will find yourself on a small stony beach, no more than 4 metres wide. Enter the water and enjoy a slow surface swim along this narrow gorge for 8-10 minutes, admiring what nature can achieve. Just before the exit to the gorge descend, **you now have two choices. One;** head towards the open sea, turn slightly to your left and swim in a northerly direction down to 19m, in front of you will see a drop off and to your right the reef will rise to a plateau at 14m, go over the drop off and descend to the sea bed at 33m or your chosen depth.

A diver just outside the entrance to Cathedral Cave.

Once you have explored this area follow the reef around keeping it on your right, up and over the large boulders and slowly into the cave, your dive time should now be 20-25 minutes. **Two;** of course you can follow the coastline reef all the way to the cave which is possible at a depth of 6m. If you wish, here you can complete a safety stop if required if you intend to surface within the Dome. If you do surface it will be safe to remove your regulator for there is a crack in the cave above sea level which allows fresh air inside the Dome. With the light penetration from the cave entrance and the light from the crack, turning the surface water inside the Dome to a vivid blue, this makes a brilliant photograph even from below the surface. Now descend and leave the cave entrance on the north side, there is a plateau with a maximum depth of 20m to explore, when you decide to head back to the exit point take an easterly bearing to the coastline reef, turn right at your chosen depth and follow it into the gorge. From its entrance to the exit point it will take anything from 10 to 20 minutes, depending on time taken to explore. Of course you can plan your own dive routes from the gorge to the cave and back again.

LEFT: *Inside Cathedral Cave one can see the vivid blue colours of the surface water below the Dome of the cave.*

PGL AERIAL PHOTOS

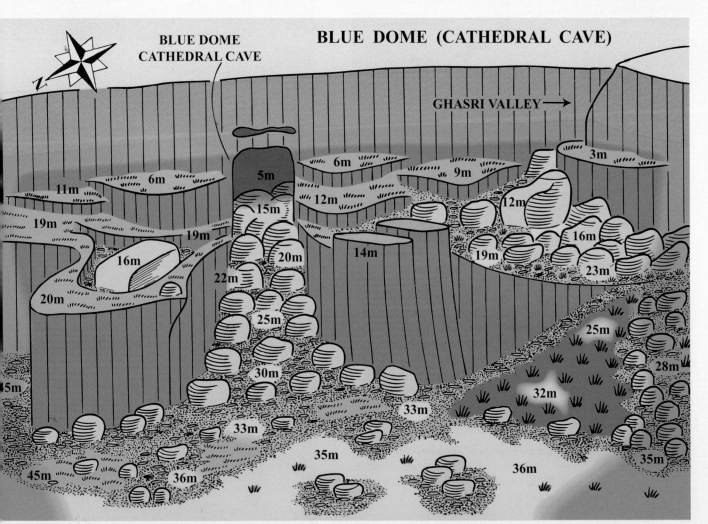

1. The Bristol Beaufighter

The Bristol Beaufighter built was in Filton and Weston-Super-Mare England, the Mk1 was first taken into service in July 1940. It was a twin engine 2-3 seater long range fighter, strike and torpedo aircraft, she had a wing span of 18 metres and almost 13 metres in length, armed with 4 x 20mm Hispano cannons in the fuselage nose, 6 0.303" machine guns in the wings and one machine gun in the dorsal position. One 18" torpedo externally under the fuselage also eight rocket projectiles could be carried as an alternative to the wing guns. Using a gyro angling device and a radio altimeter the Beaufighter could make precision attacks at wave top height with her torpedoes or rockets, add to this her long range and ability to undertake combat during darkness made her a formidable fighter aircraft.

Beaufighter on the wartime runway at Ta'Qali which is now the site of the craft village also home to the Malta Aviation Museum, in the background Mdina also known as the Silent City.

PHOTO: BY KIND PERMISSION OF FREDRICK GALEA, MALTA AVIATION MUSEUM

On the 17th March 1943, nine Beaufighters of 272 squadron took off to join up with nine others from 39 squadron on a shipping strike off Point Stelo, on the same day the convoy MW 23 arrived in Malta safely from Alexandra with much needed supplies for the islands.

Beaufighter 'N' with her pilot Sgt. Donald Frazee and his observer Sgt. Sandery, started to climb to 1500 feet and turned left to search for other aircraft to form up with. At this time the aircraft began to vibrate violently. The observer reported smoke coming out of his heating pipe, the pilot throttled back each engine in turn, this did not help, by this time he could hardly read his gauges due to the vibration. Their air speed was around 130 mph and they were losing height at

RIGHT: *One of the engines of the Bristol Beaufighter remains almost intact.*

PHOTO: ALEXANDER ARISTARKHOV, SUBWAY DIVE CENTRE

The wreckage of the Beaufighter laying on the sand at 42m.

PHOTO: JESPER KJØLLER, DYK MAGAZINE

three to four hundred feet a minute. At 600 feet the pilot informed his observer they would have to ditch, he tried to keep a steady course while throttling back completely shortly before impact. There was a slight swell and the aircraft hit the water at about 100 mph, they both managed to get out and apart from minor

A side view of the Beaufighter showing what remains of the undercarriage and tyres .

PHOTO: ALEXANDER ARISTARKHOV, SUBWAY DIVE CENTRE

bruises they were both uninjured. By the time they had both floated away from the aircraft, within 15 seconds she had disappeared beneath the waves. Within five minutes they were picked up by a Maltese fishing boat and five minutes after that their rescue launch arrived.

THE DIVE

The Beaufighter now lies upside down on a sandy seabed at 38m, which makes her an experienced divers dive. As you descend you will be able to see what remains of the aircraft, the main fuselage, the wings and undercarriage. This is an excellent dive for the photographer as divers normally stay around the wreckage and with a 20 mm wide angle lens you will be able to capture all. Remember that good buoyancy is essential, even touching the sand away from the wreckage will create a cloud and it could drift towards and over the wreckage to the disappointment of the photographer and the other divers.

2. HMS *Hellespont*

This Robust-class deep sea rescue paddle wheeled steamer tug was built by C & W Earls Shipbuilding & Engineering Co. Hull England and launched on the 10th May 1910. Having spent her first working years based at Haulbowline Dockyard, Queenstown, Ireland, she came to Malta in 1922 and for the next twenty years she worked in the seas around the Maltese Islands.

Three Robust-class paddle wheeled steamer tugs were built one of which was the Hellespont.

PHOTO BY KIND PERMISSION OF SUBWAY DIVE CENTRE

On the night of the 6/7th April 1942 during an air raid she was sunk by German/Italian aircraft, later salvaged, then towed outside Grand Harbour and scuttled three miles off Riscasoli Breakwater lighthouse. She now lies on a sandy seabed in an upright position at a depth of 45m; the visibility is normally quite good. The metal fittings for the wooden paddles are still in place but the paddles are long gone. An interesting dive with lots to see and explore, including the engine room where the piston rods and boiler are still in place. There is plenty of natural light for photography. A stunning wreck which has remained remarkably intact.

3. HM Drifter *Eddy*

Built in Aberdeen, Scotland by Alexander Hall Engineering Co Ltd and launched on 6th August 1918. Her first attachment was to a squadron conducting mine clearing duties along the south coast of England at the end of World War I. After the war she was transferred to the Mediterranean fleet and based mostly in Malta. At the outbreak of World War II the *Eddy* was re-commissioned and joined the 403rd Minesweeping Group in Malta. She was armed with a small three pound gun at the bow and a Lewis gun above the wheelhouse. She was fitted with an anti-magnetic cable around her side at water level due to the fact she had a metal hull. Her duties included sweeping the approaches to Malta's Harbour's so that the much needed supply ships would not be sunk by enemy mines. Unfortunately the *Eddy* was not destined to survive the war.

The forward section of HM Drifter Eddy on the seabed, the damage caused by a mine can be seen.

PHOTO: HUBERT BORG, SEA SHELL DIVE COVE DIVE CENTRE

On the 24th May 1942 she left Grand Harbour under cover of darkness to sweep for mines laid by the Italian E boats. Whilst on her way back to port the following day at 16.40hrs she struck a mine and sank with a loss of eight crew members, the skipper and ten others survived. She now lies upright on a sandy seabed approximately 1.3km off St. Elmo point on the north coast of Malta, at a depth of 56m. There is a large hole on the starboard side which was caused by the mine. The main deck and superstructure have collapsed over the years. Beware there is a lot of sediment inside which will quickly stir up and reduce visibility. It is known that four persons have lost their lives on this wreck, but research has shown that their bodies have been recovered.

4. HMS *St. Angelo*

An auxiliary British tug built by Scott Bowling, this ship originally named HMS *Egmont*, not quite sure when she arrived in Malta. Her harbour duties included, to serve as harbour transport for the Royal Navy Officers carrying personnel from Fort St. Angelo to other

An unusual photograph on HMS St. Angelo.

PHOTO: DMIRTY VINOGRADOV, SUBWAY DIVE CENTRE

destinations. During the war she undertook sea rescue duties and later on as a minesweeper, she was sunk on the 30th May 1942 and now lies upright on a seabed of boulders and sand at a depth of 55m. Permission must be obtained from the Harbour Master before diving this wreck, due to the close proximity of the entrance to Grand Harbour and the shipping lanes.

HMS *St Angelo* was one of four mine sweepers sunk in this area during May and June 1942

5. Schnellboot *S-31* (E-boat)

Built by Lurssen at Vegesack Beckedorf Germany launched in October 1939 the *S-31* had three Daimler-Benz diesel engines, 3 propellers, a maximum speed of 38 knots and a range of 800 sea miles. An armament of 2 torpedo tubes 2 x 20mm guns and a crew of 24 men. Intelligence from the Luftwaffe indicated that HMS *Welshman* was making a solo run from Alexandria to Malta. During the late evening of the 9th May 1942 the German 3rd MTB Flotilla of seven boats left Augusta on the island of Sicily at 2200 to intercept the mine layer HMS *Welshman*. By 0414 the following morning the MTB's were laying mines in Maltese waters; afterwards they regrouped to search for the British war ship. Suddenly the S-31 exploded probably due to hitting one of her own mines which had cut loose from the mooring ring causing it to rise to the surface and drift

into the path of the S-31. She sank at 0438 on the 10th May 1942; half the crew lost their lives. She now lays approximately one mile from Grand Harbour entrance with a

The torpedo inside its launching tube of the Schnellboot S-31.

PHOTO: DMITRY VINOGRADOV, SUBWAY DIVE CENTRE

maximum depth of 73m fully intact with torpedoes in the tubes ready for launch. Good Trimix dive.

HMS Welshman supported the island of Malta during the long siege in World War II. The island population resisted strongly and were collectively awarded the George Cross, the highest decoration for civilian bravery. Welshman brought food and essential supplies many times; her role was featured in the UK movie *The Malta Story*.

6. Italian E-boat

This Italian E-boat is believed to have struck one of its own mines which it was laying off the entrance to Grand Harbour to sink allied shipping bringing supplies to the siege islands of Malta and Gozo. She quickly sank and now lies on a sandy seabed a short distance to the east of Delice larga Forca reef, which is approximately one mile north of Zonqor Point at a depth of 45m. It is surrounded by other wreckage and debris from the war years.

7. HMS *Southwold*

HMS *Southwold* was a Hunt-class destroyer built in Cowes in 1941 by J.S. White of which the Royal Navy had 86 in the fleet. With a tonnage of 1050, 86 metres in length and a beam of 9.5 metres and a top speed of 29 knots. She had a crew of 168 and an armament of 3 x 2 barrel 4 inch guns, a number of anti-aircraft guns and submarine depth charges. After completing her trials and work outs she started service as a convoy escort round the Cape to Mombassa. She was then sent to the Mediterranean to join the 5th Destroyer Flotilla escorting convoys between Alexandria, Tobruk and Malta. In these waters the British were heavily outnumbered by the Italian cruisers and destroyers and on 22nd March 1942 the Italians attacked the convoy MW10. So the British laid a smoke screen to prevent the Italians from taking proper range. They began to dash in and out of the smoke screen firing damaging salvoes at their superior opponents and then doubling up behind the smoke before the Italians could take range.

The engagement was broken off that morning, but the Italian fleet approached again in the afternoon. The British ships emerging out of the smoke screen succeeded in hitting the

Two divers approach the bows of HMS Southwold *lying on her starboard side at a depth of 70m.*

PHOTO: DMITRY VINOGRADOV, SUBWAY DIVE CENTRE

A Hunt-class destroyer, a sister ship to HMS Southwold.

Two of the rear guns of HMS Southwold *which have been covered by marine growth over the years.*

PHOTO: DMITRY VINOGRADOV, SUBWAY DIVE CENTRE

Italian ship *Littorio* with a salvo which started a fire on the battleship. The Italians responded and the British cruiser *Cleopatra* was hit and was severely damaged. A quick counter attack by the British destroyers including the *Southwold* emerging swiftly out of the smoke blanket hit *Littorio* again by torpedo and also managed to hit the cruiser *Giovanni delle Bande Nere*. The Italians withdrew. This was recorded for history as the Second Battle of Sirte. The Luftwaffe took over the attacks as they were determined to prevent the convoy from reaching Malta. When it was a mere twenty miles from Malta they sank the *Clan Campbell*.

On the 23rd March 1942 another merchant ship the *Breconshire* was hit a few miles off Delimara Point, the weather was deteriorating and she started to drift helplessly towards the shore. The crew on the *Breconshire* managed to anchor the ship 1.5 miles off Zonqor Point. The next day *Breconshire* was dragging its anchors on the sandy bottom, *Southwold* was ordered to tow her but while trying to pass a line to the disabled ship a floating mine exploded under her engine room. One officer and four ratings lost their lives, all power and electrical services were lost and the engine room flooded. She was taken in tow but it was unsuccessful the damage was so severe she sank. HMS *Southwold* lies approximately 1.5 miles off Marsascala Bay on a sandy seabed in two sections, the bow is the largest and the stern lies some 300 metres away. The depth varies from 65 to 75m. Good dive planning and safety cover is required for this extended range or tri-mix dive.

8. Le *Polynesien*

Le *Polynesien* was built for 'The Company of Maritime Freight' at Cirtat in France and launched on the 18th April 1890 by the then president of the Republic of France. She was 152 metres in length with a gross tonnage of 6659, with a maximum speed of 17.5 knots. This ship was designed to carry 252 passengers and easily recognisable by her two distinct black funnels and low profile in the water. She began service in 1891 and operated between France and Australia. In 1914 *Le Polynesien* started its work for the French Ministry as a troop ship. In the early hours of the 10th August 1918 she was part of a convoy approaching Malta, at 10-30 am she was torpedoed by 'U' boat UC22. It took only thirty five minutes for the vessel to sink with a loss of ten lives.

The forward section of the SS Le Polynesien *sunk in World War I.*   PHOTO: HUBERT BORG, SEA SHELL DIVE COVE DIVE CENTRE

Nick-named the 'plate' ship due to the number of artefacts still aboard, she lies on a sandy seabed almost intact, with depths ranging from 53 to 70m. The wreck is found listed on the port side at an angle of 45° the upper starboard side is the shallowest part of the dive there are two deck guns which can be found, one at the bow and one at the stern. The engine room which took the direct hit of the torpedo is quite severely damaged. Often there are strong currents over this wreck so proper planning and safety cover is required for this extended range or tri-mix dive.

When the SS Le Polynesien *was used as a troop ship she was armed*   PHOTO: HUBERT BORG, SEA SHELL DIVE COVE DIVE CENTRE

Part of the deck of this huge liner Le Polynesien.

PHOTO JOSEPH FARRUGIA

The Blenheim bomber laying almost in tact on a sandy seabed surrounded by small reefs.

9. Munxar Cave/Reef

Munxar Point is situated to the south of St. Thomas Bay on the east coast of Malta. The reef runs out almost one and a half miles to the outer Munxar Rock which is 9m below the surface and marked by a cardinal buoy, this is the most easterly point of Malta. The dive starts just to the west of this buoy where the reef is 10m, once over the ledge in places it drops away to 45m. When you have reached a depth of 25m follow the wall round to the east and you should find an enormous cave where the roof almost reaches the top of the reef, the walls are covered in flora and fauna.

At a depth of 35m there is a spectacular arch and surrounding craggy rocks some of which are covered in old fisherman's nets. Beware of the occasional currents on this underwater headland. Both the reef and cave can be completed on the same dive or you can dive them separately.

10. Bristol Blenheim

At least nine Blenheim squadrons operated out of Malta during 1941-42. The Bristol Blenheim mark 1V serial No.Z7858 (code M) started service on the 30th August 1941 allocated to the 18th squadron the following month and in October it was flown to the Middle East. On 13th December 1941 five Blenheims from 18 Squadron took off from Luqa airport to attack Argostoli Harbour, Kefelonia, Greece. One of them was the Z7858 Blenheim with its crew, pilot Frank Jury, D.J. Mortimer, air gunner, and Tom Black navigator.

During their flight to their target they were attacked by a Macchi C200s, which prevented it from even reaching its objective. Air gunner Sgt Dennis Mortimer was helpless to react as the mid-upper turret with its twin .303 Browning machine guns had jammed and could not be rotated. Something, probably a bullet or metal fragment, struck the pilots head causing a nasty cut. The outcome could have been far worse were it not for the pilots unusual habit of wearing a steel helmet during operations!

The bombers port engine was also damaged causing the propeller to spin off. After pursuing his quarry for many miles, the Italian broke contact. The Blenheim was left with smoke pouring from the destroyed engine and only about 30 metres above sea level; she continued towards Grand Harbour, then turned and headed south. When a Maltese fishing boat was spotted just off shore, it was decided to ditch nearby. The Blenheim touched down tail first, Sgt. Thomas Black was the only casualty being knocked unconscious, despite its battering she remained intact and floated allowing the crew to escape, all three were quickly rescued. A Royal Air Force Sea Rescue launch went to the crash site after making sure the crew were safe. In his book 'Call – out' Frederick Galea reveals that a launch arrived to find the aircraft still afloat, they attempted to tow it but before this could be achieved, Z7858 sank. The other four aircraft returned safely to Malta.

THE DIVE

This Blenheim bomber now lies on a sandy seabed surrounded by small reefs at a depth of 42m, less than a kilometre off Xrobb-il Ghagin on the Delimara peninsular in the south of Malta. It is now a highly rated dive and this World War II aircraft lives up to its reputation. The wings and engines are upright and mostly intact, although the propeller is missing off the portside engine and some of the rear fuselage lays a few metres in front of the wreckage. Very popular with

Diver over the portside wing which is still supported by the engine and is now covered in marine growth.

PHOTO: JONATHAN THOMAS, DIVE DEEP BLUE DIVE CENTRE

diving photographers, most position their buddies over the starboard side engine.

A number of pieces are missing from the aircraft, almost certainly down to early amateur salvage attempts. Only the depth and difficulty in finding this aircraft has stopped further destruction to the Blenheim, so please take care, do not touch and leave it as it is for others to admire.

The starboard side engine and propeller of the Blenheim Bomber which lies at 42m

11. Benghajsa Reef

Benghajsa patch/reef is located to the western side of the entrance to Marsaxlokk bay. This reef runs out in a south easterly direction for 1.5km, the end is marked by a cardinal buoy. Here on the outer side of the end of the reef there is a pinnacle only 6m below the surface. Be aware that this reef is located on the western side of the entrance to the Free Port and Marsaslokk Bay; also there are often currents on the point of this, the most southerly reef of the Maltese Islands.

Once under the water the dive takes a northerly direction towards the shore, there are dramatic vertical drop offs to 50m plus, this is an excellent dive but the sea conditions must be perfect. The marine life here is very good and seeing large shoals of fish feeding off the point of the reef is a must. A dive for experienced divers.

12. Il Mara

This dive site is located half way between Ghar Hasan caves and Fort Benghajsa with the high cliffs as a background, there is a huge rock jutting out of the cliffs, below this rock is a small ledge at 8m where the dive boat will anchor. A very pretty and interesting area to explore with a wide variety of marine life which have made their home not only on this reef but in the many vehicles which have been pushed over the cliffs and ended their days below the waves. This is not a popular site for divers, so the chance of seeing large fish is quite good.

13. Filfla Island

The Island of Filfla once used for target practice by the Armed Forces is now a nature reserve.

Filfla is a small un-inhabited island about 3km south of Ghar Lapsi once used for target practice by the Armed Forces of Malta; it is now a protected nature reserve. This island was made famous as the opening backdrop for the film 'The Count of Monte Cristo'. A special permit is required to visit or dive this area and is issued by the Malta Maritime Authorities. This off-shore island is seldom dived and if you wish to do so then pre-plan with your dive centre well in advance.

14. Migra Ferha (Dingli Cliffs)

Migra Ferha (see shore diving) is the only place where shore diving can take place along Malta's southwest dramatic coastline of Dingli Cliffs, if you have the energy and determination to descend and climb over 100 steps each way. The cliffs make these dive sites very isolated with Ghar Lapsi 9km to the east and Gnejna Bay 6km to the north. Of course you can boat dive this area, but due to its location it is rarely dived and arrangements must be made well in advance with your chosen dive centre. This area normally offers excellent visibility with depths exceeding 50m with vertical drop offs and huge boulders and here you really do have a chance of seeing large fish.

15. *Scot Craig*

A diver looks for conger and moray below the hull of the Scot Craig.

This wreck is located at Ic-Cumnija, 500 metres north of Anchor Bay on the west coast of Malta. The *Scot Craig* started its life as a passenger/car ferry operating on the river Thames; although relatively small she could carry up to six cars as well as passengers. During the filming of 'Popeye' the movie, *Scot Craig* was used as Popeye's boat. After the completion of the film she helped in the construction of the Anchor Bay jetty, she was scuttled in such a way as to be used as a breakwater. She was re-floated and moved out of the bay, now she sits upright on a sandy seabed at a depth of 21m

A diver explores the wreck of the Scot Craig which lies on a seabed of sea grass, small shingle and sand at 20m.

almost totally in tact. During this dive you will most probably see a number of eels, groupers, octopuses and the occasional stingray or tun shell on the sand.

The Scot Craig is an interesting dive with many areas to explore above and below the main deck.

16. Devils Reef

Situated on the south side of RasIl-Qammieh below the high cliffs of Marfa ridge is Qammieh Point, this is a really good dive site with a drop off to almost 50m, then gently slopes away even deeper. On the southern side of the wall is a cave which contains stalactites, this ancient cave once above the surface is now completely submerged. Keep an eye out for the marine life such as dentex, amberjacks, grouper and barracuda. Please take note that this dive is for the very experienced only, and should be planned with great care for safety.

17. Qammieh Point

Qammieh Point is at the western end of Marfa Ridge, this ridge is the last of the high ground on the north end of the island of Malta. The views towards Gozo and Comino are quite breathtaking. This is an excellent boat dive on the reef which runs out in a westerly direction for almost 900 metres from Qammieh Point.

On both sides the reef drops away almost vertically, to 50m on the north side and 60m on the south side, moving away from the reef the depth quickly increases to 100m plus. Closer in and on the reef, especially on the north side are many large boulders at shallower depths with hiding places underneath their edges where one might encounter octopus or large scorpion fish resting on the seabed. The most picturesque part of the dive is reasonably close to the reef, further out the seabed quickly becomes sandy and here you will find flying gurnards and rays.

18. Smugglers Cave/Reef

This dive site is situated below the cliffs of Rdum L-Ahmar, which is on the north side of Marfa Ridge. This site with its gentle slopes makes it an easy dive with a sandy seabed, areas of small rocks and sea grass. Further out the rocks become more rugged, this makes an interesting dive with lots of places to explore. There is a shallow cave at the base of the cliffs approximate

Looking almost pre-historic the spiny lobster (Palinurus elephas) can be found on rocky walls and within pipes and holes on wrecks. PHOTO: VICTOR FABRI, SUBWAY DIVE CENTRE

The conger (Conger conger) is very variable in colour depending on habitat and depth. Mostly nocturnal found in both shallow and deep waters, your eels normally found near the shore. PHOTO: COLIN STEAD

depth 3m. Maximum depth 16m. Marine life normally found around this reef are red mullet, painted combers, flying gurnards, saddle bream, scorpion fish and in the small overhangs cardinal fish.

19. Sikka Il Bajda (White Reef)

White reef is the English meaning for this off shore reef which is sometimes referred to as Hoofers Reef. It is approximately 2.5km off Rdum L-Ahmar on the easterly side of Marfa Ridge on the north coast of Malta, a huge rocky outcrop, almost the size of Comino which rises to within 10m of the surface.

The immediate depth around the outer side of this reef is 25m, but on the inside depths of 30m are possible. To the north and south of this reef there are a number of much smaller reefs. Very few dive boats come here due to its location. Normally the visibility and marine life are good here. Calm seas are a must for this dive.

20. HMS *Stubborn*

HMS *Stubborn* was a 1940 S-class British submarine launched in November 1942 and commissioned in January 1943. A maximum displacement of 990 tons and a length of around 70 metres with a beam of 7 metres and carried a full crew of 48. Carrying maximum fuel capacity of 92 tons gave her a range of 6,000 miles, with a speed of almost 15 knots on the surface and 9 knots below. She had an armament of 6 forward torpedo tubes and one rear tube, a 3 inch gun and a 20mm Oerlikon gun. During the early part of 1943 she operated out of Lerwick on the Shetland Islands, patrolling the Norwegian Sea from the Norwegian coast to the Jan Mayen Islands. During the summer she headed south patrolling around the Scilly Isles. In September and October of that year she was back in the Norwegian Sea, during her operations she was involved in towing and supporting the X craft which attacked the battle ship *Tirpitz*. In the late evening of

TOP: *The conning tower of the submarine HMS* Stubborn *which lies at 57m.*

PHOTO: J.P. BRESSER, DIVE DEEP BLUE

LEFT: *HMS* Stubborn *entering harbour.*

PHOTO: RN SUBMARINE MUSEUM, GOSPORT

ABOVE LEFT: *The bow of HMS* Stubborn *showing her three starboard side torpedo tubes.*
ABOVE RIGHT: *The stern torpedo tube of HMS* Stubborn.

PHOTOS: J.P. BRESSER, DIVE DEEP BLUE

11th February 1944 *Stubborn* sighted a convoy of 7 ships, she broke off for an attack, 6 torpedoes were fired and two hits were claimed; then a total of 34 depth charges were dropped before she left the area. HMS *Stubborn* returned the next day and a further convoy was sighted of 5 ships, again 6 torpedoes were fired and two hits were claimed. A total of 36 depth charges were dropped and the submarine was damaged, she sank three times after coming to the surface, the third time she passed the 500 feet mark.

This time she really did have a guardian angel watching over her, for a further 16 depth charges were dropped whilst she was on the seabed. Due to her damage it was almost two hours and after many unsuccessful attempts before she was able to surface. During the next seven days which it took *Stubborn* to reach Lerwick she was escorted by 4 destroyers, a Norwegian Patrol boat and an air escort of Beaufighters, sometimes being towed and sometimes under her own steam she made it. After a refit in Devonport she returned to Holylock and on the 18th March 1945 she left for Freemantle Australia, via Gibraltar, Malta, Port Said, Suez, Aden and Ceylon, arriving in Freemantle on the 1st June 1945, she then saw action in the Pacific.

HMS *Stubborn* recorded the deepest dive made during the war by a British submarine, reaching 540 feet. She endured one of the worst attacks of the war and suffered the loss of her complete tail fin which held the aft hydroplanes and rudder. This loss was caused by depth charges, but principally from hitting the seabed at 540 feet. During the return voyage from Australia it became evident that the hull aft had suffered more distortion than was originally thought. *Stubborn* was one of the few British submarines that had art work painted on her conning tower during the war, it was a mules head. She was sunk on the 30th April 1946, as an Asdic target two miles off Qawra Point on the north coast of Malta.

THE DIVE

This excellent boat dive to a depth of 57m is for experienced divers only. Descending the shot line through the crystal blue waters and when the *Stubborn* comes into view you will see that she sits almost upright on a sandy seabed. This wreck is remarkably well preserved with its conning tower, torpedo tubes and propellers, there are two open hatches, but please do not enter. For the photographer, even at this depth, normally the visibility will allow you to take some decent shots.

21. The *Imperial Eagle*

Built in 1938 by J. Crown and Sons Ltd Shipbuilders in Sunderland England, weighing 257 gross tonnes with an approximate length of 45 metres. Named *New Royal Lady*, she was requisitioned by the Royal Navy for transport duties, attached to the US Navy, and then transferred to port defence duties. In 1947 she was sold to John Hall, Kirkcaldy for service on the Firth of Forth and re-named *Royal Lady*. Later in 1947 she was sold on to General Steam Navigation Co. Ltd. London for

A diver explores what remains of the upper deck of the Imperial Eagle, *for the many marine creatures that will make this artificial reef their home, for it lies within the area of Malta's first marine park.*   PHOTO: JON MITCHELL, DIVE DEEP BLUE

Thames dock cruises and re-named *Crested Eagle*. In 1957 she was purchased by Magro Bros. Malta, after modification to carry 70 passengers and 10 cars, she was re-named *Imperial Eagle* and carried out this service between Mgarr Harbour in Gozo and Marfa Harbour in Malta until the mid 1970's after which time she was used for storage. She was scuttled some 500 metres off Qawra Point on the 19th July, 1999, and has come to rest in an upright position at an approximate depth of 38m. An ideal extended range dive with an added extra in the Statue of Christ, a short distance away.

On the bridge of the Imperial Eagle – *still in its original place is the ships' wheel.*

The Imperial Eagle *moored along side Marfa Quay, Malta, where she sailed from to Gozo.*

PHOTO: BY KIND PERMISSION OF ALEX DUNCAN, ISLE OF WIGHT

ABOVE LEFT: *After being re-floated and made environmentally safe the* Imperial Eagle *was towed out of Grand Harbour during the morning of the 19th July, 1999*
PHOTO: CHARLIE SCICLUNA

ABOVE RIGHT: *The last few moments before the* Imperial Eagle *sinks slowly beneath the waves where she came to rest with those famous words 'The Eagle has landed'.*
PHOTO: BY ANDY PROBERT

LEFT: *The bow and the bridge of the* Imperial Eagle *which lies north east of Qawra Point.*
PHOTO: JONATHAN THOMAS, DIVE DEEP BLUE

Hermit crab (Dardanus arrosor) on rigid sponge
(Petrosia ficiformis).

MAIN PICTURE: *Two divers over statue of Christ.*
INSET: *The statue of Christ just off Qawra Reef is within a short distance of the wreck of the Imperial Eagle.*

PHOTO: ALEXANDER ARISTARKHOV, SUBWAY DIVE CENTRE

Dive boats – just a sample

This is just a small selection of the large variety of boats which are available to visiting divers.

Gozo Boat Diving Sites

1. Fesse Rock

This rock is situated some 400 metres outside the entrance to Mgarr ix Xini on the south coast of Gozo. The column of rock rises almost 15 metres out of the sea; below the surface the vertical sides plunge impressively down to almost 50m, where the base is surrounded by large boulders sitting on a sandy seabed. The vertical sides of the column are littered with holes and small fissures, these areas are covered in soft and hard corals and many tube worms. Fire worms, starfish coloured nudibranch and of course octopuses are just some of the marine life which have made this reef their home. Looking out into the blue on the southwest side you may see passing shoals of barracuda, dentex and amberjacks. Moving carefully around the algae covered boulders you may spot one of the large groupers that roam this area. On the inside of this rock the shoals of salema fish are easy to recognise, with their blue and gold stripes, passing from one part of the reef to another feeding as they go.

A group of divers encircle Fesse rock where the depth plummets to 50m.

Fesse Rock has so much to offer all grades of diver who can control their buoyancy, and for those who do not dive there is always snorkelling. Most experienced divers descend the vertical column until they reach 50m then slowly circumnavigate the column until they reach shallower depths.

2. Newwiela Point

This little headland is the most southerly point on the island of Gozo, situated 1km to the west of Mgarr ix Xini. Along the coastline here the vertical cliffs plunge into the blue sea and below the surface there are interesting drop offs and large algae covered boulders to explore, a good place to look out for large groupers. Just a short distance away from the cliffs the seabed drops to 100m plus, good buoyancy is a must to explore this dramatic reef. Normally the marine life in this area is quite good

The moray (Muraena helena) likes to hide in holes and fissures, the teeth are sharp and the bite can be very dangerous. PHOTO: VICTOR FABRI, SUBWAY DIVE CENTRE

3. Ta'Cenc Reef

Beneath these vertical cliffs not far from the exclusive Ta' Cenc hotel and to the west of Newwiela Point is the Ta' Cenc reef. If there is no south westerly swell there is a small plateau where the boat will be able to anchor. This plateau with a depth of only 8m is the perfect place to end your dive and complete any safety stops. Close to the shallow reef the seabed drops away to depths of 20 to 35m. There are many holes and fissures to explore hoping to find that elusive large octopus. Here you will be able to admire the shoals of salema fish moving from one area of the reef to another; great opportunity for the photographer.

Divers explore one of the many beautiful reefs to be found around Gozo.

A diver enjoys the spectacular reef – maybe the nearest feeling to being in space.

4. Sanap Cliffs

Just around the corner from Dawra Tas-Sanap this dive site is sheltered from the north westerly seas. Below the vertical cliffs there is a small ledge at 8m where the boat can anchor, which you can explore at the end of your dive while completing any safety stops required. The dive takes place along a vertical wall which drops off from the ledge to the west of the shallow reef. On this side there is an interesting cave covered in kidney sponges and calcified red seaweed. To the east of the ledge behind the indentation in the cliff is a second cave with small reefs on each side. On the walls of the reefs look out for the long tentacles of the sea anemones and brown spotted sea slugs, the most common of the nudibranchs. In the darker areas the rock faces are covered by a carpet of orange corals and golden zoanthids, using a torch will show off their vivid colours. The maximum depth of this dive is 45m and the average visibility sometimes is 40 metres plus.

5. Dawra Tas-Sanap

This dive site is the first sheltered inlet to the southeast of Xlendi Bay and has an underwater landscape to please all divers. A shallow reef, drop offs, massive boulders, an arch and most of the time dentex and

groupers roam this area. If all is calm the boat will anchor on the shallow reef which has an average depth of 8m. There is a deep cave and a natural arch in the surrounding cliffs, which has been created by the sea over thousands of years. There is a massive semi-circular cavern at the base of the archway, below this area there are many large boulders, to both sides and above the walls are vertical. After you have reached your maximum depth (45m) return to 15m and enjoy the wonderful sight of the big arch in the sunlight and the large shoals of salema fish moving across the reef. Now you can return to the shallow reef for your safety stops and the boat. This is a great dive with much to explore.

6. Ulysses Cave

Located just over 1km west of Xlendi Bay this is a huge cavern which has been carved by the sea out of the giant vertical cliffs. Just below the surface the walls are covered with a brilliant green algae interspersed with areas of hard and soft brightly coloured corals. Resting on the ledges will be many red scorpionfish and in the fissures, lobsters, small morays and the roaming fire worms always looking for their next meal. The rock formation here is quite spectacular and next to the large opening is a smaller cave with room for two divers.

The painted comber (Serranus scriba) likes to live on rocky seabeds close to posidonia grass.

You can surface within this unique cave with its fresh water spring which is mixed with the sea water creating a misty blue halocline. It is an excellent place for a night dive when there is a whole host of marine life to be discovered in the beam of your torch. The maximum depth here is 45m

7. Zurzeip Reef

This dive site is midway between Wardija Point and Xlendi Bay, here the sea conditions can be choppy and sometimes there is a slight current. The best time to do this dive is in the afternoon when the sun moves over towards the west. There is a plateau here at the base of the cliffs with a depth of only 5m where the St.

Andrews mooring buoy is located. Moving towards the edge of the plateau there is an interesting drop off, armed with a good torch it will be possible to discover the real colours of the marine life seeking refuge in the dark holes and fissures. The rocks near the surface are covered with hard and soft corals, many damsel fish swim on the edge of this reef, which is close to their hiding places should a large predator appear. Normally the visibility is excellent here. The average depth is 30m.

8. Wadrdija Point

Below the headland of Wardija Point where the sheer faced cliffs change direction from east to north making this the most south westerly corner of Gozo. Due to its location the sea can be quite rough and there are possible currents. This dive is nearly always done as a deep dive. The drop offs are very dramatic, down to depths of 50m plus. You may be lucky and spot the large fish such as tuna, amberjack and barracuda which all feed in the currents off this headland.

9. Fungus Rock

This large limestone rock dominates Dwejra Bay, originally named 'The Generals Rock' famous for the rare shrub like fungus discovered by the Knights of St. John which was used for its healing properties. Fungus Rock was guarded by the Knights and they built an early form of cable car to the mainland.

An oval bodied fish with short head and big eye the cardinal fish (Apogon imberbis) likes to hide under overhangs and in caves.   PHOTO: VICTOR FABRI, SUBWAY DIVE CENTRE

The fascinating rock wall drops vertically to a depth of 45m where you find the area covered in sizeable boulders, often sitting one top of the other. These provide excellent habitat for large groupers. From the north-eastern corner of the rock as you begin your slow ascent you will find that the underwater features become more interesting, as ledges and gullies present themselves for closer inspection. You will find the walls are covered with yellow, golden and red corals and among the marine life that have made this reef their home are tube worms, starfish, fire worms and nudibranch and in the larger overhangs many cardinal fish.

The pilot fish (Naucrates doctor) appear in small shoals, swimming near the surface in open water. Often found under the raft-like bunches of palm leaves used in lampuki fishing.

10. San Dimitri Point

San Dimitri Point is the most westerly point of Gozo; here the impressive cliffs rise out of the shimmering blue waters to a height of 80 metres. While admiring the beauty of this area you will realise that the boat is your only exit. Below where the boat will anchor is a shallow plateau with an average depth of 6m, great area for safety stops if required. The first part of the drop off is more of a steep slope leading down to house sized boulders with vertical walls; here you might spot groupers resting on the algae covered ledges. Put these underwater landscapes together with excellent visibility, large shoals of barracuda and truly spectacular fish such as dentex and tuna passing by in the blue makes this a fantastic dive.

A diver relaxing in the shallow depths surrounded by bubbles from ascending divers at this excellent dive site of San Dimitri Point.

The excellent visibility at San Dimitri Point, Gozo.

Grouper (Epinephelus guaza).

PHOTO: VICTOR FABRI, SUBWAY DIVE CENTRE

San Dimtri Chapel and in the background is Gozo's only inshore lighthouse.

The Lamp of San Dimitri – a legend

The legend of San Dimitri Point is that there was an old widow who lived with her son near to the chapel of San Dimitri. When Turkish invaders came and captured her son, taking him away to become a slave, she ran to the chapel praying to San Dimitri to return her son to her. The painting in the chapel came alive, and San Dimitri on his white horse rode out of the picture to follow the Turkish ships, rescuing the boy and returning him to his mother. Then San Dimitri vanished back into the painting. As a thanksgiving the mother and son promised to light an oil lamp under the painting every day until they died. However one day a big tremor shook the surrounding cliff side; the earth subsided and the chapel sunk to the bottom of the sea. The area has a reputation for abundant fish life, because they are attracted to the lamp of San Dimitri, which still shines to this very day!

Research for this legend kindly carried out by Marthese Matusiak

The arrow urchin (Stylocidaris affinis) is almost spherical with large primary spines surrounded at the base by smaller ones.

PHOTO: GRAHAM OWEN

12. Ta' Camma

The vertical cliffs above water extend below the surface to the rocky seabed. Boulders of various sizes are home to groupers, while many fissures, cracks and small caves in the wall offer refuge to smaller species of marine life. Look out for the Narval Shrimp with their antennae protruding from their hiding places.

13. Hallq Hamiem

A massive cave which shows above the surface, this impressive cave dominates the cliff off Hekka Point. Starting the dive from this cave which is only 6m deep

The seabed around Gozo is covered with boulders of various sizes which create arches, tunnels and overhangs; these make ideal hiding places for the local marine life.

11. Weid Ir-Raheb

A small rocky ledge at 5m, the edge of which drops sharply away to 20m, where you will find the seabed is covered with boulders of various sizes. The highlight of this dive is the completely submerged cave, at the rear of this cave is a narrow passage leading to a second underwater chamber. Take you time to explore this cavern before going out into the blue to check on the marine life passing by.

The cuttlefish (Sepia officinalis) whose colours are variable, individuals are capable of rapid colour change, especially when threatened, it also may take the colour or patterning of its background.   PHOTO: IAN FORDER, SUBWAY DIVE CENTRE

A dusky grouper (Epinephelus guaza) is a solitary fish which lives in crevices, holes and caves.

PHOTO: VICTOR FABRI, SUBWAY DIVE CENTRE

then continuing in a northerly direction until reaching a rocky ledge dropping down to 20m. Here the seabed is completely covered with massive boulders.

14. Hekka Point

This dive starts from a brilliantly coloured cavern which is completely submerged, the top of which is just below the surface and its stony base at 15m. Out of the cavern follow a steep wall to the right which leads to a massive completely submerged cave full of corals, this is by far the highlight of the dive and worth spending time to explore.

The view to the outside blue of the ocean is breathtaking and a chance to see the big fish such as dentex tuna and shoals of barracuda passing by.

15. Tac-Cawla (Gudja Cave)

For unknown reasons this dive site has never offered an abundance fish life but the underwater scenery makes up for it. The dive normally starts by entering the cave, depth 8m. After just a few metres in, the floor of the cave shelves steeply away to a depth of 30m. Just below the entrance, a massive arch stretches down from 16m right to the seabed, making an ideal and spectacular exit from this cave.

Once out of the cave and over the drop off where massive boulders litter the seabed, there are a further four caves, their lengths vary from 40 to 120 metres and in one you can surface.

16. Il-Margun

At this dive site which is to the west of Forma Point you will see a sharp indent in the cliff, dominated by two massive caves stretching almost from the top of the vertical cliff right down to the sea and below. The sloping seabed here is completely covered in boulders of all sizes. The fish life in this area is quite prolific, as you would expect.

17. Forma Point

This dive site has vertical drop offs on both sides of the headland, also there are two caverns to the east side, with massive boulders littering the seabed. The hard and soft corals which line the walls of these caves are quite spectacular. This area is not normally dived as much as the more popular sites so maybe there is more chance of spotting an elusive giant grouper.

18. Billinghurst Cave

This spectacular cave is situated on the north coast of Gozo not far from Reqqa Point. The cave/tunnel entrance is approximately 30 metres wide and 20 metres high; the distance to the cavern is 130 metres. This cave has a maximum depth of 27m and at this point the roof of the cave is 17m. The ceiling of this huge cavern, in which you can surface, is almost 10 metres high and has a diameter of approximately 20 metres.

The entry point for Billinghurst cave when undertaken as a shore dive, the exit is at Reqqa Point.

Further in there is a second cave, the entrance is at a depth of 14m and is approximately 40 metres in diameter, with a maximum depth of 20m. On entering the main cave, the walls are abundant with anemones, sponges, hard and soft corals. About 30 metres in you will begin to lose all natural light and you will have to travel almost another 100 metres to the cavern.

Divers enter the Billinghurst cave which is situated on the north coast of Gozo. PHOTO: JONATHAN THOMAS, DIVE DEEP BLUE

It was in 1984 a group of divers from St. Andrews University SAC were exploring what they called Booming Cave and the Railway Tunnel, when they reached the cavern they found a plastic bag containing a soggy book, which read 'We are Billinghurst SAC and we have invited others to sign the book and leave a message'. It was around this time it became known as Billinghurst Cave.

After a number of dive trips to Gozo, St. Andrews discovered the bag and book were missing, so it was duly replaced. A number of years passed and in 1993 St. Andrews University returned to leave a new Billinghurst Visitors Book, all the dive members signed the book and it was left in the cavern, is it still there? I am not sure. There was talk that the book would be replaced with a plaque in 2004, but I am sure it never happened.

If cave diving is your thing, then Gozo is the place, for there are many to suit all tastes, but possibly Billinghurst is the icing on the cake. In my opinion this is a boat dive and should not be attempted from the shore; divers should be experienced in cave diving and planning.

19. Calypso Tunnel/Cave

Just a short distance to the west, from the seaside resort of Marsalforn, is the lovely Xwejni Bay. The landmark here is the large lump of sandstone which has been shaped over the years by the wind and sea. The reef wall where the dive site is located is a continuation of the same wall at the Double Arch and lies some 100 metres off the reef below the sandstone landmark. On the face of this vertical wall there are two narrow horizontal cracks at 21m, below at 35m is a spectacular arch.

A diver passes through one of the 'eyes' in Calypso cave.

Divers can easily pass through all these openings into a semi cave area, this is due to two very large holes in the roof, and looking back the holes resemble a face. This is a very impressive and interesting dive with a maximum depth of 35m. You can of course shore dive this site if sea conditions are very good, but in my opinion the boat is the best option.

20. Qala Quarry

This dive site is located 1km north of the most easterly point of Gozo. The seabed is covered in a very fine shingle/sand and Posidonia (sea grass) banks which litter this area. Small reefs, patches of stones and small boulders makes this an excellent area for the smaller marine habitants such as spider crabs, shoe lobsters and small scorpion fish resting on the sea grass.

You may see painted combers and if you are lucky the pilot fish which like to dart around the divers as if playing tag. Depths here average 16m and a maximum of 30m, due to the seabed covering the visibility here is normally very good.

The common starfish (Echinaster sepositus) lives in shallow waters among seaweed, almost up to the shore.

The divers are leaving Calypso cave, where as you can see the holes resemble a face.

TOP: *Lantern Point, Comino.* ABOVE: *A dive boat is anchored just in front of the Santa Marija Caves, Comino.*

Comino Boat Diving Sites

1. Lantern Point

This spectacular dive takes place at the most southwest point of the island of Comino, sometimes called Lighthouse Point. There is a small narrow peninsular of land and this is where the lantern (light) has been placed to warn shipping of the danger. To the south of this point where your boat will anchor is a large plateau/reef with an average depth of 8m. This peninsular of land continues under the water where a ridge runs out in a southerly direction for about 100 metres, on the east side of it, is the plateau, on the westerly side is a drop off. The area below the drop off is covered with massive boulders with an average depth of 30m and a maximum depth of 50m; this is really a fantastic dive. Your dive will start at the entrance to the chimney, depth 4m, which is just below the lantern. Moving down the chimney, which runs through the limestone rocks and exits at 18m., now it is time to explore the areas around the massive boulders down to your chosen depth. Here you should be able to spot groupers, dentex out in the blue, and around the boulders moray eels, octopus and cuttlefish. When it is time to ascend move up and over the boulders to the base of the vertical drop off, then continue up to the ridge, once here you have a chance to see shoals of barracuda. The top of this reef is spectacular and is a great opportunity for photography, following the ridge will lead you onto the plateau where you started your dive. Take your time to explore this area below the boat for there is much to see including bubbles being released from the chimney through the porous limestone rock rushing to the surface forming a curtain, good for an unusual photograph. I consider this to be one of the best boat dives in the Maltese islands.

A diver descending through the chimney to the outer reef at Lantern Point.

The octopus (Octopus vulgaris) usually hides in holes and has excellent camouflage it releases a cloud of black ink when threatened.

2. Lantern Point West

Sometimes this dive site is referred to as inner Lantern Point and is suitable for all levels of diver. On some occasions it is a second choice and only normally used when the anchorage at Lantern Point is too rough. This dive can begin anywhere along the wall, which drops down to around 15m where there are many large boulders. From there as you head out from the wall the boulders begin to drop away to depths of 20, 30m and beyond. The ever present damsel fish are here in abundance, also cuckoo wrasse which during spring time in it's mating colours, the vivid blue seems to form an outline around the fish. Ornate wrasse can be easily spotted by their blue marbled markings on the forehead. At depths of 30m you will begin to notice the calcified seaweed due to the absorbance of light, at 40m the boulders give way to a sandy seabed. If possible you should consider doing this dive in the afternoon as you will get direct sunlight onto the reef.

3. Crystal Lagoon

This sheltered dive site is only just around the corner and south of the famous Blue Lagoon. A very popular second dive and is suitable for all levels of diver, the lagoon itself is a nursery for young fish. The boat will normally moor up against the small jetty or just beside the tunnel. Once you have entered the water and descended on to the sandy seabed, your dive plan will normally take you through the tunnel and around the headland and back into Crystal Lagoon. There are fields of Posidonia (sea grass) on the sandy seabed away from the reef. Possible marine life you will find here are flying gurnards, red mullet, dabs and spiny starfish. Average depths for this dive are 12m with a maximum of 15m.

Atlantic blue fin tuna (Thunnus thynnus) migrates is shoals at the surface in summer, keeps to greater depths in winter.

PHOTO: JOSEPH FARRUGIA

Diver on the outer reef at Lantern Point - possibly the best dive on Comino.

MAIN PICTURE: *Divers return from the outer reef, ascending through the chimney to the plateau where their boat is anchored.*

4. Alex's Cave

Alex's cave is situated within the largest islet to the south of the Blue Lagoon, another very popular second dive, which is suitable for all levels of diver. It has a very nice swim through and a superb internal cave, a reasonably easy and pleasant dive which is within the 20m range. The cave which goes back approximately 35 metres will be more interesting and enjoyable if you take a torch along with you. At the back of the cave is a chimney where you can surface when the sea conditions are calm.

This serves as a great first cave dive for the intermediate diver and has an average depth of 9m. The seabed within the cave and surrounding area is sand/fine shingle, moving away from the reef there are areas of Posidonia (sea grass). Around the entrance to the cave and in the small holes you may find octopus and small morays.

The cardinal fish (Apogon imberbis) is found on rocky bottoms with plenty of crevices, the male incubates the eggs in its mouth.   PHOTO: VICTOR FABRI, SUBWAY DIVE CENTRE

pull these tentacles back into the tube for protection. As these are delicate creatures please do not to touch. This dive is well protected from the northwest wind and seas.

6. The Canyon

Situated on the northwest coast of Comino not far from the Comino Hotel, on the headland is a mini inlet which is the start of the canyon, it has near vertical sides with many small walls and drop offs. In the rocks are small narrow tunnels and the seabed is made up of rocks, boulders, sand and Posidonia (sea grass) on a gently undulating bottom. There are the remains of a traditional Maltese fishing boat (Luzzu) which have become wedged in the rocks but this is rapidly being broken up. This is a very good second dive with a maximum depth of 20m and suitable for all levels of diver, also it is very popular as a night dive.

Alex's cave which is not far from the Blue Lagoon makes an interesting second dive.   PHOTO: GRAHAM OWEN

5. Cominotto Reef (Anchor Reef)

This dive is located on the north west side of the island of Cominotto, which is on the opposite side of the Blue Lagoon to Comino. The name Cominotto means Little Comino, the diving is just as dramatic and scenic as Comino. The dive begins where what looks like a large V has been carved out of the shoreline, this V shape continues down to a depth of 10m where there is a ledge from which there is a drop off down to 25m. You can follow this wall for about 200 metres where at a depth of around 38m is a relic of Malta's war history, a World War II anchor, which is encrusted in sponges and soft corals.

There are lots of nooks and crannies to explore along the wall, you may find the head of a moray poking out, awaiting for some unsuspecting prey. I hasten to add that that divers are generally not on the menu. Tube worms can also be found here, their fan like tentacles sifting the water for tasty morsels. If you place your hand too close to them they instinctively

Salpa maxima is one of the planktonic organisms abundantly found in the Mediterranean.

7. Comino's Delight

The opportunity to fish feed at this dive site always seems to be there.
PHOTO: SEAN HILL, MEDIADIVE

8. Santa Marija Reef

Located on the north side of Comino on the same headland where the Comino caves are in the north Comino channel. Suitable for all grades of diver with a maximum depth of 22m., the dive boat will anchor in 10 metres. This dive site covers a large area with two main guide routes; your guide will select which route according to your group's qualifications. There are numerous gullies, caverns, swim-throughs and small caves to explore. An excellent dive for the photographer as there are lots of opportunities for the wide angle cave shots. The large swim through to the north has a large colony of red anemones in its roof, schools of salema fish that feed on the algae, red mullet, saddle bream, painted combers and cuttlefish are just some of the marine life that have made this reef their home.

The triggerfish (Balistes carolinesis) feeds on small organisms, as its mouth does not open widely.
PHOTO: KEVIN DEBATTISTA, SUBWAY DIVE CENTRE

9. Comino Caves (Santa Marija Caves)

Almost the perfect dive? This dive site is situated on the rugged north east coast of Comino. With its interconnecting caves/caverns and the fantastic feeling of close contact with the saddled bream in a feeding frenzy makes this a very popular dive with most divers. Your dive boat will anchor in the little 'L' shaped bay, where you will be able to see some of the caves from the surface, below the boat the gentle undulating seabed is made up of sand, Posidonia (sea grass) and some small boulders. Normally planned as a second dive and with an average depth of 10m, even moving away from the reef wall will only give you a maximum depth of 16m. Once in the water and descending, the saddle bream will be there to greet you expecting to be fed; this is quite unique to this dive site. Your dive will normally start at the entrance to the first cave

A diver enters the Comino caves from the entrance where the boat is moored.

which is quite large, here the depth is about 10m, moving inside and once off the sand the rocky floor starts to rise and will give you the impression that the cave is a dead end. Follow it through and turn right, you will then see an enormous exit, now take your time to explore this area within the cave and take some photographs, you cannot fail to be impressed with these interconnecting caves.

When you return to the area below the boat you will be able to feed the fish or if you have a camera take some exceptional photographs of the fish feeding and being almost unable to see your buddy due to the number of fish surrounding him. I have been diving this site for almost twenty five years and each time it still gives me a buzz. I do not normally feed the fish myself, but this practice has been carried out here for as long as I can remember. The photographic opportunity with the light blue of the sea, the hundreds of silver fish on a sandy seabed is too good to miss. Whether you feed the fish, take photographs or just watch this spectacular show I cannot see how you will not be impressed.

10. Elephant Rock

Sometimes referred to as the Santa Marija Tunnel, situated on the north east coast of Comino and sheltered from any south westerly seas. This 30 metre long tunnel which runs through the headland is the highlight of the dive, once again do take a torch or you may be disappointed. Here the seabed is littered with boulders and is mostly sand also small areas of Posidonia (sea grass). Inside the tunnel the floor is partly covered in calcified seaweed, which look like red rose petals, the walls are covered in red and yellow sponges. At the entrance and exit of the tunnel, if you look closely on the reef, you may be able to spot the small yellow, black faced blenny and the red blenny, normally one is not far from the other.

This tompot blenny (Parablennius gattorugine) looks as though he has just had lunch!

PHOTO: VICTOR FABRI, SUBWAY DIVE CENTRE

11. Sultan Rock

The dive is located off the south east coat of Comino in the south Comino channel; this dive site is sheltered from any north westerly seas. Around this rock the seabed is littered with massive boulders, sand/shingle and areas of Posidonia (sea grass). In March 1889 the ironclad battleship HMS Sultan with a gross weight of over 9,000 tons ran aground, this incident happened during torpedo practice. During the following years she was heavily salvaged and virtually no wreckage remains, although from time to time artefacts are found. The marine life here is mostly small such as several species of wrasse, painted combers, red mullet, saddle bream and if you are lucky John Dory. Occasionally there are currents around this dive site and has a maximum depth of 18m.

Lizardfish (Synodus saurus) lives close to shore but in deep water, has numerous needle-like teeth.

PHOTO: SEAN HILL, MEDIADIVE

Two beautiful nudibranchs (Hypselodoris valenciennesi) of which there are many varieties. When you happen to find one please do not touch.

PHOTO: COLIN STEAD

The eggs laid by the female seahorse (Hippocampus hippocampus) are collected by the male and carried in a pouch until they hatch.

PHOTO: VICTOR FABRI, SUBWAY DIVE CENTRE

TOP: *Mdina – The Silent City, Malta.* ABOVE: *Golden Bay, Malta*

Malta

Malta is about 27km long and, at its widest point is approximately 14.5km. although towards the north of the island there is a place where both coastlines can be observed. There are no mountains in Malta and the rivers are mostly dry, but after short heavy rain falls they carry the water to the sea. The island's coastline is characterised in mainly two different ways; most of the south and southwest coastline is dominated by dramatic sheer cliffs rising from the sea. On the other hand the south east to the north coast, is not so dramatic but reasonably flat and in most areas the land gently runs down to the sea. It is on this coastline that the capital Valletta with its two harbours is situated as well as many residential areas. The Island is characterised by a series of low hills with terraced fields on the slopes. The airport is Luqa, which is 6km from Valletta.

Places of interest

There are many place of interest to visit in Malta and too numerous to mention within these pages for the whole of the island is steeped in history. The following are a few places to wet your appetite.

The Port des Bombes was built in 1721 and forms part of the outer bastion on the main road into Floriana and Valletta. Originally it had a single arch the second was added by the British in the 19th century to cope with the increase in traffic.

Valletta

Valletta, the capital was built by Jean de la Valette, French Grand Master of the Order of the Knights of St. John of Jerusalem, after the epic siege of 1655. Within its limited boundaries is reflected some of Malta's rich heritage of archaeology history, architecture, art and culture. The island's historic Grand Harbour, being one of the finest natural ports in Europe, and the three Cities of Vittoriosa, Cospicua and Senglea, all of which can be viewed from the Upper Barracca Gardens. This is also a vantage point to view the many ships from all over the world that visit Malta. To mention all the many places of interest within this city would fill this book so here are just a few that you may wish to see.

Auberge de Castille

This impressive building was originally built by Gerolamo Cassar but was remodelled in the baroque style by Domenico Cachia. The building which is laid out around an inner courtyard was formerly the British military HQ and is now the office of the Prime Minister.

The front view of the Auberge de Castille where the Prime Minister has his office.

Republic Street

The main axis of Valletta is Republic Street, which runs along the middle of the peninsula from the City Centre to Fort St. Elmo. It is the place the Maltese go to stroll and meet people So as well as the number of historically interesting buildings to be seen, Republic Street offers a glimpse of the true southern European style.

Republic Square in Republic Street, Valletta with the National Library in the background.

Republic Square

Republic Square is the real centre of Valletta with its charming street cafes. It was formerly called Queens Square and still has a statue of Queen Victoria to recall the period of British rule.

Upper Barracca Gardens

From the terrace of the Upper Barracca Gardens is a superb view of Grand Harbour and the Three Cities. This has been a public garden since the 18th century. There are also the Lower Barracca Gardens from which the Siege Bell can be closely seen.

The Upper Barracca Gardens as seen from Senglea.

St. John's Cathedral and Museum

One of the most compelling sights in the Maltese Islands – a real must for all those sensitive to great art and the appeal of history – is the Conventual Church of the Order of St. John in Valletta. It is a veritable treasure house full of the most impressive works of art dating from the 16th century right down to the 19th century. Within the interior are many coloured marble tombstones, frescoes and numerous treasure-filled chapels. Attached to the Cathedral itself, the St. John's Museum is noted for its unique collection of precious Flemish tapestries, church vestments and other interesting objects of art.

The Cathedral of St John built between 1573 & 1577 by Girolamo Cassar and is considered to be his masterpiece. Plain outside but beautiful inside.

National Library

The building was erected in the late 18th century, but the library was founded in 1555 for the use of the chaplains of the Order of St. John and was housed in the premises adjoining the conventual church. It was opened to the public in 1750 its stock of books was

rapidly increased by donations and by the end of the 18th century it possessed some 80,000 volumes. Like other institutions in Valletta it suffered from the plundering activities of Napoleon's troops, and after their departure was left with only 30,000 volumes. It was reopened in its new building in 1812 and now has around 300,000 volumes.

Built in 1731 the Manoel Theatre is one of the oldest in Europe still showing regular performances

The Manoel Theatre

This little theatre in Old Theatre Street is a real jewel because of its cultural history as well as its architectural design. It was built in 1731 in the time of the Grandmaster Monoel de Vilhena, whose name it bears, initially it was called 'The Theatre of the People', later becoming 'The Royal Theatre' and finally in 1868 as a tribute to its founder 'Manoel Theatre'. The acoustics within the theatre are internationally recognised as unique and is one of the oldest theatres showing regular performances in Europe.

A view of Senglea from Valletta with Dockyard Creek in the background.

The Grandmaster's Palace

A grand and beautiful building, it is today the seat of the President and Parliament of the Republic of Malta. You can still visit important parts of the palace, such as the Armoury; besides this the Grandmaster's Palace is a treasure trove of sights for the determined sightseer.

Mdina – The Silent City

In days gone by this ancient walled city was the capital of Malta, but now it is known as the Silent City. Once through the main gate of this Medieval City you will find yourself going back in time with its palaces, cathedral, museums and narrow streets leading to the ramparts, where on a clear day the views are quite breathtaking.

Crowning a hilltop at the centre of Malta is the beautiful city of Mdina, also known as the Silent City. The magnificent cathedral dome and the surrounding city walls can be seen from quite a distance.

Mosta – The Mosta Dome

The Maltese architect Giorgio Grognet de Vasse designed Mosta Dome, which is the parish church of Mosta and the first stone was laid in 1833. The dome is one of the largest unsupported domes in the world. During World War II a 500 lb. bomb fell through the Mosta dome, even with the shock of penetrating the roof and then hitting the floor the bomb did not explode. At this time there was congregation inside and even to this day people talk about the bomb that did not explode. A replica of the bomb can be seen in the church

Built between 1833 & 1860 the church of St Mary in the town of Mosta, is much better known as the Mosta Dome. A large unsupported dome, its sheer size will not fail to impress.

Vittoriosa – National Maritime Museum

This museum on Vittoriosa Wharf was opened in 1991 and is housed in what was a former Royal Navy bakery. It highlights the most important moments of Malta's maritime history; exhibits include two ceremonial barges, several models of sailing ships as well as a number of authentic guns and cannons.

Dockyard Creek with the building in the background which now houses the National Maritime Museum.

Dockyard Creek

This quiet little creek is now home to a Marina where many boats visit from all over the world. It is often used as a backdrop for film sets, one of them being the Count of Monti Christo. There are many bars and restaurants to visit in the area.

The Vedette on Senglea Point where the watchfulness of the men once posted here are symbolised by carvings of two eyes and two ears.

A traditional Maltese gondola in Dockyard Creek, in the background Senglea and Valletta.

Marsaxlokk – fishing village

The Turkish forces invaded here in 1565, Napoleon landed here in 1798 and more recently in 1989 George Bush and Mikhail Gorbachev had their historic meeting outside the bay. But for visitors this is much better known as Malta's largest fishing village; a fish market is held here every Sunday and a street market is held daily on the seafront promenade. In the harbour you will see many Maltese colourful fishing boats; almost always an eye is painted on the bow of the boats to protect the fishermen from the evil eye of the Devil. This is a tradition which goes back to Phoenician times.

At the Sunday fish market you can purchase the best of what can be found in the Maltese waters. A taste of Malta at its very best.

Wied iz Zurrieq –Blue Grotto

Situated on the southwest coast of Malta these grottoes are at the base of the sheer cliffs that rise from the blue sea near the pretty little village of Wied iz Zurrieq. In order to visit them you will need to take a trip in one of the many brightly coloured small boats, which run trips from the inlet below the village.

There are many sea caves along this rugged coastline on the south-west of Malta and these are the spectacular sea caves of the Blue Grotto.

PHOTO: JON MITCHELL. DEEP BLUE DIVE CENTRE

The slipway and inlet where the small brightly coloured boats leave to visit the picturesque Blue Grotto.

Hagar Qim – Mnajdra – Neolithic Temples

Hagar Qim (stones of prayer) and Mnajdra (view) are two of the finest Neolithic temple complexes in the Maltese archipelago. Quite close to Wied iz Zurrieq, they are about 1,000 years older than the famous pyramids of Giza. Huge rocks, several tons in weight were used in the construction of these temples. Even today with modern techniques and tools this would not be an easy task. How these enormous loads were moved, or lifted, 5,000 or 6,000 years ago remains a mystery.

Evening entertainment

One of the many venues on the Waterfront on Pinto Wharf, Valletta to relax and enjoy a meal.

For those who like the high nightlife with restaurants, bars and disco music, Paceville, St. Julians has all these, plus nightclubs, cinemas and ten pin bowling. For those who like an evening at a more leisurely pace then Valletta, Sliema, Bugibba, St. Pauls Bay, Mellieha, and to the south, Marsascala and Marsaxlokk are possible venues. But of course there are many places away from the main tourist areas where there are excellent restaurants and friendly bars where you can spend a most enjoyable evening. A taste of Malta at its best.

Ta'Qali – Aviation Museum

The Malta Aviation Museum Foundation is a voluntary, non-profit making organisation and was set up in November 1994 joining together various associations with the aim to create a display of unique exhibits related to Malta's rich aviation history. Ta'Qali which is the site of one of the well-known wartime airfields where British fighter aircraft were based during World War II and is situated below Mdina and Rabat, if you have an interest in history and aircraft you will find a visit worth while. Ta'Qali is being turned into a national park and this is where to find a crafts village and a football stadium together with the museum. The museum is run entirely by volunteers and is not a business concern; it is open for seven days a week and is easily reached by bus.

Hawker Hurricane llaZ3055 flew off HMS Ark Royal *to reinforce Malta in June 1941 during Operation Rocket. Ditched in the sea about a mile off shore from the Blue Grotto on the 4th July 1941 and recovered in September 1995. Presently being restored to taxiing condition at the Malta Aviation Museum.*

Douglas DC-3 Dakota, built 1944 and entered RAF service in the Far East in 1945. Flew with the RAF until 1950 when it moved to civvy street becoming G-AMPT Reliance with Eagle Aviation at Blackbushe Airport in the UK.

The above information was supplied by the Malta Aviation Museum.

The Royal Malta Golf Club

Sir Henry D'Oyley Torrens founded the Royal Malta Golf Club when he was posted as Governor and Commander in Chief of Malta in September 1888. Within one month he founded the club with a club house in St. Anne's Ditch and a nine-hole course laid out around the outer and inner ditches of Valletta's fortifications. Pictures of this unique course hang in the present club house. The club moved to its present location in 1904, onto a course built on reclaimed marshland, designed by the sappers of the Royal Engineers. The club was run by the British Forces until 1971 when it was handed over to a Maltese civilian management committee and became known as the Marsa Sports Club. The running of the club at present is entrusted to a Board of Management for general policy and finance, while the Captain's Committee is entrusted with all matters relating to the game of golf and members facilities. There is ample space for visitors to play on the course, either as individuals or as a group upon the payment of green fees, equipment hire is available. There is a bar and restaurant which overlook the course.

Why not spend a day at this green oasis in the middle of Malta? Open to non-members and equipment is available for hire.

Trotting horses. The Marsa Racecourse is home to the beautiful trotting horses; meetings are held here during the season and prove to be very popular, not only with the Maltese but also with tourists.

TOP: *The Citadel, Victoria (Rabat), Gozo.* ABOVE: *Mgarr Harbour, Gozo.*

Gozo

Gozo, the island of the nymph Calypso, is smaller than its sister island Malta; it is approximately 15km long and 7km at its widest point. It has a character quite distinct from Malta and the countryside is greener and more spectacular. Flat-topped hills characterise the landscape whilst almost all the coastline has rugged cliffs, penetrated by steep valleys and beautiful bays. Life here moves at a leisurely pace moving around farming and fishing. Gozo is more rustic and quieter than Malta and the charm of the island makes itself apparent as soon as you land. It is an island where time seems to have stood still, so if you are looking for a restful time then Gozo will suit you.

Places of interest

There are many places of interest to visit on this beautiful island of Gozo and many tastes are catered for, with its dramatic coastline, towns, small villages with their many churches and its history. The following, are a few places, which you may be interested in visiting

The Citadel

The Citadel, also known as 'Gran Castello' owes its origins to the late medieval era, and was re-fortified by the Knights in the 17th century to provide refuge and defence against the numerous attacks by the Turks and Corsairs during that time. It was built at a most strategic point on a hill in the centre of the island above the capital Victoria, it offers stunning views and the steep uphill walk is well worth the effort. Malta can be seen 6km away across the rim of bright water, even Sicily is visible on very clear days.

There are a number of museums within the Citadel: Cathedral, Natural History & Folklore are just a sample

The impressive Cathedral which stands within the Citadel.

The Cathedral

The Cathedral in the Citadel designed by Lorenzo Gaf'a was built between 1697 and 1711. At the time it was constructed, money was short and would not run to a dome. The Italian painter Antonio Manuele, who created a wonderful impression that the flat roof was a dome, brilliantly overcame this problem.

One of the many cannons situated along the bastions of the Citadel, which is also known as Gran Castello.

Marsalforn is a small fishing village which lies to the north of the Citadel in Victoria. To the northwest of Marsalforn, is Xwejni Bay.

Victoria – Rabat

The old name Rabat simply means 'the city'. On the occasion of the jubilee of Queen Victoria in 1897 the official name was changed in Her Majesty's honour. Even today, many locals still call it by its original name, Rabat. The town is picturesque. To stroll along the streets and look at the colourful shops and above all to see the market is alone worth a trip to Gozo. St. George's Church built between 1672 and 1778, is very interesting to visit. The paintings in the dome are the works of Battista Conti of Rome; other paintings are by Giuseppe Cali, Stefano Erardi and Mattia Preti. Paolo Azzopardi carved the richly decorated statue of St. George in the year 1841. The area surrounding the Church itself is steeped in history showing objects and indications of former cultures and settlements dating back to Roman days.

On the southern outskirts of Victoria this fertile valley leads down to Xlendi Bay.

Some of the shops and market stalls which Victoria in Gozo has to offer.

Ta' Pinu – National Shrine

The origin of Ta' Pinu goes back to June 22, 1883 when a peasant woman, Carmela Grima, heard the voice of the Blessed Virgin in a little old chapel. In the following years many miracles and acts of grace were manifested. It was believed that the prayers said in the little chapel saved Gozo from the plague, which had stricken Malta at the time. It was therefore decided to build a larger and more magnificent church on the site in honour of the Blessed Virgin. A collection from amongst the Gozitans, including those living abroad, together with donations contributed by community members and much physical work, enabled the people to start construction work in 1920. In 1931 Ta' Pinu was consecrated and in 1932 Pope Pius X1 gave it the status of Basilica. The original 16th century chapel was fully integrated into the new church and with its fine tower built in the Romanesque style stands out like a rock greeting the visitor. There is a ferry operating between Gozo and Malta called Ta' Pinu which was launched in the year 2000.

Ta'Pinu sanctuary dominates the countryside between Gharb and Ghammar, a Romanesque centre of pilgrimage that was given basilica status in 1932.

Marsalforn – popular resort

This fishing village on the north coast has developed over the years into Gozo's most popular seaside resort. Once again it is very quiet and peaceful, a very pleasant place to sit at one of the bar/restaurants on the quayside. From here it is just a short drive along the coast road to Reqqa point, where you will be able to view the shapes that have been created in the sand stone cliffs by the wind and sea, also the many salt pans which are still in use today.

The little bay and harbour at Marsalforn where there is a wide selection of restaurants, bars and cafes. Many dive boats leave from here for the north coast of Gozo.

Xlendi – picturesque bay and village

Tucked away in the south of the island, this long narrow bay dominated by towering cliffs on one side and if you fancy a climb the view is worth the effort. On the other side of the bay are some hotels and apartments, along the waters edge are footpaths leading to seats where one can sit and watch the world go by. At the back of the bay is a small sandy beach with a little harbour with restaurants, café's and shops. My wife and I consider this to be one of the most picturesque villages on the island.

The headland at the entrance to Xlendi Bay which is only part of this pretty seaside village.

Dwejra – Inland Sea

This proposed World Heritage site on Gozo's western coastline where the land meets the sea; nature has created a number of wonders for the visitor to see. This area is not normally referred to as Dwejra, but the Inland Sea, the Azure Window and the Blue Hole. Many well known movies have been made here using this area as a backdrop.

The Inland Sea where one of my favourite places to sit is at the small waterside café watching the world go by.

The Inland Sea

Set in a deep recess in the rock coastline, the Inland Sea is an area of shallow water, which is approximately 100 metres across, linked to the sea outside through a narrow tunnel in the cliffs. Boat trips are available here, which will take you through the tunnel out to the open sea, from this vantage point, you can view the dramatic coastline and the Azure Window. On the land the soil shows myriads of prehistoric shells and the remains of other marine animals, which make this area a rich source of information for people interested in history and geology. The oldest salt pans in Gozo are to be found here.

This 80 metre tunnel is used by many small motor boats taking tourists to view the coastline from the open sea, therefore when diving here it is essential to keep to the sides.

Azure Window

Waves and rough seas breaking on the rocks over thousands of years created the Azure Window. On the top of a giant column of rock, with a diameter of about 40 metres rests a huge ledge of rock about 100 metres long and 20 metres high, forming a giant window/arch through which the azure waters of the sea can be seen beyond.

Rough seas and waves over the years have created the impressive Azure Window. This area has been used on many occasions as a backdrop for major films.

The Blue Hole

Situated right in front of the Azure Window, this almost circular hole with its crystal clear waters, some 20 metres in diameter and 15m deep, with a large window below the water allows divers to exit into the open sea.

Fungus Rock

Known also as the General's Rock, Fungus Rock stands proudly in the sweeping bay alongside the Inland Sea. It was here that Fungus Gaulitanus, a fungus much prized by the Knights for its medicinal powers, once grew. This rare plant for centuries was kept under constant guard and anyone caught stealing it was instantly put to death. Due to its height, the Fungus Rock was almost unreachable from the sea; therefore the Knights constructed a hoist resembling a funicular, on the watchtower. This tower known as 'Qawra Tower' can still be seen. Sadly, it has been proved in recent years that the fungus has no known medicinal powers.

Fungus Rock stands proudly in the sweeping bay.

Ggantija – Prehistoric Temples

The megalithic temples of Ggantija near the village of Xaghra are an outstanding example of the prehistoric monuments to be found on the Maltese Islands. These are considered to be the oldest free standing structures yet discovered in the world. Ggantija means 'giant woman' and the huge stones of these two temples, according to the latest analysis, were built around 3600 BC, earlier than the first pyramids in Egypt which was 2800 BC, and Stonehenge in England around 2400 BC.

The entrance to the megalithic temples of Ggantija where thousands have visited over the years.

A Taste of Gozo

One of the greatest pleasures when visiting any country is its local cuisine, the food and the wine. In Gozo this is particularly enjoyable because everything sold in the markets or served in its restaurants, is fresh from the fields or the sea. This is after all a rural and fishing community.

The fields are abundant with Mediterranean produce like green peppers, aubergines and courgettes, and each day a wide variety of fish is brought into the tiny harbours only an hour or so after the catch.

Most waterfronts in Gozo have a wide selection of restaurants, cafes and bars.

To go with these is Gozo's delicious crispy bread as well as Gozo wines, which are served young and chilled. There are some very attractive restaurants nestling in the small bays where you can dine next to the waters edge with a view of the fishing boats. Others to be found are perched high up within the ancient bastions of the capital city of Victoria, with spectacular views of the terraced countryside.

Look also for the intimate weathered courtyards with worn flagstones and old walls covered in flowers, where small tables and candlelight provide the most romantic of settings. Sometimes compromise on the setting and search out the family run bars, which specialise in local dishes and by balancing your budget you will also get an enjoyable first hand taste of Gozitan cuisine.

A typical evening out in a restaurant enjoying local produce and friendly service.

Comino

Comino is the smallest island in the Maltese archipelago and for anyone who loves the sea, peace and tranquillity, this is the place. The waters are crystal clear with safe bathing even for young children. The superb Blue Lagoon is not only excellent for swimming but also one of the most wonderful sights of the Maltese Islands.

Comino's total area measures about 2.5sq kms and has only eight permanent residents. There is no traffic, no noise and for most of the year its rock landscape is covered with wild flowers and thyme. There is a modern hotel dedicated to everything Comino has to offer, it also has a resident policeman and a parish priest to look after the tiny Island's welfare.

Crystal Lagoon on the island of Comino with Cominotto and the Blue Lagoon in the background.

The quay at Marfa, Malta where most of the boats pick up divers to go to the Comino and Gozo dive sites.

Acknowledgements

I would like to thank the people below who have assisted me in one way or another in producing this book, without their help it would not have been possible.

Dr. Michael Refalo - The High Commissioner for Malta in London

Malta Tourism Authority

Members of the Armed Forces of Malta
Commander AFM Brigadier Carmel Vassallo, RCDS
Air Wing Commanding Officer Lieutenant Colonel Claudio Spiteri
Major Ivan M.Consiglio, Staff Officer-Public Information
With a special mention to Major Joseph Abdilla (retired)

Chris Gray, a friend and dive buddy, who had the original idea that I should produce a book

Bent Matusiak – a friend and dive buddy – and his wife Marthese for their help, genuine hospitality and friendship

Ian Gaunt for his tireless work on colouring the illustrations, without his input the book would not have been printed

George Lanham for the professional way in which he has designed the book

Darren Foreman, friend, dive buddy and my computer expert

Paul & Mariella Mizzi – The Foto Grafer, Malta (aerial photographs)

Atlantis Dive Centre – Brian & Stephania Azzopardi, John (Jack) Dabill

Dive Deep Blue Dive Centre – Jon Mitchell, Jonathan Thomas

H2O Divers – Stephen Clough, Marietta Borg, Marcus Grant, Sara Kilminster

Maltaqua Dive Centre – Agnes & Mike Upton, Simone Brinch-Iversen, Anna Catania

Subway Dive Centre – Olga Pelshe. A special mention to Lina Fabri for her never-ending help, patience and lovely sense of humour

George Zammit Briffa, Manager, Captain Morgan Cruises Malta

Diving Instructors – Antonio Anastasi, Martin Hall, Gerrard De Waal.

Adrian Buttigieg – Underwater portrait photographer

Members of Horizon Divers BS-AC 1121, who have assisted me with the book and visited me while in Malta, with a special mention to Dave Henighan and Gareth Jones

David Mallard for his painstaking task of research on the *X 127* Lighter

Evarist Bartolo for his assistance and support

Malta Maritime Authority – Joseph Roger Sammut, Joseph Bianco, Charlie Scicluna (retired)

The staff of Fuji in Qormi, Malta

CIANCIO (1913) Co. Ltd.
FUJI *TECH* Centre, Malta
(356) 21 480 500

Daniel Debono   Director
Mario Ciancio   Director
Christine Ciancio Director
Neville Aguis   Manager
Adrian Aquilina   Printer Operator

PHOTOGRAPHY

Victor Fabri
Subway Dive Centre

Jesper Kjoller
DYK Magazine

Sharon Metson
H2O Divers

Ian Forder
Subway Dive Centre

Alexander Aristarkhov
Subway Dive Centre

Kevin Debattista
Subway Dive Centre

Joseph Farrugia

Gavin Galea
Meldives Dive Centre

J. P. Bresser
Dive Deep Blue Dive Centre

Colin Stead

Marilyn Hiatt
www.mphphotography.co.uk

Sean Hill
www.mediadive.com

Hubert Borg
Sea Shell Dive Cove Dive Centre

Graham Owen

Dmitry Vinogradov
Subway Dive Centre

August Janker
Atlantis Dive Centre

Alan Porter
NDS Dive Centre

Alan James
Photography. Bristol, UK

Derek Chircop

All photographs in this publication which are credited, the copyright remains with the photographer.

Are You Diving With A ....

Professional Diving Schools Association

Member ??

I wish I HAD!!!

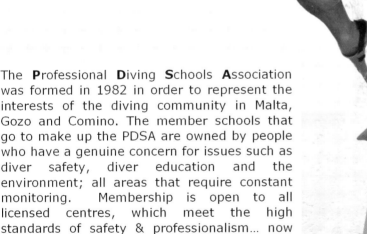

The **P**rofessional **D**iving **S**chools **A**ssociation was formed in 1982 in order to represent the interests of the diving community in Malta, Gozo and Comino. The member schools that go to make up the PDSA are owned by people who have a genuine concern for issues such as diver safety, diver education and the environment; all areas that require constant monitoring. Membership is open to all licensed centres, which meet the high standards of safety & professionalism... now expected throughout the diving world.

Please look out for the PDSA Logo when selecting your Diving Centre on the Maltese Islands.

All Our Members Run Professional Diving Schools

Together... Safeguarding Malta's Diving Future

Malta, Gozo, Comino

www.pdsa.org.mt

Dive centre locations

1 Atlantis Diving Centre, Qolla Street, Marsalforn, Gozo

2 Gozo Aquasports, Rabat Road, Marsalforn, Gozo

3 Calypso, The Seafront, Marsalforn, Gozo

4 Aquaventure, Mellieha Bay Hotel, Mellieha, Malta

5 Meldives, Tunny Net Lido, Mellieha, Malta

6 Sea Shell Dive Cove, Mellieha, Malta

7 North East Diving Services, St. Pauls Bay, Malta

8 Maltaqua, Mosta Road, St. Pauls Bay, Malta

9 Scubatech, Alka Street, St. Pauls Bay, Malta

10 Subway, Pioneer Road, Bugibba, Malta

11 Buddies, Pioneer Road, Bugibba, Malta

12 Dive Deep Blue, Ananija Street, Bugibba, Malta

13 Underwater World, Tourist Street, Bugibba, Malta

14 Starfish, Corinthia Resort, St. Georges Bay, Malta

15 Divewise Services, Dragonora Point, St Julians, Malta

16 AquaOasis, George Borg, Oliver St., St Julians, Malta

17 Dive Systems, Tower Point, Exiles, Sliema, Malta

18 H2O Divers, Tower Road, Fortizza, Sliema, Malta

19 Dive Shack, Qui-Si-Sana, Sliema, Malta

20 Oxygene.Tigne Seafront, Sliema, Malta

21 Dive Med, Zonqor Point, Marsascala, Malta

22 H2O Divers, Raddison SAS, Golden Sands, Malta

23 Paradise Diving, Paradise Bay Hotel, Cirkewwa, Malta

24 H2O Divers, Riviera Resort Hotel, Marfa Bay, Malta

25 Dawn Divers, Ramla Bay Hotel, Cirkewwa, Malta

26 Comino Island Dive Centre, Comino

27 Frankies, Mgarr Road, Xewkija, Gozo

28 Moby Dives, Triq Il-Gostra, Xlendi Bay, Gozo

29 St. Andrews Divers Cove, Xlendi Bay, Gozo

Full details of the above dive centres can be found in alphabetical order commencing on page 211.

Malta dive centres

Dawn Dives

Open every day all year round!

Escorted diving:
All sites in this book - and more!
Group rates available!
Courses:
Beginner to Instructor!
Equipment:
Sales, service and rental!
Air and Nitrox available!

To book or for more information
e: info@dawndivesmalta.com
visit: www.dawndivesmalta.com
call: 00 356 2152 0245

featured picture is the anchor at Cirkewwa

PADI INTERNATIONAL RESORT ASSOCIATION
GOLD PALM

P.A.D.I.

5 Star Gold Palm Centre
DSAT Technical Centre

Hotel or Apartment
Diving Packages.

Malta/Gozo/Comino Trips

Introduction Dives.
Guided Dive Packs.
Courses /Specialties.

**The Adventure
Starts Now !**

BS-AC

**Premier Centre &
Technical Centre**

Facilities include:
Dive Shop.
Equipment Rental.
Car parking.
Pool & Sundeck
A Warm Welcome !

DIVE DEEP BLUE LTD.
Deep Blue Lido, 100 Annanija Str., Bugibba/Qawra. Malta.
Tel:(+356)21 583946 Fax:(+356)21 583945
Internet:http://www.divedeepblue.com   email:dive@divedeepblue.com

---

PADI 5 Star Diving Centre
Zonqor Point
Marsascala
MALTA
Tel: +356 21639981
Mob: +356 99887118
99494269

DIVE MED.

PADI 5 Star Dive Center

Full Range of Diving Services for All...

Beginners   Technical Divers   Renatals   NITROX
Equipment Maintenance   Boat Trips
Instructor Training
Advanced Divers

www.divemed.com - info@divemed.com

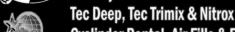
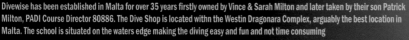

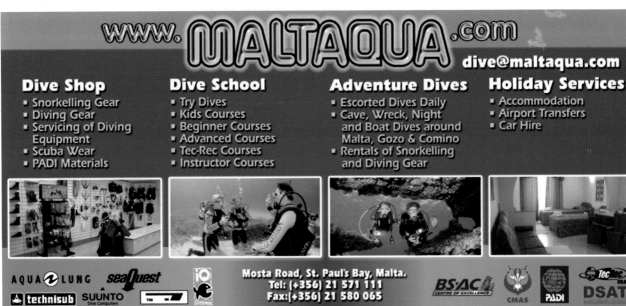

Malta dive centres

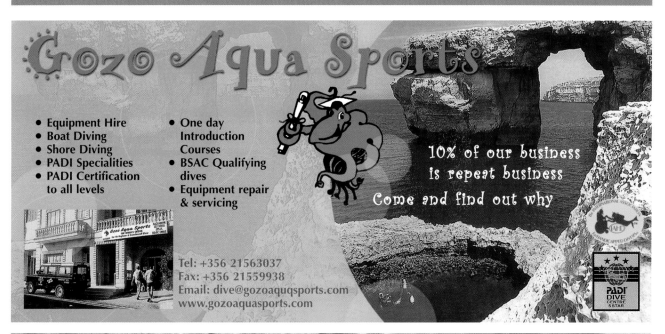

Diving in Malta

Malta's warm clear and tideless waters offer a wealth of diving opportunities to beginner and expert divers alike, year round. After a flight of just over 3 and a half hours, divers can experience crystal clear deep blue waters with unbelievable submarine topography, fish life and wrecks, the numbers of which have increased following the Maltese government's Artificial Reef Programme. English is widely spoken, meaning there are plenty of English speaking instructors and getting by is easy.